Zend Framework 2 Cookbook

A guide to all the ins and outs of Zend Framework 2 features

Josephus Callaars

[PACKT] open source *
PUBLISHING   community experience distilled

BIRMINGHAM - MUMBAI

Zend Framework 2 Cookbook

First published: December 2013

Production Reference: 1121213

Published by Packt Publishing Ltd.

Livery Place
35 Livery Street
Birmingham B3 2PB, UK.

ISBN 978-1-84969-484-1

www.packtpub.com

Cover Image by Prashant Timappa Shetty (sparkling.spectrum.123@gmail.com)

Credits

Author
Josephus Callaars

Reviewers
Armando Padilla
Diego Sapriza
David Weinraub

Acquisition Editor
Joanne Fitzpatrick

Lead Technical Editor
Balaji Naidu

Technical Editors
Pratik More
Pooja Nair
Anita Nayak

Project Coordinator
Abhijit Suvarna

Proofreaders
Bridget Braund
Lesley Harrison

Indexer
Hemangini Bari

Graphics
Disha Haria
Yuvraj Mannari

Production Coordinator
Adonia Jones

Cover Work
Aditi Gajjar
Adonia Jones

About the Author

Josephus Callaars is a software developer whose passion began like so many other developers at the appropriate age of twelve. Being intrigued by mathematics and software languages such as Assembler and Java, he quickly found out that his career was to be found in the abstract side. Since 2003 he has been developing software applications commercially, and always tried to stay up-to-date with the latest technologies.

Josephus has been passionate about developing ever since, and always thought it could be done better every time. He is a Zend Certified Engineer and is regularly to be found in the open source community, where he is always on the lookout for new things to learn.

I would like to thank my wife for supporting me in everything and deciding to not kick me out of the house just yet. I would also like to thank my parents for always believing in me, and teaching me the value of hard work.

About the Reviewers

Armando Padilla has over 10 years of experience in the PHP ecosystem, working with some of the best at Yahoo where he assisted with Shine, World Cup, and Winter Olympics, also as a scalability expert, he helped the RiotGames' web-scalability team by supporting the demands of its web-based gaming community. He has written two PHP books, *Beginning Zend Framework* and *Pro PHP Application Performance*, and now spends his time as the Sr. Engineering Manager at Disney Interactive.

> I would like to thank Alba Luz Guevara and my baby Amanda Luz Padilla for giving me the time to tech review this book.

Diego Sapriza is a Senior Software Engineer at CASE who loves technology and applying it to solve business-related problems. Diego lives in Uruguay where he oversees the CASE web development team as well as setting the direction and strategy for how the company delivers software development solutions.

He specializes in web technologies such as PHP, MySQL, Sphinx, JavaScript, jQuery, Python, and many more. He is also an expert in Linux Server Administration. Pulling from his experiences as a manager, CTO, developer, and consultant in the IT industry, Diego maintains his vast knowledge of web technologies through extensive research and development of the latest advancements in the field. As a result he ensures that custom applications designed for clients are focused on effective solutions and improving the built environment.

A self-proclaimed libre software evangelist, Diego spends his time near the beautiful beaches of Uruguay taking pictures and spending time with his family.

David Weinraub is a Zend Certified Engineer (ZCE) specializing in application development on the LAMP (Linux, Apache, MySQL, PHP) stack. He is passionate about clean code, structured architecture, SOLID object-oriented principles, and DRY. He has experience with Zend Framework, Slim, Lithium, MongoDB, PHPUnit, Vagrant, and a range of associated technologies.

David earned his Ph.D. in Mathematics from the State University of New York, Albany, for his work on Hopf algebras. He lives in Phuket, Thailand with his wife and two wonderful children.

Also, he's a sucker for astronomy/cosmology.

www.PacktPub.com

Support files, eBooks, discount offers and more

You might want to visit www.PacktPub.com for support files and downloads related to your book.

Did you know that Packt offers eBook versions of every book published, with PDF and ePub files available? You can upgrade to the eBook version at www.PacktPub.com and as a print book customer, you are entitled to a discount on the eBook copy. Get in touch with us at service@packtpub.com for more details.

At www.PacktPub.com, you can also read a collection of free technical articles, sign up for a range of free newsletters and receive exclusive discounts and offers on Packt books and eBooks.

http://PacktLib.PacktPub.com

Do you need instant solutions to your IT questions? PacktLib is Packt's online digital book library. Here, you can access, read and search across Packt's entire library of books.

Why Subscribe?

- ▶ Fully searchable across every book published by Packt
- ▶ Copy and paste, print and bookmark content
- ▶ On demand and accessible via web browser

Free Access for Packt account holders

If you have an account with Packt at www.PacktPub.com, you can use this to access PacktLib today and view nine entirely free books. Simply use your login credentials for immediate access.

Table of Contents

Preface

A couple of years ago I was introduced to Zend Framework 1 by a friend of mine, and since then I have been a fan. Although the first framework was a real bulky framework with not much documentation, I feel that the second version of the framework improved greatly. The incredible toolshed full of features, makes this framework (personally) one of the best frameworks to work in.

But as we all probably know, because of its incredibly vast library of features the learning curve can appear very steep. That is why I felt the need to write about all the important parts of the framework, in bite-size pieces that don't overwhelm someone (you in this case) who wants to learn it.

What this book covers

Chapter 1, Zend Framework 2 Basics, talks about how we can set up a small application and run it. The dependency injection and configuration are also handled.

Chapter 2, Translating and Mail Handling, explains the importance of internationalization and localization, and the overall handling of sending and receiving of mails in our applications.

Chapter 3, Handling and Decorating Forms, demonstrates how forms are created. After that it talks about filtering, validation, and decoration of forms.

Chapter 4, Using View, covers one of the most important parts of the framework that will be discussed here, setting and rendering of the View.

Chapter 5, Configuring and Using Databases, gives out the configuration and explanation of databases that will give us an insight into how we can fully utilize them in our application.

Chapter 6, Modules, Models, and Services, mainly discusses how modules are built up, models can be hydrated, and services are defined.

Chapter 7, Handling Authentication, delves into the different ways of authenticating users and how we can create our own authentication method.

Chapter 8, Optimizing Performance, discusses the use of caching and the methods available to cache output, opcode, and how to use plugins.

Chapter 9, Catching Bugs, teaches us how to debug applications, handle exceptions, and log stuff.

Appendix, Setting up the Essentials, shows where we can find the documentation, how to set up a development environment, and shows how the composer works.

What you need for this book

To follow the book in the best possible way I would recommend using a Linux-based web server, as most of the recipes are more Linux oriented than Windows. If you are a Windows user you'll probably be better off installing a virtual machine with Linux on it, or installing a Zend Server community edition to make sure your machine is compatible for Zend Framework 2 development (you can also do this without Zend Server, but it is just more convenient).

Who this book is for

Zend Framework 2 Cookbook is for PHP developers who are fairly advanced in PHP programming. It will also be useful for developers who have a keen interest in expanding their knowledge outside the boundaries of simply scripting pages together. As unit testing and MVC will be discussed, it is beneficial for the reader to know what these technologies are, although experience with developing applications is not necessarily essential.

Conventions

In this book, you will find a number of styles of text that distinguish between different kinds of information. Here are some examples of these styles, and an explanation of their meaning.

Code words in text, database table names, folder names, filenames, file extensions, pathnames, dummy URLs, user input, and Twitter handles are shown as follows: "We can either get the flags from a message by using the `getFlags()` method, or by using the `hasFlag()` method."

A block of code is set as follows:

```php
<?php
echo $this->dateFormat(
    // Format the current UNIX timestamp.
    time(),

    // Our date is to be a LONG date format.
    IntlDateFormatter::LONG,

    // We want to omit the time, defining this is
    // optional as the default is NONE.
    IntlDateFormatter::NONE
);
```

When we wish to draw your attention to a particular part of a code block, the relevant lines or items are set in bold:

```
SampleModule/
  config/
    module.config.php
  language/
  src/
    SampleModule/
      Controller/
        IndexController.php
  view/
    samplemodule/
      index/
        index.phtml
  Module.php
```

Any command-line input or output is written as follows:

php composer.phar update

New terms and **important words** are shown in bold. Words that you see on the screen, in menus or dialog boxes for example, appear in the text like this: "After we have done all that we can, click on **OK** and you can choose a location to save our file."

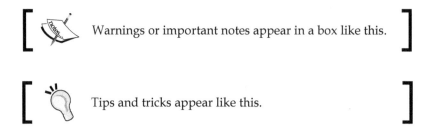

[Warnings or important notes appear in a box like this.]

[Tips and tricks appear like this.]

Reader feedback

Feedback from our readers is always welcome. Let us know what you think about this book—what you liked or may have disliked. Reader feedback is important for us to develop titles that you really get the most out of.

To send us general feedback, simply send an e-mail to feedback@packtpub.com, and mention the book title via the subject of your message.

If there is a topic that you have expertise in and you are interested in either writing or contributing to a book, see our author guide on www.packtpub.com/authors.

Customer support

Now that you are the proud owner of a Packt book, we have a number of things to help you to get the most from your purchase.

Downloading the example code

You can download the example code files for all Packt books you have purchased from your account at http://www.packtpub.com. If you purchased this book elsewhere, you can visit http://www.packtpub.com/support and register to have the files e-mailed directly to you.

Errata

Although we have taken every care to ensure the accuracy of our content, mistakes do happen. If you find a mistake in one of our books—maybe a mistake in the text or the code—we would be grateful if you would report this to us. By doing so, you can save other readers from frustration and help us improve subsequent versions of this book. If you find any errata, please report them by visiting http://www.packtpub.com/submit-errata, selecting your book, clicking on the **errata submission form** link, and entering the details of your errata. Once your errata are verified, your submission will be accepted and the errata will be uploaded on our website, or added to any list of existing errata, under the Errata section of that title. Any existing errata can be viewed by selecting your title from http://www.packtpub.com/support.

Piracy

Piracy of copyright material on the Internet is an ongoing problem across all media. At Packt, we take the protection of our copyright and licenses very seriously. If you come across any illegal copies of our works, in any form, on the Internet, please provide us with the location address or website name immediately so that we can pursue a remedy.

Please contact us at copyright@packtpub.com with a link to the suspected pirated material.

We appreciate your help in protecting our authors, and our ability to bring you valuable content.

Questions

You can contact us at questions@packtpub.com if you are having a problem with any aspect of the book, and we will do our best to address it.

1
Zend Framework 2 Basics

In this chapter we will cover:

- ▶ Setting up a Zend Framework 2 project
- ▶ Handling routines
- ▶ Understanding dependency injection
- ▶ Using configurations to your benefit
- ▶ The EventManager and Bootstrap classes

Introduction

In this chapter we will go through a basic Zend Framework 2 application, from download, to setup, to running it. If you are unfamiliar with how Zend Framework 2 works, and the best way to install it, you can use this chapter as a reference. Further on in the chapter, we will get somewhat deeper in the framework by looking at the **dependency injection** (**DI**) and how it can help us code more efficiently. Lastly we will go more into the details of the configuration options, the `EventManager` and `ModuleManager`.

Setting up a Zend Framework 2 project

Nothing is more exciting than setting up a new project in our favourite framework. Every time we start a new project we begin with a clean slate.

Getting ready

Before you can set up a new Zend Framework 2 application you need to make sure you have the following items ready:

- A web server such as Apache running PHP Version 5.3.3 or higher that you can reach from a web browser
- Git

If you don't have everything ready as mentioned, you are best off reading the topics mentioned in the *See also* section of this recipe (every topic we explain in this chapter is called a recipe) before you continue reading here.

We are assuming that Zend Framework 2 will be used on a Linux-based platform running an Apache 2 web server; this means that commands might not directly work on a Windows platform. Windows users, however, can set up a virtual machine with Linux on it to make full use of the book.

To install a virtual machine on Windows, we can use an application called Oracle VM VirtualBox, which is freely available. We can go to `www.virtualbox.org` and download plus install the latest version of VirtualBox, we can go to VirtualBoxes (`http://virtualboxes.org/images/ubuntu`) and download a preconfigured virtual machine from there.

All we have to do on the VirtualBoxes website is click on the latest Ubuntu (which is a distribution of Linux) link in the list, please take note of the username and password displayed there as we will need it later to login. Once the image is downloaded, it can be made ready by following the instructions in the documentation that can be found on the VirtualBoxes site (`http://virtualboxes.org/doc/register-and-load-a-downloaded-image`).

Assuming the image is imported we can easily start up the virtual machine and put in our username and password that has been supplied with the downloaded virtual machine.

Once logged in to the virtual machine we need to make sure Git is installed, which can be done easily by typing in the following command (mind that the dollar sign is the command prompt, and not the command we actually need to type):

```
$ sudo apt-get install git
```

If Git wasn't installed, the system will ask you to install Git, which can be done by pressing the *Y* key, followed by the *Enter* key, on the other hand if Git was already installed, than it will not do anything and tell you it already is installed.

How to do it...

First of all, we need the Zend Framework 2 skeleton so we can easily create a new project. A skeleton is a template structure that can be used to start developing with an application, and in this case it creates a template for us to develop within Zend Framework. Fortunately doing this is relatively easy, and almost never causes any problems, and when it does, it is usually related to Git not being able to retrieve the code. When Git isn't able to retrieve the skeleton, please make sure there are no spelling mistakes in the command, and that Git has outside access (we can test this by typing `ping Github.com` and see whether we get a response back).

The method we are going to use to retrieve the skeleton is called **cloning**, through a version control system called Git. Cloning the source code will make sure we always get the latest version that the developer (in this case Zend itself) has put online.

Cloning the skeleton

We can clone the skeleton—and almost everything else on Github for that matter — through use of the following command:

```
$ git clone git://github.com/zendframework/
  ZendSkeletonApplication.git
```

Moving the skeleton

Once finished we can go into the newly created folder called `ZendSkeletonApplication`, and copy and paste everything in there over to our web server document root. On a Linux system this is usually `/var/www` (this is also the case when we use Zend Server, as described in the *Appendix, Setting up the Essentials*). We can do this, for example, by typing the following commands:

```
$ cd ZendSkeletonApplication
$ mv ./* /var/www -f
$ cd /var/www
```

Initializing the Composer

When everything is copied over, we are going to initialize the project by typing the following command:

```
$ php composer.phar install
```

Now the **Command Line Interface** (**CLI**) of PHP executes `composer.phar`, which will in this instance, download and install the Zend Framework 2 library and set up a simple project for us to be able to work in.

This command can take a long time before it is successfully executed, as Composer needs to do a lot of things before it tells you that Zend Framework 2 is ready for use, we won't go into the details of the workings of Composer here, as it is already discussed in the *Appendix, Setting up the Essentials*.

Once this command has been completed we need to make sure our web server document root is changed to match the layout of the skeleton. It is common practice that Zend Framework 2 uses the `public` folder as a main landing point for the application. The structure of the Zend Framework 2 skeleton allows us to bind the user to the `public` folder, while all our logic is safely outside the public area.

In essence this means we need to `root` or `jail` the web server in using the `public` folder first before we can actually see anything that we just installed. We want to `root` or `jail` the web server because we don't want the outside world to be able to abuse our web server more than necessary, and rooting or jailing makes sure that the web server itself has no access to any other folders than what it is jailed to, thus making our server a bit more secure.

In my personal case this means changing the Apache 2 configuration. In most Linux-based systems it will be the Apache web server that is serving our web requests.

The easiest thing that you can do is find your web server configuration (usually located in `/etc/apache2` and append the DocumentRoot with `/public`. For me this would change the document root from `/var/www'` to `'/var/www/public`.

 If you are using Apache, you need to check if the `AllowOverride` setting is set correctly, this can be found in the same section as your document root and should reflect the following:

```
AllowOverride FileInfo
```

Finally we need to restart the Apache web server, which can be done by the following command if you are logged in as a root user or invoke it by prepending the command with `sudo`, which tells the server that we want to execute it as a super user.

```
$ apache2ctl restart
```

Now we are able to check our browser and see what we have actually done. We now simply go with a web browser to the project created by typing in the URL, in my case this would be the following:

```
http://localhost/
```

This will result in the following screen:

Congratulations, you have now set up a basic Zend Framework 2 application.

How it works...

After getting the basic Zend Framework 2 skeleton working, it is the perfect time to install the ZFTool. The ZFTool is a utility module that comes in handy when we want to list the current modules in our project, or add a new module, or even set up a new project. It also contains an extremely useful class-map generator that we can use in the somewhat more advanced areas of Zend Framework 2.

We can install this utility by using the following commands:

```
$ cd /var/www
$ mkdir -p vendor/zftool
$ cd vendor/zftool
$ wget https://packages.zendframework.com/zftool.phar
```

Although we already set up our Zend Framework 2 skeleton through the composer, it might be a fun thing to show you how you can easily set up a new project through the ZFTool.

```
$ cd /var/www
$ php vendor/zftool/zftool.phar create project new-project
```

The preceding command will create a new Zend Framework 2 skeleton project in the folder `/var/www/new-project`. In turn this means that the document root for our new project should be set to `/var/www/new-project/public`.

To complete the Zend Framework 2 application in our new-project, we can simply go to the new-project directory and execute the following command:

```
$ cd new-project
$ php composer.phar install
```

Another handy command of the ZFTool is the creation and display of modules in our project. The ZFTool can easily display a list of modules that we currently use (with larger applications we tend to lose sight of the modules) and the ability to create a new skeleton module for our application. To see a list of the current modules used in our application we can use the following command:

```
$ php ../vendor/zftool/zftool.phar modules
```

To create a new module named `wow-module` in our project based in the directory `/var/www/new-project` we can use the following command:

```
$ php ../vendor/zftool/zftool.phar create module wow-module
  /var/www/new-project
```

Giving the path to the application is optional, but if we are using it with multiple projects on the same machine, it is best to make sure that we have the right path for our project.

And now for the last and probably the most useful command in the ZFTool box, the class-map generator. A class-map file is a file that has all the classes of a project with their respective paths declared, which makes it easier for the PHP auto loaders to load the class file. Normally class files are found in paths that we know of, creating a small lag because the auto loader actually needs to search for the file. With a class-map file, however, this is not the case as the auto load can immediately find the file required.

Class-mapping is a big issue in Zend Framework 2 because a bad class mapping can make a good application terribly slow, and to be completely fair Zend Framework 2 can use all the speed it can get.

What the class-map generator does is create a file that contains all the classes and paths that can be autoloaded. That way we don't have to worry about where the classes are located.

To generate a new class-map file, we can use the following command:

```
$ php zftool.phar classmap generate <directory> <file> -w
```

The command requires us to give in two different parameters:

- `<directory>`: The directory that needs to have the classes indexed. For example, this can be a new library you added to the `vendor` directory.

- `<file>`: This is the class-map file the ZFTool needs to generate. Our auto loader in Zend Framework 2 needs to pick this file up, so we need to make sure that the ZFTool can find the file. If you don't specify a file, it will create a file called `autoload_classmap.php` in the current working directory.

Most of the time it is necessary to append a class-map file instead of overwriting it, if you want to append it you can simply change `-w` with `-a`.

An example of a class-map file is the `autoload_namespaces.php` file in the `vendor/composer` directory, and it looks a little bit like this:

```php
<?php
return array(
    // Every class beginning with namespace Zend\ will be
    // searched in this specific directory
    'Zend\\' => array(
        __DIR__ . '/../zendframework/zendframework/library'
    ),
    'ZendTest\\' => array(
        __DIR__ . '/../zendframework/zendframework/tests'
    ),
);
```

Downloading the example code

You can download the example code files for all Packt books you have purchased from your account at `http://www.packtpub.com`. If you purchased this book elsewhere, you can visit `http://www.packtpub.com/support` and register to have the files e-mailed directly to you.

There's more...

There are also other ways of installing the ZFTool, some are just as easy as using the composer, so we'll cover two other methods of installing the ZFTool. That way we give ourselves the broadest options available to use.

Another method of installing ZFTool is by utilizing git, and thus cloning the source code from the repository itself. This however gets the current master version, which can be a bit buggy.

```
$ cd vendor
$ git clone https://github.com/zendframework/ZFTool.git
$ cd ZFTool
$ php ./zf.php
```

Instead of `zftool.phar` we have now got the `zf.php` file at our disposal, which can be used in exactly the same way. Now we have covered all the different options on installing ZFTool.

See also

- ▶ The *Making sure you have all that you need* recipe in the *Appendix, Setting up the Essentials*

- ▶ The *Downloading Zend Framework 2 and finding its documentation* recipe in the *Appendix, Setting up the Essentials*

- ▶ The *Composer and its uses within Zend Framework 2* recipe in the *Appendix, Setting up the Essentials*

- ▶ Apache web server `http://apache.org/`

- ▶ PHP website `http://php.net`

Handling routines

An important aspect (if not the most important one) is the routing within Zend Framework 2. In its most basic form routing tells the framework how the user should get from page A to page B, and what needs to be done to arrive at that destination. That is why we generally think this is the most important part to understand if you are just starting out.

How to do it...

To define a route we can simply go into one of the configuration files and add the router configuration to there.

Setting up routing

Let's look at our simple (`Segment`) configuration as follows (file: `/module/Application/config/module.config.php`):

```
return array(
    // Here we define our route configuration
    'routes' => array(
```

```php
    // We give this route the name 'website'
    'website' => array(

        // The route type is of the class:
        // Zend\Mvc\Router\Http\Segment
        'type' => 'segment',

            // Lets set the options for this route
            'options' => array(

                /*
                    The route that we want to match is /website
                    where we can optionally add a controller name
                    and an action name. For example:
                        /website/index/index
                */
                'route' => '/website[/:controller[/:action]]',

                /*
                    We don't want to accept everything, but this
                    regex makes sure we only accept alpha-
                    numeric characters and a dash and underscore.

                    In our instance we want to check this for the
                    action and the controller.
                */
                'constraints' => array(
                    'controller' => '[a-zA-Z][a-zA-Z0-9_-]*',
                    'action' => '[a-zA-Z][a-zA-Z0-9_-]*'
                ),

                /*
                    We want to make sure that if the user only
                    types /website in the URL bar it will actually
                    go somewhere. We defined that here.
                */
                'defaults' => array(
                    'controller' => 'Website\Controller\Index',
                    'action' => 'index'
                ),
            ),
        ),
    ),
);
```

With this basic configuration we can easily define routes in our application, and in this instance we have configured a route that responds to the `/website` URL. When we would go to the `/website` URL, we would be routed to the `Website\Controller\ Index::indexAction` by default. If we however use the route `/website/another/ route`, we would be routed to the `Website\Controller\Another::routeAction`, as we have defined that the controller and action can be parsed behind that. If we omit the route path and put in `/website/another`, we would be redirected to the `Website\ Controller\Another::indexAction`, as that is used by default by the framework.

The preceding example has only one really major drawback, which is, when we decide to use anonymous function in the configuration to create more dynamic routes, we would not be able to cache the route as closures are not serializeable by the cache.

However, there is another method of declaring the route, and that is in the code. The need to create the route functionality in the code could (obviously everyone has their own reasons and requirements) arise because we want to cache the configuration in a later stage (as we cannot cache anonymous function, for example) or when we want to load up a route dynamically from a database.

Let's take a look at the `/module/Application/Module.php` example:

```php
<?php

// We are working in the Application module
namespace Application;

// Our main imports that we want to use
use Zend\Mvc\ModuleRouteListener;
use Zend\Mvc\MvcEvent;

// Define our module class, this is always 'Module', but
// needs to be specifically created by the developer.
class Module
{
  public function onBootstrap(MvcEvent $e)
  {
    // First we want to get the ServiceManager
    $sm = $e->getApplication()->getServiceManager();

    /*
      Say our logged in user is 'gdog' and we want
      him to be able to go to /gdog to see his profile.
    */
    $user = 'gdog';
```

```
// Now get the router
$router = $sm->get('router');

// Lets add a route called 'member' to our router
$router->addRoute('member', array(

    /*
       We want to make /$user the main end point, with
       an optional controller and action.
    */
    'route' => '/'. $user. '[/:controller[/:action]]',

    /*
       We want a default end point (if no controller
       and action is given) to go to the index action
       of the index controller.
    */
    'defaults' => array(
        'controller' => 'Member\Controller\Index',
        'action' => 'index'
    ),

    /*
       We only want to allow alphanumeric characters
       with an exception to the dash and underscore.
    */
    'constraints' => array(
        'controller' => '[a-zA-Z][a-zA-Z0-9_-]*',
        'action' => '[a-zA-Z][a-zA-Z0-9_-]*'
    ),
    ));
    }
}
```

Naturally there are more ways of adding a route, but the method mentioned in the preceding code for adding a route displays a canny way of dynamically adding a route. What we created there is that whenever Gdog goes to his profile, he can simply type in `http://example.ext/gdog` and end up on his profile.

Even more wonderful is that if our friend Gdog wants to see his friends, he is able to do that by just typing in for example, `http://example.ext/gdog/my/friends`, which will resolve to the `Member` module and then go to the `My` controller, lastly executing the `Friends` action.

Using SimpleRouteStack

This route stack is—as the name implies—the simplest router around and is basically a list with routes that is being parsed to see which route matches, by default this type of router is not used in Zend Framework 2. The general rule of thumb is that if we want to add a route with a high priority, we give it a high index number for example, 100, or 200. If we want to give the route a very low priority, we would give it an index number of, for example, 5 or 10.

Giving priorities to routes comes in handy when we have very specific routes (which usually have a high priority) and less specific routes (low priority). If we, for example, want to make / website/url redirect to a completely different module, controller, and action, but not affect the other website routes, we need to give the /website/url route a higher priority so that when it is found, it will not search for the lower priority routes.

If we, by accident, turn the priorities around, we would find our /website/url always redirect to the route that contains all the /website routes.

SimpleRouteStack uses a Zend\Mvc\Router\PriorityList class to manage its routes priorities.

We need to consider routing before we want to start creating our application, as when the application grows we might get into trouble with our routing if we haven't considered 'how to route' beforehand. It would therefore be wise for us to 'sitemap' the application before coding the routes to make sure we have a correct route list and are not creating any conflicting routes.

The SimpleRouteStack class has a number of methods defined that are very useful for us:

- getRoute($name) / getRoutes($name): This will retrieve the current route—if a name is provided—or routes that are defined in our SimpleRouteStack. If we are unsure about the routes we have defined, this would be a good place to check first.

addRoute($name, $route, $priority) / addRoutes($routes): We can use this to add a new route or an array of routes to our route type by simply adding it through this method. A route requires a name, route (which can be a string or an instance of RouteInterface) and if we fancy a priority, we can give that as the third parameter.

hasRoute($name): If we would want to check whether a specific route already exists, we can search using its name and find out if it does or doesn't.

- removeRoute($name): When we are tired of a route we can simply give its name and remove it from the list. This can be particularly handy if we want for example to have a module override a certain /login when the user has logged in to route to/user.

- SimpleRouteStack: Does not have a functionality to have multiple routes with the same priority. If there is a route with a priority already defined, it will prioritize the last route added as the route with the highest priority.

Using TreeRouteStack

Routers are not restricted to using the URI path to find out how to route a request. They can also use other information such as the query parameters, headers, methods, or hostnames to find a match.

How it works...

In Zend Framework 2, we will generally use routing that is based on a request URI, which contains path segments that should be queried. Routes are matched by a router, which utilizes `RouteStack` to find the match to the query made by the router. We use `RouteStack` because we want a decent way of managing our different routes. With Zend Framework 2 there are loads of route types provided, but only two flavorless routers namely `SimpleRouteStack` and `TreeRouteStack`.

When we are defining a router, we need to make sure we understand how it works. Although creating lists with different paths is simple enough, it is wise to remember that the Zend Framework 2 router generally works with the **Last In First Out** (**LIFO**) concept, which means that a route that would be used often would be registered last, and a route that is less common would be registered earlier in the router stack.

There's more...

Besides the two standard route types, Zend Framework 2 comes with a whole scale of route types that are more specialized to the Internet navigation or even through the console.

Namespace – Zend\Mvc\Router\Http

A wonderful set of HTTP routers can be found in the `Zend\Mvc\Router\Http` namespace and we will take a quick look at the different classes that reside within this namespace.

The Hostname class explained

The `Zend\Mvc\Router\Http\Hostname` namespace will try to match its routing against the hostname defined in the configuration. For example, if we define the route to be `something.example.ext`, our router will make its routing decision based on the full URL. But, if we add a single colon at the beginning of that same route, for example: `:something.example.ext`, the router would base its route on the `something` variable, which could be anything from `aardvark.example.ext` to `zyxt.example.ext`.

The Literal class explained

The `Zend\Mvc\Router\Http\Literal` class will literally match the path we give in. For example, if we put a route in there, which is `/grouphug`, the route will only resolve to that URL, and nothing else.

Methods explained

The `Zend\Mvc\Router\Http\Method` class is used when we want to match against an HTTP method instead of a segment or path. This could be, for example, a `POST`, `DELETE` and so on. The method is also called `verb` by Zend Framework 2, which means that instead of a `route` parameter, it requests a `verb` parameter when adding the route, which is an excellent way to create RESTful APIs.

The Part class explained

The `Zend\Mvc\Router\Http\Part` class is used to describe `child_routes` in our routing configuration. This means that—although never used directly—we can define that `/user/profile` is being redirected to use the `UserController`, with the `profile` action.

Let's consider the following configuration:

```
return array(
    // We begin our router configuration
    'router' => array(

       // Define our routes
       'routes' => array(

          // We are defining a route named 'Example'
          'Example' => array(
             'type' => 'Literal',
             'options' => array(

                /*
                  This route will resolve to /recipe
                  which will resolve to the Example
                  module's IndexController and execute
                  the IndexAction.
                */
                'route' => 'recipe',
                'defaults' => array(
                   '__NAMESPACE__' => 'Example\Controller',
                   'controller' => 'Index',
                ),
             ),

             'may_terminate' => true,

             /*
```

```
    Here we begin to define our Part route,
    which always begins with the
    'child_routes' configuration.
  */
  'child_routes' => array(
    'client' => array(
      'type' => 'Literal',
      'options' => array(

      /*
        This child route (or Part)
        will resolve to /recipe/foo
        and will call the fooAction in
        the IndexController.
      */
      'route' => '/foo',
      'defaults' => array(
        'action' => 'fooAction'
      ),
    ),
  ),
 ),
 ),
 ),
 ),
);
```

Regex explained

The Zend\Mvc\Router\Http\Regex class would be used when we have a complex routing structure that requires us to dynamically create the route. This would, for example, come in handy when we look at News sites, where posts are built up like /archive/some-subject-2013.html. This fairly complex route (as some-subject-2013.html is dynamic in our case) would require a Regex router that can resolve the Controller, Action, and in our case also the output format.

Let's consider the following example:

```
// We begin our router configuration
'router' => array(

  // Define our routes
  'routes' => array(
```

```
        // We are defining a route named 'Archive'
        'Archive' => array(
          'type' => 'Literal',
          'options' => array(

            /*
              This route will resolve to /archive
              which will resolve to the Archive
              module's IndexController and execute
              the IndexAction.
            */
            'regex' => '/archive/(?<id>[a-zA-Z0-9_-
   ]+)(\.(?<format>(html|xml)))?',
            'defaults' => array(
                '__NAMESPACE__' => 'Archive\Controller',
                'controller' => 'Index',
                'action' => 'indexAction',
                'format' => 'html',
            ),
            'spec' => '/archive/%id%.%format%',
          ),
        ),
      ),
    ),
```

In the preceding example, it is important to note that `/archive/%id%.%format%` tells us that we will receive two parameters in our method called `indexAction` that is, `id` and `format`.

The Scheme class explained

The `Zend\Mvc\Router\Http\Scheme` class is always using the `defaults` parameter and will accept only one other parameter, which is called `scheme` and can only contain one of the following options, that is, `http`, `https`, and `mailto`.

The Segment class explained

The `Zend\Mvc\Router\Http\Segment` class is probably one of the most-used routers that we would use, as you can dynamically define the route and controller for any module by using, for example, `/:controller/:action`, which is easily recognizable by the colon separation. We can define any `constraints` to the segment by configuring only the use of alphanumeric characters or another definition that we would like to use.

An example of `Segment` is given in the first example in the *How to do it...* section.

Understanding dependency injection

When we talk about the dependency injection, or in short DI, we talk about the simple task of, for example, injecting data in object or methods at initialization when needed by one or other higher up classes, which either modify or dispose off the object after use. The DI is probably the most complex feature in Zend Framework 2 to understand. Unfortunately because DI's over complexity in debugging and performance and the Service Locator (explained in *Chapter 6, Modules, Models and Services*). However, although it is not the best tool in the shed, we must try to learn it, because when mastered it could prove to be a very powerful tool to create a very maintainable piece of code.

If we come across a situation where it is necessary for us to input a lot of parameters in classes because of objects deeper in the code are dependent on them is probably the most annoying and un-maintainable piece of code that we can find in even the most professional environment. We need to think mainly about objects that are used more than once in an application, and always required to instantiate again.

How to do it...

Let us take a look at the following example and assume that `FirstClass` is the only class that we will actually need further in the code:

```
namespace OneNamespace
{
  class FirstClass
  {
    private $secondClass;
    public function __construct(SecondClass $secondClass)
    {
      $this->secondClass = $secondClass;
    }
  }

  class SecondClass
  {
    private $thirdClass;
    private $vehicle;
    public function __construct(ThirdClass $thirdClass, $vehicle)
    {
      $this->thirdClass = $thirdClass;
      $this->vehicle = $vehicle;
    }
```

```
    }
  }

  namespace AnotherNamespace
  {
    class ThirdClass
    {
      private $first_name;
      private $last_name;

      public function __construct($first_name, $last_name)
      {
        $this->first_name = $first_name;
        $this->last_name = $last_name;
      }
    }
  }

  // Let us now create the example through the classic
  // method.
  $thirdClass = new AnotherNamespace\ThirdClass("John", "Doe");
  $secondClass = new OneNamespace\SecondClass($thirdClass,
    'Motorcycle');
  $firstClass = new OneNamespace\FirstClass($secondClass);
```

Both the preceding examples give either variables that are only used to instantiate another class and/or add complexity in reading the code. Although they both are correct, the use of DI can, in this case, make the configuration of both the classes much easier.

Initializing the DI at call-time

Let's take a look at this DI example, considering that we have the same classes as the preceding example:

```
  namespace OneNamespace
  {
    class FirstClass
    {
      [..]
    }

    class SecondClass
    {
```

```
        [..]
      }
    }

  namespace AnotherNamespace
  {
    class ThirdClass
    {
      [..]
    }
  }

  // Instead of configuring all the classes, we will now
  // simply configure the Di, and only instantiate the
  // class that we want to use.
  $di = new \Zend\Di\Di();
  $lister = $di->get(
      'OneNamespace\FirstClass',
      array(
          'first_name' => 'Jane',
          'last_name' => 'Doe',
          'vehicle' => 'Car',
      )
  );
```

In the preceding example, we simply say to the DI that `AnotherNamespace\ThirdClass` has two parameters in its `__construct` method. The DI will then utilize `Reflection` to find out what parameters are present there, and will then give any class that has a `first_name`, `vehicle`, or `last_name` parameter in its constructor that parameter.

Of course we will see a potential flaw here, as you might need to utilize multiple instantiations, one can presume that at some point the same parameter name will be used. In our example, it would cause a problem if another class also has a `$first_name` parameter but requires a different input, as the DI will simply give the one that is in its list.

> If we use DI to instantiate our classes and all we need the constructor for is to set our variables, we can easily remove the constructor altogether as the DI doesn't use the constructor to initialize the variables. Instead the DI will just set the properties of the values.

One good thing about this is that this can flaw only happens when we use the DI at a call-time level, and not in a global configuration level as we will see now. That is why it isn't recommended to use the DI at call-time level at all.

Initializing the DI through a Configuration object

What we also can do to create a more specific (or accurate) initialization of our object – and to make sure classes with the same property names don't conflict – is initializing the DI with a configuration object.

The idea behind this is that we first create a configuration object (or array) that defines which classes need which properties set, and then use that to initialize the DI, which in its turn finds out when it needs to initiate what.

Take a look at the following example, which shows you the exact thing we just explained:

```php
<?php
// We are assuming that we are using the same classes as
// in the previously shown examples.
namespace OneNamespace
{
  class FirstClass
  {
     [..]
  }

  class SecondClass
  {
     [..]
  }
}

namespace AnotherNamespace
{
  class ThirdClass
  {
     [..]
  }
}

// After defining our classes we now begin to create our
// configuration array which we will use to initialize
// the DI.
$configuration = array(

  // We want to use this specific configuration at
  // initialization of our class.
  'instance' => array(
```

```php
    // We specify the class name to use here
    'SecondClass' => array(

      // We want to use this as a parameter
      'parameters' => array(

        // The property name to fill is vehicle.
        'vehicle' => 'Airplane'
      ),
    ),

    'FirstClass' => array(
      // Again we want to use this as a parameter
      'parameters' => array(

        // The property name to fill is first name and
        //last name.
        'first_name' => 'Neil',
        'last_name' => 'deGrasse Tyson',
      ),
    ),
  ),
);

// We want to instantiate the Di\Configuration now.
use \Zend\Di\Configuration;

$diConfiguration = new Configuration($configuration);

// Now instantiate the Di itself, with the configuration
// attached.
$di = new \Zend\Di\Di($configuration);

// And to get the object we want to use, we just do the
//same as before.
$firstClass = $di->get('OneNamespace\FirstClass');
```

To make everything even nicer, we would just put the Zend\Di\Configuration of the DI in the bootstrap of our module, so that we can use it easily throughout the namespace. This way we can simply put the configuration of the DI in our module.config.php and let the framework take care of it.

How it works...

The DI or dependency injector is an important, and most of the time overlooked feature of Zend Framework 2. The DI makes our lives a lot easier by automatically finding the classes we need in our application.

With all its complexity however, comes a couple of features we should be wary of.

The DI only gives out one instance of an object

This means that every `get()` call will result in the same instantiation over and over again. If we would like a new instance, we would need to call `newInstance()` as the DI implements the singleton pattern, which means that all the data persists every time we call the `get()` method unless we force a new instance of the DI.

Defining either all properties, or using a Fully Qualified (FQ) setter parameter

When our class has more properties than we define, we will find out that the DI will use the last value for every other property in the class. Of course this is unwanted, and if we wrote the class ourselves we should consider refactoring the configuration and/or class.

However, when there is no other way we can define the right properties only by using a **Fully Qualified (FQ)** setter parameter.

In our configuration we would then define a very specific property name, for example, `class::method:paramPos`. If we take our `ThirdClass` example from earlier on, this would then be `ThirdClass::setFirstName:0` and `ThirdClass::setLastName:0` respectively.

There's more...

There is loads more we can learn about the DI in Zend Framework 2. The following list provides a very short and compact description of other interesting DI components:

▶ `RuntimeDefinition` (default), `CompilerDefinition` and `ClassDefinition`: These definitions are used to determine how to configure our objects. Although the default one usually does the job, it can't hurt to see what the other two Definitions do, because they all have their pros and cons.

▶ `InstanceManager`: Used to define the configuration, specifically the `Aliases`, `Parameters` and `Preferences`.

Using configurations to your benefit

Configurations play a crucial role in the workings of Zend Framework 2, therefore it is essential to know how it works.

How to do it...

Go through the following sections to use configurations to your benefit:

Creating a global configuration

When beginning to code in Zend Framework 2 there is some misunderstanding as to what the different configuration files do. By default we have multiple configuration files, and it might not always be simple to understand where things need to go. That is why we like to apply a simple rule:

> Is the configuration necessary throughout all our modules? If yes, place your configuration in the `config/application.config.php` file. If not, place your configuration in the `config/global.php` file at the module where it belongs.

The configuration that we usually place in the `global.php` file can be, for example, the caching method and configuration, the database configuration. Normally we would like to place items in there that are environment related, but nothing that is security sensitive.

Let's take a look at a bad example of `global.php`:

```php
<?php
return array(

    // We want to create a new database connection
    'db' => array(

        // The driver we want to use is the Pdo, our
        // favorite
        'driver' => 'Pdo',

        // This is our connection url, defining a MySQL
        // connection, with database 'somename' which is
        // available on the localhost server.
        'dsn' => 'mysql:dbname=somename;host=localhost',

        // This is exactly what we should NOT do in this
        // file, shame on you developer!
        'username' => 'terribleuser',
        'password' => 'evenworsepassword',
    ),
```

```
    // We need a database adapter defined as well,
    // otherwise we can't use it at all.
    'service_manager' => array(
      'factories' => array(
        'Zend\Db\Adapter\Adapter' =>
    'Zend\Db\Adapter\AdapterServiceFactory',
      ),
    ),
  );
```

It is terrible practice to put the username and password in the `global.php` file. The `global.php` file is to be put in our version control, and therefore should contain only configuration items that are required to globally run the application, not specific information that is relevant per environment, such as database usernames and passwords.

Creating configuration that only works for a local machine

One of the benefits of the ultra-many configuration files in Zend Framework 2, is that you are able to override your global configuration with your local configuration. This certainly comes in handy when developing and you find yourself in a position where your details are slightly different in configuration than your production environment.

Let's assume that we have the following `/config/autoload/global.php` configuration file:

```php
<?php
return array(

  // We want to create a new database connection
  'db' => array(

    // The driver we want to use is the Pdo, our
    // favorite
    'driver' => 'Pdo',

    // This is our connection url, defining a MySQL
    // connection, with database 'somename' which is
    // available on the localhost server.
    'dsn' => 'mysql:dbname=somename;host=localhost',
  ),

  // We need a database adapter defined as well,
  // otherwise we can't use it at all.
  'service_manager' => array(
```

```
    'factories' => array(
      'Zend\Db\Adapter\Adapter' =>
  'Zend\Db\Adapter\AdapterServiceFactory',
    ),
  ),
);
```

As we can see in the preceding example, we create a nice and simple MySQL database connection to our `somename` database which resides on the localhost. But as good developers we have not defined our username and password in here. That is where the `/config/autoload/local.php` file comes in.

Let's take a look at how our `local.php` might look like:

```
<?php
return array(
  'db' => array(
    'username' => 'awesomeuser',
    'password' => 'terriblepassword',
  ),
);
```

If we are using a version control system (please say yes), we should not commit this file, not only for security reasons but also because this is a local configuration file and wouldn't be necessary on a live system, as we would create a new one with the right details for that environment.

Editing your application.config.php file

If we look at our default `config/application.config.php` file we have only a few properties set, but loads of inline comments, which really come in handy when we can't remember the exact name or description of a property any more.

The main configuration that we will be changing the most in our application as we develop is the `modules` property. This specific property is a simple array with the different module namespaces that we have (and want to use) in our application. At default this looks somewhat like this:

```
<?php

return array(
  // This should be an array of module namespaces used
  // in the application.
  'modules' => array(
    'Application',
  ),
  [..]
```

When we add or remove a module, this line needs to be modified as well and one can even suggest modifying this before starting a new module or removing one. The reason for this is simple, when we forget to modify this file when removing a module it will generate a `500 - Application Error` when visiting the application in our browser. And because this configuration file is read quite early in the instantiation, it can sometimes be hard for the developer to pinpoint why the application fails to load all of a sudden.

How it works...

If we look at the `index.php` file in the `public` folder, we can see that we parse our initial configuration file to the Zend Framework MVC Application with the line `require 'config/application.config.php'`. This then loads up the main configuration file, which in its turn defines all our properties.

A nifty property in the `application.config.php` file is the `config_glob_paths` property. Any additional configuration files are by default read by finding files in the `config/autoload` folder as well, using a very specific file pattern namely; `*global.php` and `*local.php`. The order in which this is defined is also very important.

When we say `*global.php`, we can define anything from `somemodule.global.php` to `menu.global.php` to just `global.php`, as the file pattern (also named `GLOB_BRACE`) searches for anything that matches that. The same happens for `*local.php`.

The order this is defined is very important as said before because we want our global configuration to be loaded before our local configuration, otherwise there would be no point in overriding our global configuration, would there?

There's more...

To summarize the configuration files:

- `config/application.config.php`: Modules can be added and removed here, and very low level configuration happens here.

- `config/autoload/some-module.global.php`: Used to override your default values of your module configuration. Make sure not to put sensitive information in here, but hostnames and database names should go in here.

- `config/autoload/some-module.local.php`: You can put your usernames and passwords and other configuration items that are very specific to your local environment here.

- `module/SomeModule/config/module.config.php`: Module specific configuration happens here, use only default values and make sure nothing too specific will be entered here.

The EventManager and Bootstrap classes

We will be showing off one of the most beautiful features of Zend Framework 2: The EventManager.

How to do it...

The `EventManager` and `Bootstrap` classes are an essential part of our application, this recipe is all about how to use those two tools:

Using the bootstrap

The bootstrap is in our case the start of a module, whenever a module is requested it will use the `onBootstrap()` method located in the `Module.php` file. Although the method is not required, we usually want this method in our module as it is an easy method of making sure that some instances already exist or are configured before venturing further in our client request.

Starting a session

Sessions are a wonderful way of saving information about a user on a temporary basis. Think about saving the information of a logged-in user, or history on the pages they have been. Once we begin creating an application we find ourselves saving a lot of things in the session.

The first thing we need to do is modify the `/module/Application/config/module.config.php` file, and add another section called `session` to it. Let's assume that we have a completely empty module configuration:

```php
<?php
return array(
  'service_manager' => array(
    // These are the factories needed by the Service
    // Locator to load in the session manager
    'factories' => array(
      'Zend\Session\Config\ConfigInterface' =>
'Zend\Session\Service\SessionConfigFactory',
      'Zend\Session\Storage\StorageInterface' =>
'Zend\Session\Service\SessionStorageFactory',
      'Zend\Session\ManagerInterface' =>
'Zend\Session\Service\SessionManagerFactory',
    ),
    'abstract_factories' => array(
'Zend\Session\Service\ContainerAbstractFactory',
    ),
  ),
```

```
    'session_config' => array(
      // How long can the session be idle for in seconds
      // before it is being invalidated
      'remember_me_seconds' => 3600,

      // What is the name of the session (can be anything)
      'name' => 'some_name',
    ),
    // What kind of session storage do we want to use,
    // only SessionArrayStorage is available at the minute
    'session_storage' => array(
      'type' => 'SessionArrayStorage',
      'options' => array(),
    ),
    // These are session containers we can use to store
    // our information in
    'session_containers' => array(
      'ContainerOne',
      'ContainerTwo',
    ),
  );
```

And that is it. Sessions are now useable in our controllers and models. We have now
created two session containers that we can use to store our information in. We can
access these containers in any Controller or Model that has a service locator available by
doing the following (file: /module/Application/src/Application/Controller/
IndexController.php):

```
<?php

namespace Application;

use Zend\Mvc\Controller\AbstractActionController;

class IndexController extends AbstractController
{
  public function indexAction()
  {
    // Every session container we define receives a
    // SessionContainer\ prefix before the name
    $containerOne = $this->getServiceLocator()
  ->get('SessionContainer\ContainerOne');
  }
}
```

Using the EventManager class

The `EventManager` class is possibly one of the nicest features in the framework. When used properly, it can make our code a lot more dynamic and maintainable without creating spaghetti code.

What it does is relatively simple, for example; a class might have a method called `MethodA`. This `MethodA` has a list of listeners, which are interested in the outcome of that class. When `MethodA` executes, it just runs through its normal procedures, and when finished it just notifies the `EventManager` a specific event has occurred. Now the `EventManager` will trigger all of the interested parties that this event has taken place, and the parties in their turn will execute their code.

Got it? Don't worry if you don't, because this example code might clear things up (file: /`module/Application/src/Application/Model/SwagMachine.php`):

```php
<?php
// Don't forget to add the namespace
namespace Application\Model;

// We shouldn't forget to add these!
use Zend\EventManager\EventManager;

class SwagMachine
{
  // This will hold our EventManager
  private $em;

  public function getEventManager()
  {
    // If there is no EventManager, make one!
    if (!$this->em) {
      $this->em = new EventManager(__CLASS__);
    }

    // Return the EventManager.
    return $this->em;
  }

  public function findSwag($id)
  {
    // Trigger our findSwag.begin event
    // and push our $id variable with it.
    $response = $this->getEventManager()
```

```
                          ->trigger(
                    'findSwag.begin',
                    $this,
                    array(
                       'id' => $id
                    )
              );

              // Make our last response, the final
              // ID if there is a response.
              if ($response->count() > 0)
                 $id = $response->last();

              // ********************************
              // In the meantime important code
              // is happening...
              // ********************************

              // ...And that ends up with the
              // folowing return value:
              $returnValue = 'Original Value ('. $id. ')';

              // Now let's trigger our last
              // event called findSwag.end and
              // give the returnValue as a
              // parameter.
              $this->getEventManager()
                    ->trigger(
                       'findSwag.end',
                       $this,
                       array(
                          'returnValue' => $returnValue
                       )
                    );

              // Now return our value.
              return $returnValue;
        }
   }
```

As we can see we created a little class with two event triggers, `findSwag.begin` and `findSwag.end`, respectively on the beginning of the method, and one on the end of the method. The `findSwag.begin` event will potentially modify the `$id`, and the `findSwag.end` event only parses the `returnValue` object, with no modification possible to the value.

Now let's see the code that implements the triggers (file: `/module/Application/src/Application/Controller/IndexController.php`):

```php
<?php

namespace Application\Controller;

use Zend\Mvc\Controller\AbstractActionController;

class IndexController extends AbstractActionController
{
  public function indexAction()
  {
    // Get our SwagMachine
    $machine = new SwagMachine();

    // Let's attach our first callback,
    // which potentially will increase
    // the $id with 10, which would
    // make it result in 30!
    $machine->getEventManager()
            ->attach(
        'findSwag.begin',
        function(Event $e)
        {
          // Get the ID from our findSwag()
          // method, and add it up with 12.
          return $e->getParam('id') + 10;
        },
        200
    );

    // Now attach our second callback,
    // which potentially will increase
    // the value of $id to 60! We give
    // this a *higher* priority then
    // the previous attached event
    // trigger.
    $machine->getEventManager()
            ->attach(
        'findSwag.begin',
        function(Event $e)
        {
```

```
            // Get the ID from our findSwag()
            // method, and add it up with 15.
            return $e->getParam('id') + 40;
        },
          100
    );


        // Now create a trigger callback
        // for the end event called findSwag.end,
        // which has no specific priority,
        // and will just output to the screen.
        $machine->getEventManager()
                 ->attach(
            'findSwag.end',
            function(Event $e)
            {
               echo 'We are returning: '
                  . $e->getParam('returnValue');
            }
        );


        // Now after defining the triggers,
        // simply try and find our 'Swag'.
        echo $machine->findSwag(20);
    }
}
```

As we can see attaching triggers to events is pretty straightforward. And – if the events are properly documented – can come in handy when we want to, say, modify parameters going into a method (like we did with the `findSwag.begin`), or just outputting the results to a log (like `findSwag.end`).

When we look at what is on our screen, it should be something like this:

We are returning: Original Value (60)

Original Value (60)

The result consists of the top line being the output from the `findSwag.end` trigger, while the value `60` comes from the highest priority trigger, the one with priority `100` (as that is considered a higher priority than `200`).

Changing the View output

Sometimes it is necessary that we have different View outputs, for example when we need to build ourselves a REST service or a SOAP service. Although this can be arranged much simpler by a controller plugin, it is an example on how to hook into the `dispatch` event, and see what is going on there.

Without further ado, let us take a look at the following code snippet:

```
Module.php:
namespace Application;

// We are going to use events, and because we use a MVC,
// we need to use the MvcEvent.
use Zend\Mvc\MvcEvent;

class Module
{
  public function onBootstrap(MvcEvent $e)
  {
    // Get our SharedEventManager from the MvcEvent $e
    // that we got from the method
    $sharedEvents = $e->getApplication()
                      ->getEventManager()
                      ->getSharedManager();

    // Also retrieve the ServiceManager of the
    // application.
    $sm = $e->getApplication()->getServiceManager();

    // Let's propose a new ViewStrategy to our
    // EventManager.
    $sharedEvents->attach(

        // We are attaching the event to this namespace
        // only.
        __NAMESPACE__,

        // We want to attach to this very specific
        // event, the Dispatch event of our controller.
        MvcEvent::EVENT_DISPATCH,
```

```
          // The callback function of the event, used when
          // the event we attached to happens. In our
          // callback we also want our local variable $sm
          // to be available for use.
          function($e) use ($sm)
          {
            // Get our alternate view strategy from the
            // ServiceManager and attach the EventManager
            // to the strategy.
            $strategy = $sm->get('ViewJsonStrategy');
            $view = $sm->get('ViewManager')->getView();
            $strategy->attach($view->getEventManager());
          },

          // We want to give this a priority, so this will
          // get more priority.
          100
      );
  }
```

As we can see it is relatively simple to attach a callback function to the `EventManager` object. In this example we are using `McvEvent::EVENT_DISPATCH` as the event we want to hook in to. So what basically happens is that whenever a controller executes the `onDispatch()` method, this event will be triggered as well. This means that through events we can modify the outcome of a method without actually needing to modify the code.

How it works...

The EventManager class works through a couple of different methods, namely the Observer pattern, the Aspect-Oriented Programming technique (or AOP) and the Event-Driven architecture.

The Observer pattern explained

Simply said the Observer pattern means that there are several interested parties, called listeners that want to know when the application triggers a certain event. When a specific event is triggered, the listeners will be notified so that they can take their necessary actions.

Aspect-Oriented Programming (AOP) explained

If we want to explain what AOP is, we could say that in short it stands for writing clean code that have only function and are as isolated from the rest of the code as possible.

Event-driven architecture explained

The benefit of an Event-driven architecture is that instead of creating bulks of code that need to check every condition, we can easily hook ourselves to different events, which in essence will create a more responsive application.

There's more...

The `EventManager` object is queried through a `PriorityQueue`, which tells us that an important event will generally get a lower value, while an unimportant event a higher value. For example, the highest priority might get priority `-1000` while a quite low priority might get 40. The `EventManager` class then gets the queue through a **FIFO (First In, First Out)** concept, meaning the higher the priority, the lower the number.

2
Translating and Mail Handling

In this chapter we will cover:

- ▶ Translating your application
- ▶ Localizing your application
- ▶ Sending mail
- ▶ Receiving mail

Introduction

An application wouldn't be an application if it couldn't react to the users. One simple but effective way of reacting is obviously displaying text and sending e-mails. Over the last couple of years internationalization (i18n) and localization (l10n) have become increasingly important. Nowadays users expect to be greeted in their language, and even receive automated e-mails from applications in a normal day's work.

Translating your application

In this recipe we will be using the **Zend Framework 2** skeleton as a base, but we will create a new module to show how it all works.

Getting ready

For this recipe, we assume that you have a working Zend Framework 2 application/skeleton in place. To ensure that we can actually run the code that we produce in the recipe, we need to make sure that the `intl` and `gettext` extensions in PHP are enabled.

For translating the strings we will be using **Poedit**, a cross-platform open source application used for translating `gettext` catalogs. The current version is 1.5.5 and can be found at `http://www.poedit.net/` website. We are using gettext as this is a widely used internationalization and localization system for writing multilingual applications. The files generated by Poedit have the extensions `.po` or `.mo`. The `.po` file is used for editing; let's say this is an uncompiled translation file. The `.mo` file is the compiled translation file, which is used in our application.

How to do it...

In this recipe we will talk about getting our application translated, something that is of much use in applications nowadays.

Setting up and checking the essentials

We will assume that we have at least a basic module set up, containing a simple `IndexController` that outputs a simple View.

First thing we want to do is make sure we have a language directory in our module structure as shown in the following code:

```
SampleModule/
  config/
    module.config.php
  language/
  src/
    SampleModule/
      Controller/
        IndexController.php
  view/
    samplemodule/
      index/
        index.phtml
  Module.php
```

In this directory all the `gettext` files will be stored, which will make it easier for us to control them. Now, we have set up a simple folder structure, we need to make sure the module configuration also knows what we are doing. Now, we open up the `module.config.php` and add the following lines to the array:

```
// We want to have our translator available through the
// ServiceManager.
'service_manager' => array(
  'factories' => array(
    // Make our translator available in the
    // ServiceManager so we can retrieve it under the
    // 'translator' key.
    'translator' =>
  'Zend\I18n\Translator\TranslatorServiceFactory',
  ),
),

// Now to configure the Translator
'translator' => array(
  'locale' => 'en_US',

  // We would like using file patterns when matching
  // i18n files, as that makes our lives so much easier,
  // this is default in the skeleton.
  'translation_file_patterns' =>array(
    array(
      // The type of i18n we want to use is gettext.
      'type'     => 'gettext',

      // Here we define our i18n file directory, this is
      // the directory we just made.
      'base_dir' => __DIR__ . '/../language',

      // We want to match our i18n files through this
      // pattern, what will be for example 'nl_NL.mo'.
      'pattern'  => '%s.mo',
    ),
  ),
),
```

With the above configuration we have set up our module exactly the way we need it to look That's it; our module is now set up to use i18n.

Translating strings in the controller

Once we have set up the translator, translating strings couldn't be simpler. In the following example (file: /module/Application/src/Application/Controller/IndexController.php) we will translate the strings in the controller, but this is not good practice if used in the real world and is only shown here as an example:

```php
<?php

// Set our namespace
namespace Application\Controller;

// We need to use the following abstract on our
// controller
use Zend\Mvc\Controller\AbstractActionController;

// Begin our index controller class

class IndexController extends AbstractActionController
{
  // We can use this property to translate the strings,
  // or do some other translator related stuff.
  public $i18n;

  // Lets attach the setLocale to the dispatch event, so
  // it will be run before the action logic is executed
  public function setEventManager(EventManagerInterface $events)
  {
    // Instantiate the i18n through our ServiceLocator.
    parent::setEventManager($events);

    // We want to use this controller in our event
    $c = $this;

    // Attach our locale setting to the dispatch event
    $events->attach(
      'dispatch',

      // Variable $e is a Zend\Mvc\MvcEvent
      function ($e) use ($c)
      {
        // Put our translator in a local property
        $c->i18n = $this->getServiceLocator()
                        ->get('translator');
```

```php
        // while we are here, let's change the locale
        // to Dutch.
        $c->i18n->setLocale('nl_NL');
      },

      // Make sure this event is triggered before the
      // action execution
      100
    );

    // Return our selves
    return $this;
  }

  public function indexAction()
  {
    // Now simply translate this string with our i18n.
    $myTranslatedString = $this->i18n
                                ->translate("And how about me?");

  }
}
```

Translating strings in the View

Translation in the view is even simpler than the controller (and that was pretty simple already). The only thing we need is the string that we want to translate, and that's it. We do the following alterations to the `index.phtml` file:

```php
<?php
  // Translate and display this text.
  echo $this->translate(
      "Hello, I am a translated text!"
  );
```

Translating strings with Poedit

Once we have installed Poedit, we need to set a couple of settings before we can start translating strings. Gettext works with files that are called catalogs. Catalogs are files that represent the source and translated text for one specific language.

First of all we should create a new catalog. After typing the first tab with the project name and language we want to translate (for example, nl-NL), we should go to the second tab called sources paths. That path should contain the path to the sources we would like to translate and is most likely per module, which means the base path should be the module directory.

In the third tab there should be a couple of identifiers to which Poedit can identify which strings should be translated or not. Because we will be using the `translate()` method, we need to make sure that at least the word 'translate' is in the list, we can keep the rest in there however as they won't do any harm.

After we have done all that we can, click on **OK** and choose a location to save our file. This file needs to be saved in the languages directory within the module, and should have a name pattern, for example, `nl_NL.po`, `en_GB.po`, `en_US.po`. The naming convention for the file is `[language]_[COUNTRY]`; some countries (for example, Belgium and Canada) have multiple state languages which also need to be defined.

Once saved, press the **Update** button, which will result in the code being scanned for translatable strings. Now a new list appears with all the strings that can be translated. We can easily put our translation in the **Translation** box and save.

If we have done all that, our screen might look similar to the following screenshot:

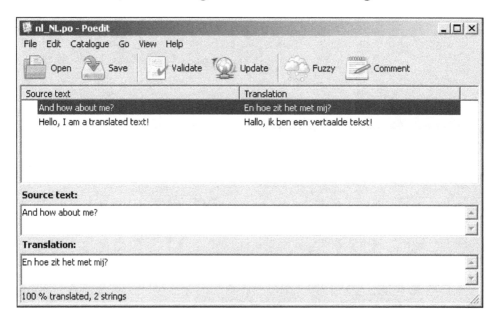

Congratulations, we have now successfully created an i18n application!

How it works...

There are multiple ways of translating strings in ZF2, and all of them are relatively easy to do.

Basic set up of translation in your module

Although the `Application` module has an already set up translation functionality, this might not be what we want to use throughout our application. For instance, if we are (and we will be) using different modules, we wouldn't like to use the translation file in the `Application` module as that would make it less dynamic.

If we would use the same `gettext` file in all our modules, and store that in the `Application` module, this would mean that if we don't use a specific module, the translations would be loaded in anyway. Of course this would mean more memory use which we shouldn't have used.

That is why it is a good idea to set up translation for every module separately.

Translation within ZF2 works, obviously, because of the `Zend\I18n\Translator\` `Translator` class. This class then looks at the configuration and loads up the relevant `Zend\I18n\Translator\Loader` which we require. If found, it will look what the current selected locale, (which we have set through `setLocale()`) is (for example, nl_NL, en_GB, en_US, and so on) and then parse the relevant translation file—`.mo` for gettext, `.ini` for INI, `.php` for PHP Array, and so on—and let is parse through the loader.

Once we call the `translate()` or `translatePlural()` method, the translator will search for the relevant untranslated string in the session. If found, it can easily return the translated string, but in the case of a string which isn't translated, it will just return the untranslated string.

There's more...

Instead of using gettext, there are also several other methods that can be used as translation files. By default ZF2 has the option to use one of the following formats:

PHP array

Although this is a viable and easy method of translating, personally I wouldn't recommend it. My personal experience is that the usage of this method limits the use of the translation files to PHP. For example, gettext is an industry standard, which can be used by many platforms and applications.

In the language directory we would name the PHP files in the format `[language]_[COUNTRY].php`, for example `nl_NL.php`. Our `module.config.php` would need an entry as shown in the following code:

```php
'translator' => array(
  'locale' => 'en_US',
  'translation_file_patterns' =>array(
    array(
      // This is the method we want to use.
      'type' => 'phparray',

      // We tell the config that our translations can be
      // found in the language directory.
      'base_dir' => __DIR__ . '/../language',

      // It will now search for files like en_US.php and
      // nl_NL.php.
      'pattern' => '%s.php',
    ),
  ),
),
```

When this is defined in the `module.config.php` file, the translation itself will work exactly the same, the translation files (for example, `nl_NL.php`) will look similar as in the following code:

```php
<?php

// We need to return an array with the translated
// strings.
return array(

  // The key is the untranslated string, while the value
  // is the translated text.
  'And how about me?'=> 'En hoe zit het met mij?',

  // More translations here [..]
);
```

Gettext

We used this format in the preceding examples, and as we could see they are easily editable by an application such as Poedit. According to Wikipedia, the most commonly used implementation of gettext is GNU gettext. Editing a gettext file is done in a so-called `.po` file where po stands for **portable object**, and once the files are compiled for use they will be placed in a `.mo` file where mo stands for **machine object**.

We can find the translation tool Poedit on the `http://www.poedit.net/` website.

Ini

The way this `ini` works is basically the same as any other method described earlier. The files in the language directory can be named `[locale].ini` (for example, `nl_NL.ini`), and in the `module.config.php` we would have an entry something like shown in the following code:

```
'translator' => array(
  'locale' =>array('en_US', 'nl_NL'),
  'translation_file_patterns' =>array(
    array(
      'type' => 'ini',
      'base_dir' => __DIR__ . '/../language',
      'pattern' => '%s.ini',
    ),
  ),
),
```

As we can see we have defined two locales in our configuration, which means that these two are our available i18n's, but our `en_US` is our fallback locale. The fallback locale is used when no suitable locale can be found. Our translation files (`nl_NL.ini`) would then be looking something like the following example:

```
translation.0.message = "And how about me?"
translation.0.translation = "En hoe zit het met mij?"

translation.1.message = "Hello, I am a translated text!"
translation.1.translation = "Hallo, ik ben een vertaalde
  tekst!"
```

We would always start a translation with `translation.X`, where X is a number which isn't used before. We should think of this as an INI array, similar to how it would work in PHP.

Localizing your application

In this recipe, we will explain localization and its uses. Localization differs from internationalization in the way that localization refers to, for example, numeric, date and time formats, and the use of currency.

How to do it...

In this recipe we will be discussing the ever so important localization of our application.

So it begins

When a user hits our website, we most likely want the user to automatically go to the right language. Although, there are several methods of doing this, we will be using a manual check to see if the language the user prefers is also in our list of languages.

We do this by a couple of simple tricks:

- First, we are getting the `Accept-Language` headers from the HTTP request
- Then we iterate through them and see if one of the languages mentioned in the header matches the language we have
- Lastly, we set the language to the language we have found, or if nothing is found, the fallback language is set

Let's see how this looks in our `Module.php` code:

```
// We will be using a modified version of the default
// Module.php which comes with the Application module on
// the ZF2 Skeleton.
namespace Application;

// onBootStrap requires a McvEvent.
use Zend\Mvc\MvcEvent;
```

First, we need to start off by declaring the namespace (in our case `Application`) as we want the framework to know where to find our code. We then want to make sure we always put all the required classes in the use declaration so that we preload these before we go further in the code.

```
// Start of our Module class
class Module
{
  // Private storage of all our local languages
  // available.
  private $locales;

  /**
   * Retrieves any locale that is available in the
   * language directory. This
   * assumes that our language directory contains files
   * in the format of en_GB.ext, nl_NL.ext.
   */
  private function retrieveLocales()
  {
```

```php
// If we haven't already got all the locales,
// please do it now.
if ($this->locales === null) {
  $handle = opendir(__DIR__ . '/language');
  $locales = array();

 if ($handle !== false) {
   // Loop through the directory
   while (false !== ($entry = readdir($handle))) {
     if ($entry === '..' || $entry === '.') {
       continue;
      }

      // We only want the front part of the filename
      $split = explode('.', $entry);

      // Split[0] should be en_GB if the file is
      // en_GB.ext.
      if (in_array($split[0], $locales) === false) {
        $locales[] = $split[0];
      }

     unset($split);
    }

    // We are done, now close the directory again
    closedir($handle);
  }

  // Make sure the locale is available for next time
  $this->locales = $locales;

  unset($handle, $locales);
 }

 // Return our available locales
 return $this->locales;
}
```

In the `retrieveLocales()` method we are parsing through the languages directory and assume our filenames are called `en_GB.ext`. This way we can parse all the languages easily into one array:

```php
public function onBootstrap(MvcEvent $e)
{
  // Retrieve the HTTP headers of the user's request
  $headers = $e->getApplication()
               ->getRequest()
               ->getHeaders();

  // Get the translator
  $translator = $e->getApplication()
                  ->getServiceManager()
                  ->get('translator');

  // Check if we have a user that accepts specific
  // languages.
  if ($headers->has('Accept-Language')) {
    // Retrieve our locales that our user accepts
    $headerLocales = $headers->get('Accept-Language')
                             ->getPrioritized();

    // Retrieve the locales that we have in our system
    $locales = $this->retrieveLocales();

    // Make sure that our fallback has been set in
    // case we couldn't find a locale
    $translator->setFallbackLocale('en_US');

    // Go through all accepted languages, most of the
    // time this will be only 1 or 2 languages.
    foreach ($headerLocales as $locale) {
      // getLanguage retrieves languages in a en-GB
      // manner, but ZF2 only supports the underscore,
      // like en_GB.
      $language = str_replace(
        '-',
        '_',
        $locale->getLanguage()
      );
```

```
        // See if this is a language we support in our application.
        if (in_array($language, $locales) === true) {
         // We have found our *exact* match
          break;
        }
      }

      // Now set our locale
      $translator->setLocale($language);
    }
  }

  // We can just use the methods that are already in the
  // module.php, let's not repeat that code here.
  public function getConfig() {}

  public function getAutoloaderConfig() {}
  }
```

As we can see in the previous code, what we try to achieve is to see if we have an exact match with any of the language (en_GB, nl_NL) that we support. If we don't have an exact match we already made sure our fallback language (en_US) is being used.

 Please make sure that the intl extension of PHP is enabled in the configuration, otherwise this example will not work correctly.

Localizing currencies

In Zend Framework 2 localizing currencies within a View can be done through the i18n view helper, which comes standard with ZF2. The view helper, which is called CurrencyFormat, can easily be used in the view by the following method call. We do the following alterations to the sometemplate.phtml file:

```
<?php

// We always use $this for accessing a view helper.
echo $this->currencyFormat(45312.56, "EUR", "nl_NL");
```

This piece of code will give the output 45.312,56 €, as we specified to localize to a Euro currency symbol with a Dutch localization format, which in this case is dot for thousands and a comma for decimal separation. We can also leave the locale nl_NL out, and then the CurrencyFormat view helper will automatically select the default locale of the application.

Localizing date/times

To format any dates and times in our applications we can use the `DateFormat` view helper, which is just as easy to use as the currency view helper, but has a few more options to use. We do the following alterations to the `sometemplate.phtml` file.

```php
<?php
echo $this->dateFormat(
    // Format the current UNIX timestamp.
    time(),

    // Our date is to be a LONG date format.
    IntlDateFormatter::LONG,

    // We want to omit the time, defining this is
    // optional as the default is NONE.
    IntlDateFormatter::NONE
);
```

The preceding code will only display the date, which is going to be formatted as `Monday, May 14, 2012 AD`. We can omit giving any parameters, but then nothing will be displayed as the default options are `IntlDateFormatter::NONE`.

How it works...

Localization (l10n) is like internationalization (i18n), a very important aspect of a public application. We spoke about how to make sure your application can be translatable in the last recipe, but now it is time to make sure that we are able to find out how to use any l10n.

Zend Framework 2 works closely together with the i18n/l10n functionality that is already built in PHP. Although, we could use the `Locale` class of PHP separately of the ZF2 classes, it is not recommended as the ZF2 already use the Locale from PHP itself, but provide a much nicer and quicker interface to it.

In the background, however, ZF2 communicates directly with the `Locale` of PHP itself, but if we want to use the more robust functionalities, we should use the ZF2 libraries (which are handy when we are creating multilingual web applications).

Identifying the client language

The previous example code relies on the client browser sending the `Accept-Language` header. Although most modern browsers do this, it's still something that might not always work. Overall it is a pretty good tool to preselect any languages.

Instead of making everything ourselves like shown previously, there is also a very nifty module called `SlmLocale` made by *Jurian Sluiman* (`https://github.com/juriansluiman/SlmLocale`) which we can recommend for detecting and selecting the default locale.

Localizing currencies and dates

Localizing currencies and dates are usually done in View, as it basically is only formatting a piece of information. You can do it somewhere else but we should always be wary to make sure we won't localize anything in, for example, models, as they only should contain logic. In most cases the language is not part of the logic, but simply a nice way of making the view a bit more user friendly.

Sending mail

Sending e-mail through `sendmail` is usually a pretty standard way of working, as it is probably one of the most used ways of transporting e-mail (or proxying the e-mail to an SMTP server) on a Linux-based system. On most Linux servers `sendmail` is already installed and therefore it's very easy to start sending e-mail with that.

That is why we will be discussing this method of sending e-mail first, so that we can start off easy.

How to do it...

In this recipe we will discuss the method of sending mail from within our application.

Transport\Sendmail

Let's take a look at the following example of sending an e-mail through `sendmail`, and although this functionality is placed in a controller, in real life this needs to stay far away from that and be placed safely away in a model:

```php
<?php

namespace Application\Controller;

// We need the following libraries at a minimum to
// send an e-mail.
use Zend\Mail\Message;
use Zend\Mail\Transport\Sendmail;
use Zend\Mvc\Controller\AbstractActionController;

class IndexController extends AbstractActionController
{
```

```php
    public function indexAction()
    {
      // We start off by creating a new Message, which
      // will contain our message body, subject, to,
      // etcetera.
      $message = new Message();

      // Add the options we would like to give the
      // message, in this case we will be creating a text
      // message.
      $message->addFrom('awesome.coder@example.com')
              ->addTo('rookie.coder@example.com')
              ->setSubject('Watch and learn.')
              ->setBody('My wisdom in a message.');

      // Now we have set up our message, let's initialize
      // the transport.
      $sendmail = new Sendmail();

      // Although checking isValid is optional, it is a
      // great way of checking if our message would send
      //if we are getting input from outside.
      if ($message->isValid() === true) {
        // Send the message through sendmail.
        $sendmail->send($message);
      }
    }
  }
}
```

No configuration is usually required for setting up e-mail to be sent through `sendmail`, as it is a mail transport application on the local host only.

Transport\Smtp

We can easily send our e-mail through SMTP if we want (if we know our SMTP server details obviously):

```php
<?php
// Usually this sort of code is defined in the Model,
// but to test it out we can place it in the
// controller as well.
namespace Application\Controller;
```

```php
// We need these classes to initiate a SMTP sending.
use Zend\Mail\Message;
use Zend\Mail\Transport\Smtp;
use Zend\Mail\Transport\SmtpOptions;
use Zend\Mvc\Controller\AbstractActionController;

class IndexController extends AbstractActionController
{
  public function indexAction()
  {
    // First we built up a small message that we want to
    // send off.
    $message = new Message();

    // We need at least one recipient and a message body
    // to send off a message.
    $message->addTo('someone@example.com')
            ->addFrom('developer@example.com')
            ->setSubject('An example message!')
            ->setBody('This is a test message!');

    // Now we created our message we need to set up our
    // SMTP transportation.
    $smtp = new Smtp();

    // Set our authentication and host details of our
    // SMTP server.
    $smtp->setOptions(new SmtpOptions(array(
      // Name represents our domain name.
      'name' => 'ourdomain.com',

      // Host represents the SMTP server that will
      // handle the sending of our mail. This could also
      // be 'localhost' if the sending happens on our
      // local server.
      'host' => 'smtp.somewhere.com',

      // Port is default 25, which in most cases is
      // fine, but this is just to show how we can
      // change it.
      'port' => '1234',
```

```
      // Connection class is the class used for
      // authenticating with the SMTP server. Normally
      // login will suffice, but sometimes the SMTP
      // server requires a PLAIN (plain) or CRAM-MD5
      // (crammd5) authentication method.
      'connection_class' => 'login',

      // This tells the connection_class which
      // properties to set. The default three connection
      // classes only require username and password.
      'connection_config' =>array(
        'username' => 'someuser',
        'password' => 'someplainpassword',
      ),
    )));

    // We have set the options, now let's send the
    // message.
    $smtp->send($message);
  }
}
```

Transport\File

Let's take a look at an example of how to send our e-mail in to files...

```php
<?php
// Usually this sort of code is defined in the Model,
// but to test it out we can place it in the
// controller as well.
namespace Application\Controller;

// We need these classes to initiate a SMTP sending.
use Zend\Mail\Message;
use Zend\Mail\Transport\File;
use Zend\Mail\Transport\FileOptions;
use Zend\Mvc\Controller\AbstractActionController;

class IndexController extends AbstractActionController
{
  public function indexAction()
  {
```

```
    // First we create our simple message.
    $message = new Message();

    // Set the essential fields send it off.
    $message->addTo('someone@example.com')
            ->addFrom('developer@example.com')
            ->setSubject('An example message!')
            ->setBody('This is a test message!');

    // Now we will initialize our File transport.
     $file = new File();

    // Set the options for the File transport.
    $file->setOptions(new FileOptions(array(
        // We want to save our e-mail in the /tmp path,
        // this can be anything where we have write
        // permission on.
        'path' => '/tmp',

        // Define our callback, which will be ran when
        // the e-mail is being saved to our system. This
        // also called an anonymous function, as it
        // isn't defined as a normal method.
        'callback' = function(File $file) {

        // We want to return a name in which the file
        // should be saved, which should be a unique.
        return 'mail_'. time(). '.txt';
      }
    )));

    // Now send off the message.
    $file->send($message);
    }
}
```

After sending the e-mail the file transporter will create a file which might look something like `mail_453421020.txt`. We have given `/tmp` as the directory to where this file should be saved, we should look there to see if our file exists.

Of course we can do anything in the callback function, for example, we can check if a certain file exists, or pull a name from the database. The options are endless.

How it works...

Zend Framework 2 needs a minimum of two objects to make the sending of e-mails work. First is the `Zend\Mail\Message` object, which is used to completely define the message that needs to be sent. We can define `to`, `cc`, `bcc`, and `from` addresses in this object. The object is also used to set the body of the message; this can be either HTML or plain-text, completely depending on our own requirements.

Then as a second object we need a class that implements the `Zend\Mail\Transport\TransportInterface` class that handles the actual sending of the e-mail. This class only (at the moment anyway) has a `send(Mail\Message $message)` method defined that needs to be added when we implement the transport.

What happens after defining the two objects is that we give our `Message` object to our `Transport` object and tell it to send it off. How the sending is handled, is obviously determined by the `Transport` object.

Sending mail through SMTP

Transporting mail through SMTP might not sound familiar to us, but it is a common method of sending e-mail through another system. Think about a desktop e-mail client that retrieves our e-mail from another server. When we send off an e-mail from that same e-mail client, it could very well be that we will be using SMTP to send it off. In a nutshell, SMTP is sending an e-mail to another mail server that then handles our mail transportation for us.

Sending mail through files

Although not used often, there are e-mail senders that simply pick up clear text files with the complete message which needs sending from a specific directory, and send them off. And obviously if we have no way of testing our actual e-mail sending, this is also a great way of testing if the system works.

Receiving mail

Now, let's deal with the part of receiving mails.

Getting ready

In this recipe we will be giving examples on the different methods of connecting to mailbox through ZF2, and therefore it would be nice if we had access to a mailbox we connect to. Of course this is not required, but it sure adds to the fun to have an actual working mailbox.

How to do it...

We will now discuss receiving e-mail within an application, which can be useful on some occasions.

Connecting to an IMAP mail server

The first method of connecting to a mail server is through IMAP. The protocol basically lets us connect to the mail server, and looking in the different folders on the server if there are unread e-mails.

Let's take a look at our example:

```php
<?php
// Usually this sort of code is defined in the Model,
// but to test it out we can place it in the
// controller as well.
namespace Application\Controller;

// We need these classes to initiate an IMAP connection
use Zend\Mail\Storage\Imap;
use Zend\Mvc\Controller\AbstractActionController;

class IndexController extends AbstractActionController
{
  public function indexAction()
  {

    // We will create a new IMAP connection here:
    // host: user/password: The username and password
    // to use.
    $mail = new Imap(array(
    // Refers to the host where we want to connect to.
    'host' => 'imap.example.com',

    // The username/password to connect to the server
    // with.
    'user' => 'some_user',
    'password' => 'some_password',

    // Do we want to explicitly use a secure
    // connection.
    'ssl' => true,
```

```php
        // If we want to use a port that is different to
        // the default port, we can do that here.
        'port' => 1234,

        // Specify the folder we want to use, if none
        // given it will always use INBOX. This will also
        // work with the Mbox and Maildir protocol.
        'folder' => 'Some_Folder',
    ));

    // We want to parse through all our e-mails.
    foreach ($mail as $message) {
        // Display the from and subject line.
        echo $message->from. ': '. $message->subject;
      }
    }
  }
}
```

Connecting to a POP3 mail server

Let's take a look at our simple connection example:

```php
<?php
// Usually this sort of code is defined in the Model,
// but to test it out we can place it in the
// controller as well.
namespace Application\Controller;

// We need these classes to initiate a POP3 connection
use Zend\Mail\Storage\Pop3;
use Zend\Mvc\Controller\AbstractActionController;

class IndexController extends AbstractActionController
{
  public function indexAction()
  {
    // We will create a new POP3 connection here
    $mail = new Pop3(array(
      // Refers to the host where we want to connect
      // to
      'host' => 'pop3.example.com',
```

```php
    // The username/password to connect to the
    // server with.
    'user' => 'some_user',
    'password' => 'some_password',

    // Do we want to explicitly use a secure
    // connection.
    'ssl' => true,

    // If we want to use a port that is different to
    // the default port, we can do that here.
    'port' => 4321
  ));

  // We want to parse through all our e-mails.
  foreach ($mail as $message) {
    // Display the from and subject line.
    echo $message->from. ': '. $message->subject;
  }
  }
}
```

Working with flags on IMAP or Maildir connections

Flags are attributes that are attached to a message in which we can see the specific property of a message. To put it simpler, it can tell us, for example, if a message is read or answered. We can either get the flags from a message by using the `getFlags()` method, or by using the `hasFlag()` method. The flags that can be used are to be found in the `Zend\Mail\Storage` class.

Maildir++ Quota system

Let's take a look at the following example:

```php
<?php
// Usually this sort of code is defined in the Model,
// but to test it out we can place it in the
// controller as well.
namespace Application\Controller;

// We need these classes to initiate a Maildir storage
// connection
use Zend\Mail\Storage\Maildir;
use Zend\Mvc\Controller\AbstractActionController;
```

```
class IndexController extends AbstractActionController
{
  public function indexAction()
  {
    // Open up a new Maildir connection
    $mail = new Maildir(array(
      // Our mail folder on the server.
      'dirname' => '/home/user/.mymail/'
    ));

    if ($mail->checkQuota() === true) {
      // We are over quote, let's check what we are
      // using!

      // Give us extended information about the quota.
      $quota = $mail->checkQuota(true);

      // Normalise the string if we are over the
      // quota.
      $overQuota = $quota['over_quota'] ? 'Yes' : 'No';

      // Display the information.
      echo "
        -- QUOTA --
        Total quota size: {$quota['quota']['size']}
        Total quota objects: {$quota['quota']['count']}
        -- USE --
        Total used size: {$quota['size']}
        Total used objects: {$quota['count']}
        Are we over quota: {$overQuota}
      ";
    }
  }
}
```

Keeping a connection alive

The following is an example of the use of NOOP:

```
<?php
// Usually this sort of code is defined in the Model,
// but to test it out we can place it in the
// controller as well.
namespace Application\Controller;
```

```php
// We need these classes to initiate a IMAP connection
use Zend\Mail\Storage\IMAP;
use Zend\Mvc\Controller\AbstractActionController;

class IndexController extends AbstractActionController
{
  public function indexAction()
  {
    // Open up a new connection to the mail server.
    $mail = new Imap(array(
      'host' => 'imap.example.com',
      'user' => 'some_user',
      'password' => 'some_password'
  ));

  // Loop through the messages.
  foreach ($mail as $message) {
    /** Do stuff which takes a lot of time.. **/

    // Now let the server know we are still alive..
    $mail->noop();

    /** Do some more stuff..  **/

    // Let the server know again we are still here..
    $mail->noop();
    }
  }
}
```

The tricky part here is when to use `noop()`, as sometimes it is really hard to predict which process is taking the longest. That is why we created a special example to show you how easy it is to make sure that `noop()` is being carried out regularly, until we are done with our process.

We can do this by utilizing `register_tick_function`, which enables us to call a specific process on every tick. What we'll do is create a class that handles `noop()`, and executes it every 5 minutes until we say it should stop:

```php
<?php

// We can make this anything we want, we just decided on
// this though
namespace Application\System;
```

```php
// Lets call our class this
class NoopTick
{
  // This is our Zend\Mail\Storage\Imap which is a
  // static so we can call from outside the context of
  // this class without instantiating the class
  private static $imap;

  // This is the time value in seconds of the next time
  // we want to execute our noop functionality
  private static $newTime;

  // This is the amount of seconds between noop
  // executions, which in this case is 5 minutes
  private static $timeInBetween = 300;

  // This is our main method, which will only call the
  // noop method
  public static function tickTock()
  {
    if (time() >= self::$newTime) {
      // We can execute our noop now
      self::$imap->noop();

      // Now set the new time
      self::$newTime = (time() + self::$timeInBetween);
    }
  }

  // Now we want to have a method that starts up the
  // noop triggering
  public static function start($imap)
  {
    // Set our imap storage to use
    self::$imap = $imap;

    // Now we register the tick function, which executes
    // every tick of the process, we will use the class
    // NoopTicks (this class) and method 'tickTock'
    register_tick_function(array(
      'Application\System\NoopTick','tickTock'
    ));
  }
```

```
// And we now unregister our tick function again when
// we are done with our operation
public static function stop()
{
    // Unregister our tick function again, mind that we
    // don't have to provide our class name here
    unregister_tick_function('tickTock');
}
}
```

If we now are at a piece of code that requires us to execute for a long time, we can easily call the `start()` method to do the NOOP'ing for us as shown in the following line of code:

```
Application\System\NoopTick::start($imapStorage);
```

And when we are done, we simply `stop()` the NOOP'ing again as shown in the following line of code:

```
Application\System\NoopTick::stop();
```

How it works...

Mailboxes are being connected to; however we will see them in ZF2 as storage objects. Because of this we can easily parse through all the messages, and in some cases are able to manipulate messages on the storage, such as copying or moving them. We need to remember that messages are always read only, and storages are the ones that can be manipulated. It is possible, for example, to create and delete a folder, but never edit an existing message.

The only writeable functionality we have for manipulating a message is `appendMessage()`, which appends a message to the storage. But when it is stored, we are not able to edit it again.

Connecting to a POP3 server

Connecting with a POP3 server is very similar to using an IMAP server (handy, isn't it?). The only major difference is normally with a POP3 server the messages disappear from the mail server after retrieving them, unless we specifically tell the server otherwise.

About the Maildir++ Quota system

Maildir++ is an extended version of Maildir, but still compatible with the normal Maildir routine and supports quota systems. This is a very useful system because of its quota and how it stores messages (on filesystem). This is used in a lot of companies, but obviously it comes with its own troubles. For example, when trying to write/copy a message on a Maildir++ server, it can be that this will throw an exception because we are over the system quota.

That is why that – unless you know for certain Maildir++ isn't used – to implement a check for the quota before trying to do any write-based functionality.

Keeping the connection alive

Once a connection has been opened and parsing through messages is instantiated, the connection has a fair chance of closing once too much time has passed. At that point it is always wise to implement a `No Operation` command, or NOOP. This will tell the mail server that we are still there, but are just doing something else at the moment.

There's more...

There is obviously a lot more to tell about retrieving e-mails from a mail server, and it would be a great adventure to find them all out. Unfortunately, going in for all the advanced details would almost be a book in itself, so we have put down a couple of subjects which are worth exploring:

- ▶ Caching instances (see also *Chapter 8, Optimizing Performance*)
- ▶ Reading HTML messages, or multi part messages with attachments
- ▶ Advanced use of folders on IMAP/Maildir/Mbox
- ▶ Protocol class extensions
- ▶ Setting up e-mail box settings through the configuration

3
Handling and Decorating Forms

In this chapter we will cover:

- ▸ Creating forms
- ▸ Using form view helpers
- ▸ Creating a custom form element and form view helper

Introduction

In this chapter we will be discussing forms, and specifically the generation and manipulation of them. Forms are a very important part in the communication with the user, as it is one of the ways to receive information from the user. It is also a great way to use forms to do a lot of validation of the elements by combining JavaScript and PHP. If we then can make it so that it looks great as well, why would we not do that?

Creating forms

This recipe involves different ways of creating forms, and after that we will talk about how elements are added to the form. In the last part of this recipe we will discuss how to validate forms, and the best way of accomplishing this.

Getting ready...

A basic ZF2 skeleton application, with at least one module where we can work in, is necessary to create and output forms.

If we want to use form annotations, we also require `Doctrine\Common` to be initiated in the skeleton as it has the parsing engine to parse the annotations. If we are using composer (which comes with the Zend Framework 2 skeleton) we can simply update our `composer.json` by adding the following line to the required section:

```
"doctrine/common": ">=2.1",
```

 Make sure the comma on the end of the line is only there when there are still lines beneath it. If there are no lines coming after this line except for a closing brace, please refrain from adding the comma as it will fail the process.

Next is to run the composer update to make sure it gets installed, by using a command like the following:

```
php composer.phar update
```

If we are not using a composer we are best off looking at the Doctrine project website (`http://www.doctrine-project.org/projects/common.html`) to find more information on how to install this.

How to do it...

We'll first be talking about creating forms and elements, after that we'll talk about adding filters and validations.

Creating a basic form

A form always needs to be one of the following:

▸ A class that is extended from the `Zend\Form` class

▸ A class that is using the `Zend\Form\Annotation` defining method

Defining a form that is extended from Zend\Form

We will start with defining a form from the first method, by extending it from the `Zend\Form` class. This is probably the easiest way to begin if we are new in Zend Framework 2 (ZF2).

The basic idea is that our form class should extend from the `Zend\Form` class, and has at least a `__construct` method that defines our elements.

Let's take a look at the following example in the `/module/Application/src/Application/Form/NormalForm.php` file:

```php
<?php

// We define our namespace here
namespace Application\Form;

// We need to use this to create an extend
use Zend\Form\Form;

// Starting class definition, extending from Zend\Form
class NormalForm extends Form
{
    // Define our constructor that sets up our elements
    public function __construct($name = null)
    {
        // Create the form with the following name/id
        parent::__construct($name);
    }
}
```

If we now go to our controller, say `IndexController` of the `Application` module we can output the form to View by doing the following in file `/module/Application/src/Application/Controller/IndexController.php`:

```php
<?php

// Namespace of the controller
namespace Application\Controller;

// Use the following classes at a minimum
use Zend\Mvc\Controller\AbstractActionController;
use Application\Form\NormalForm;
use Zend\View\Model\ViewModel;

// Begin our class definition
class IndexController extends AbstractActionController
{
    // Set up our indexAction,  in which we want to
    // display our form.
    public function indexAction()
    {
        // Initialize our form
```

```php
    $form = new NormalForm();

    // Return the view model to the user, with the
    // attached form
    return new ViewModel(array(
        'form' =>  $form
    ));
  }
}
```

If we now take a look at our view script, we can see that we have the variable available. We will now output the form actually to the screen by the following example (`/module/Application/view/application/index/index.phtml`):

```php
<?php
  // Output the opening FORM tag: <form>
  echo $this->form()->openTag($this->form);

  // Output the formatted elements of the form
  echo $this->formCollection($this->form);

  // Output the closing FROM tag </form>
  echo $this->form()->closeTag();
```

The output of this code example will be somewhat like the following:

```
<form action="" method="POST" name="normalform"
   id="normalform"></form>
```

This tells us that the instantiating went well, and that it is fully functional. As we also can see the name that we defined (`"normalform"`) is coming back as the `name` and `id` of the form.

Defining a form that uses the Zend\Form\Annotation

Let's take a look at an empty form (`/module/Application/src/Application/Form/AnnotationForm.php`) in an annotated form:

```php
<?php

// We first define our namespace as usual
namespace Application\Form;

// We need to use this otherwise it will not parse the
// elements correctly.
use Zend\Form\Annotation;
```

```php
/**
 * We want to name this form annotationform, which is
 * why we use the tag below, defining the name.
 *
 * @Annotation\Name("annotationform")
 *
 * A hydrator makes sure our framework can 'read' the
 * properties in our object, in this case we tell our
 * annotation engine that we have an object that needs
 * its properties read. There is probably a more
 * technical, accurate way of explaining it, but let's
 * just keep it to this for now.
 *
 * @Annotation\Hydrator(
 *      "Zend\Stdlib\Hydrator\ObjectProperty
 * ")
 */
class AnnotationForm
{
  /**
   * If we want to exclude properties in our form just
   * use the Exclude annotation.
   *
   * @Annotation\Exclude()
   */
  public $id;
}
```

If we now want to begin outputting our form to our user we can do that in a similar way to the normal form (luckily). The first thing we need to do for that is actually assigning the form to the View (/module/Application/src/Application/Controller/IndexController.php) again, which is the only thing that is a bit different to the normal form creation.

```php
<?php

// Namespace of the controller
namespace Application\Controller;

// Use the following classes at a minimum
use Zend\Mvc\Controller\AbstractActionController;
use Application\Form\AnnotationForm;
use Zend\Form\Annotation\AnnotationBuilder;
use Zend\View\Model\ViewModel;
```

```
// Begin our class definition
class IndexController extends AbstractActionController
{

  // Set up our indexAction,  in which we want to
  // display our form.
  public function indexAction()
  {
    // Set up the output model
    $viewModel = new ViewModel;

    // Instantiate the AnnotationBuilder which will
    // create the actual form object
    $builder = new AnnotationBuilder();

    // Instantiate our annotated form
    $annotationForm = new AnnotationForm();

    // Now let the annotation builder create the form
    // from scratch
    $form = $builder->createForm($annotationForm);

    // Set our form to be the form variable in the view
    $viewModel->setVariable('form', $form);

    // Return the view model to the user
    return $viewModel;
  }
}
```

If we now want to output the form to our View (file `/module/Application/view/application/index/index.phtml`), we can simply do the same as we did with the other form:

```
<?php
  // Output the opening FORM tag: <form>
  echo $this->form()->openTag($this->form);

  // Output the formatted elements of the form
  echo $this->formCollection($this->form);

  // Output the closing FROM tag </form>
  echo $this->form()->closeTag();
```

The HTML output of this example would result in the following:

```
<form action="" method="POST" name="annotationform"
  id="annotationform"></form>
```

Adding elements to a Zend\Form extend form

Creating elements in this kind of form is pretty simple, let's see what it looks like with a short example (file `/module/Application/src/Form/NormalForm.php`):

```php
// Adding a simple input text field
public function __construct($name = null)
{
  // Create the form with the following name/id
  parent::__construct($name);

  $this->add(array(
    // Specifying the name of the field
    'name' => 'name',

    // The type of field we want to show
    'type' => 'Zend\Form\Element\Text',

    // Any extra attributes we can give the element
    'attributes' => array(
      // If there is no text we will display the
      // placeholder
      'placeholder' => 'Your name here...',

      // Tell the validator if the element is required
      // or not
      'required' => 'required',
    ),

    // Any extra options we can define
    'options' => array(
      // What is the label we want to give this element
      'label' => 'What is your name?',
    ),
  ));
}
```

Adding elements to an annotated form

Let's take an example of an annotated element creation:

```
class AnnotationForm
{
 /**
   * Add two filters to this element.
   *
   * @Annotation\Filter({"name": "StringTrim"})
   * @Annotation\Filter({"name": "StripTags"})
   *
   * Add a validator to make sure the string length
   * isn't going to be longer than 50, but also not
   * smaller than 5.
   *
   * @Annotation\Validator({
   *     "name": "StringLength",
   *     "options":{
   *         "min": 5,
   *         "max": 50,
   *         "encoding": "UTF-8"
   * }})
   *
   *
   * Set this element to be required.
   *
   * @Annotation\Required(true)
   *
   * Set the attributes for the element
   *
   * @Annotation\Attributes({
   *     "type": "text",
   *     "placeholder": "Your name here...",
   * })
   *
   * Set the options of this element.
   *
   * @Annotation\Options({
   *     "label": "What is your name?"
   * })
   */
   public $name;
```

Validating form input

One of the most important things of having forms is to use the data in our application, because why else would we have forms to begin with?

Let's go and create a simple model (`/module/Application/src/Application/Model/SampleModel.php`) that we can use for an example later on, but has absolutely no other use for this recipe at all.

```php
<?php

namespace Application\Model;

class SampleModel
{
  public function doStuff($array) {
    return true;
  }
}
```

As we can see this model doesn't do anything at all, but we need it later on.

We have now created our own form extension, so it is time to create our `InputFilter` class which will filter and validate the values that we are going to put in the form, and attach to our form through `setInputFilter` later on (we'll edit the file `/module/Application/src/Application/Form/NormalFormValidator.php`):

```php
<?php

// Of course our namespace first
namespace Application\Form;

// As this will be an input filter, we need the
// following imports to make it work
use Zend\InputFilter\Factory as InputFilterFactory;
use Zend\InputFilter\InputFilter;
use Zend\InputFilter\InputFilterAwareInterface;
use Zend\InputFilter\InputFilterInterface;

// Create our class, which should be implementing the
// InputFilterAwareInterface if we want to attach it to
// the form later on
class NormalFormValidator implements
InputFilterAwareInterface
{
```

```
    // This is the input filter that we will create
    protected $inputFilter;

    // This method is required by the implementation, but
    // we will just throw an exception instead of setting
    //the input filter as we don't want anyone to override
    // us
    public function setInputFilter(InputFilterInterface
    $inputFilter)
    {
        // We want to make sure that we cannot set an input
        // filter, as we already do that ourselves
        throw new \Exception("Cannot set input filter.");
    }
```

We have now started creating our input filter class, and already created one of the two required methods of `InputFilterAwareInterface`. Now, let's continue further to the point where we implement the second method, and construct the actual filter:

```
    // This is the second method that is required by the
    // interface
    public function getInputFilter()
    {
        // If our input filter doesn't exist yet, create one
        if ($this->inputFilter === null) {
            // Create the input filter which we will put in our
            // property later
            $inputFilter = new InputFilter();

            // Also instantiate our factory so we can get more
            // filters at ease
            $factory = new InputFilterFactory();

            // Let's add a filter for our name Element in our
            // form
            $inputFilter->add($factory->createInput(array(
                // This is the element is applies to
                'name' => 'name',

                // We want no one to skip this field, we need it
                'required' => true,

                // Now we are defining the filters, which make
```

```
            // sure that no malicious or invalid characters
            // are supplied
            'filters' => array(
              // Make sure no tags are in our value, which
              // could make our system vulnerable for hacks
              array('name' => 'StripTags'),

              // We want to make sure our string doesn't
              // have any leading or trailing spaced
              array('name' => 'StringTrim'),
            ),

            // Validators make the form generate errors when
            // the data is invalid, filters only filter
            'validators' => array(
              array (
                // We want to add a validator that checks the
                // length of the string received
                'name' => 'StringLength',
                'options' => array(
                  // Check if the string is in UTF-8 encoding
                  // and between the 5 and 50 characters long
                  'encoding' => 'UTF-8',
                  'min' => '5',
                  'max' => 50',
                ),
              ),
            ),
          )));
```

We just added a simple validator that makes sure the length of the string is not smaller than 5 and not longer than 50 characters, and of course in our case we also want UTF-8 characters, but obviously we can either drop this or change the character set if we need to.

We'll add a simple password field validator and filter now, but the next one after that checks if the repeat_password field is identical in value to our password field. Personally, I really like that validator because of its simplicity and yet being powerful enough to take away some manual labor.

```
      // We are doing the same trick again for the
      // password, so we can just skip over this, as this
      // was just necessary for the one after this one.
      $inputFilter->add($factory->createInput(array(
        'name' => 'password',
```

```
        'filters' => array(
          array('name' => 'StripTags'),
          array('name' => 'StringTrim'),
        ),
        'validators' => array(
          array (
            'name' => 'StringLength',
            'options' => array(
              'encoding' => 'UTF-8',
              'min' => '5',
            ),
          ),
        ),
))));

// And here is the great piece of validation we
// wanted to show off. This validator checks if the
// value of the given element is identical to
// another fields value. This way we don't have to
// manually check if the password is the same as the
// repeat password field.
$inputFilter->add($factory->createInput(array(
    'name' => 'password_verify',
    'filters' => array(
      // The usual filters, as we almost always want
      // to be sure it contains no tags or
      //trailing/leading spaces
      array('name' => 'StripTags'),
      array('name' => 'StringTrim'),
    ),
    'validators' => array(
      array(
        'name' => 'identical',
        'options' => array(
          'token' => 'password',
        ),
      ),
    ),
))));
```

After that nifty validator we will now add a simple e-mail validator, which will also have a not empty validator that checks if the field is empty or not. We will use the following code for e-mail validation:

```
// Email validator works perfectly, especially if we
// don't want to trust any client side validation
// (which we shouldn't)
$inputFilter->add($factory->createInput(array(
  'name' => 'email',
  'filters' => array(
    array('name' => 'StripTags'),
    array('name' => 'StringTrim'),
  ),
  'validators' => array(
    array (
      'name' => 'StringLength',
      'options' => array(
      'encoding' => 'UTF-8',
      'min' => '5',
      'max' => '250',
      ),
    ),
    array(
      // Don't you hate it when you get email
      // addresses that are not valid? Well, no
      // more as we can simply validate on that
      // as well.
      'name' => 'EmailAddress',
      'options' => array(
      'messages' => array(
        // We can even leave a neat little error
        // message to display
        'emailAddressInvalidFormat' => 'Your email seems to
         be invalid',
      )
      ),
    ),
    array(
      // This validator makes sure the email
      // address is not left empty. And although we
      // can simply say this field is required,
      // this will give us the opportunity to leave
      // a nice error message that is relevant to
```

```
        // the user as well
        'name' => 'NotEmpty',
        'options' => array(
        'messages' => array(
            // This message is displayed when the
            // field is empty, instead of a 'field
            // required' message as we didn't make
            // the field required
            'isEmpty' => 'I am sorry, your email is required',
        )
        ),
    ),
  ),
))));
```

Even dates are not a problem for validation, and we can make it even this good that we are only allowed to select ranges of dates as well, which in some cases (for example 18+ websites) is nice to have.

```
        $inputFilter->add($factory->createInput(array(
        'name' => 'birthdate',
        'required' => true,
        'filters' => array(
          array('name' => 'StripTags'),
          array('name' => 'StringTrim'),
        ),
        'validators' => array(
          array(
            'name' => 'Between',
            'options' => array(
              // We can define the ranges of dates
              // here, min and max are both optional,
              // as long as one of them at least exists
              'min' => '1900-01-01',
              'max' => '2013-01-01',
            ),
          ),
        ),
      ))));

      // Set the property
      $this->inputFilter = $inputFilter;
    }
```

```
      // End of our method, just return our created input
      // filter now
      return $this->inputFilter;
   }
}
```

Let's jump in immediately and take a look at a simple example that uses our `normalform` like before (`/module/Application/src/Application/Controller/IndexController.php`):

```php
<?php

// Define the namespace of our controller
namespace Application\Controller;

// We need to use the following classes
use Zend\Mvc\Controller\AbstractActionController;
use Zend\View\Model\ViewModel;
use Application\Form\NormalForm;
use Application\Form\NormalFormValidator;
use Application\Model\SampleModel;

// Set up our class definition
class IndexController extends AbstractActionController
{
   // We want to parse/display our form on the index
   public function indexAction()
   {
      // Initialize our form
      $form = new NormalForm();

      // Set our request in a local variable for easier
      // access
      $request = $this->getRequest();

      if ($request->isPost() === true) {
         // Create a new form validator
         $formValidator = new NormalFormValidator();

         // Set the input filter of the form to the form
         // validator
         $form->setInputFilter(
             $formValidator->getInputFilter()
         );
```

```
        // Set the data from the post to the form
        $form->setData($request->getPost());

        // Check with the form validator if the form is
        // valid or not
        if ($form->isValid() === true) {
            // Do some Model stuff, like saving, this is
            // just an empty model we created to show what
            // probably would happen after a validation
            // success.
            $user = new SampleModel();

            // Get *only* the filtered data from the form
            $user->doStuff($form->getData());

            // Done with this, unset it
            unset($user);
        }
    }

    // Return the view model to the user
    return newViewModel(array(
        'form' => $form
    ));
    }
}
```

How it works...

Let's understand how we achieved what we achieved.

Setting up a basic form

The preceding first example, creating a form class that extended from Zend\Form is the bare minimum to set a form up. As we can see, this form doesn't have any elements or properties set up at the moment, the only thing it defines is the name/id of the DOM element of the form object. What we did after that is first initialize the form, and then assign the ViewModel to it as that will be the View that is going to be outputted to the screen.

The only thing that we did in the example is output the <form> tag first—with all its properties, such as method, action, and etcetera. The second thing is that we do output all the elements in the form (which in this case are none), and as a last thing that we do is we output the end form tag </form>, which now ends our form declaration.

If we open up a browser and look at our code, we will see no much different than we saw before, probably an empty page. However, when we open out the source code of that page (in Firefox this is right-clicking on the page and clicking on **View Page Source**) we see that we actually did instantiate the form properly in HTML.

Our basic form instantiation is now concluded, if we want a more advanced, but more attractive as well, way of defining our form, we should continue reading the next bit as well.

Setting up an annotated form

Defining an annotated form is a bit different than a normal form, the main difference being that an annotated form is just a class with properties, which isn't extended from any other class, while the other method requires us to extend from the Zend\Form class. In the preceding example, we first created a very simple and empty form using the annotation method. We can also see that we require a Hydrator to make the Annotation Engine understand what we are on about, but we do not need to extend the class, so we are free to do what we want there.

The only thing we should be wary about is that every element that we require in our form, should have the property access set to public, otherwise technically the Annotation Engine can't pick it up. We don't have to make getters/setters for the properties (unless we want to use it for ourselves), as the Annotation Engine just uses the public properties directly.

Using the form in a controller is slightly different then a normal form, because when we would just instantiate the class and use that as a form it would end up as an error. The class needs to go through AnnotationBuilder first to actually build up the form. That is why we need to do createForm(), which then outputs a form.

This will output nothing visible, but if we then look at the page source code (in Firefox this is achieved by right-clicking on the page and then clicking on **View Page Source**) we see that we have a new form opening tag <form> and a form closing tag </form>. In between those tags you can see that our form, which was named annotationform is now set as the name and the id of the form.

Some developers find this way of defining a form a bit overdone, because in the end it might seem that we are not adding a lot of usability, which in all fairness is a bit true. It all depends on the situation when something is better than other methods, but in all fairness it is a pretty slick way of defining forms!

Adding elements to the form

If we have set up the forms in the same way as the previous method then we have two ways of defining elements to the form. The first one will be the normal method of defining a form, which is an extension of Zend\Form\Form, just like the form example in the *How to do it...* section, and the annotation form of it, like the second example of an AnnotationForm in the *How to do it...* section.

The first example assumes that we are defining `__construct()` in a form that has been extended from `Zend\Form\Form`. What it does is call the `add()` method of `Zend\Form\Form` where we give the method an array of methods (yes, you can just as well create the whole form in a configuration file!).

It is as simple as that to add an element. Obviously, there are more elements available, and all of them have their own options and attributes, but we won't go into all of those as it would be way too long to discuss.

Adding elements to an annotated form is both easy and complicated. It is easy because in the most basic idea it only requires you to add a property to the class, which is simple enough. But if you want to go further than that, and add validations or filters, it requires you to add Annotation comments above the property.

As we could see in the preceding example, the way of defining elements through annotation isn't particularly difficult, it is just that we need to know which `@Annotation` to use. When setting attributes/options or sometimes other annotations, we will see the two curly braces `{}`, which represent an object in JavaScript and is used for JSON.

Obviously, it isn't that difficult, but it requires us to have a bit of a different train of thought.

Forms, filtering, and validation

A normal form that extends from `Zend\Form\Form` creates the elements by looking into `$this->elements` of the form, where all the form elements will be stored. Once it triggers the form renderer, all these elements will be decorated into real HTML tags. In an annotated form the process of transforming the class into HTML requires one more step, which is put simply transforming the annotated class into a frame that looks like a `Zend\Form\Form` extended class. That way we can use the build form from the annotated class just like a real form object.

When we post the form (you don't necessarily need to specify a post as it is already a `POST` by default), we let the form check if the values are correct, and more importantly we want to make sure that we are getting the values that we expect.

Not only is validating forms important security wise but also filtering wise. If we put multiple filters on our elements (for example, string trim and strip tags), we would like to have that all ready for us to use instead of using the filters afterwards again. Obviously, the bigger issue is having our application protected from malicious users, and to validate the input of the user.

As we can see in the very last preceding code example, we first create the form and we will then look if the user tried posting the form. If this is true, we will set up our form validator that we created specifically for that form. We then assign the request data (this is what the user filled in our form) to the form. After we assigned the data to the form we call `isValid()` to see if the data is valid or not. If it is, we assign the filtered data with `getData()` to our sample model to save it.

Lastly, we will assign the form to the view again so we can display any validation errors that happened through the validation process. Easy!

We can also define a form solely through the configuration, this is called form creation by factory and we encourage you to see how that works, as it is also a great way of creating forms.

To add some form security, one would be looking to add a `Zend\Form\Element\Csrf` element to our form, which looks at the source of the form to make sure no Cross-site Request Forgeries (CSRF) are done. This is a unique key that is added to the form that is used in the validation process. We would even go as far as to say that it is recommended to create a base form that has the CSRF element already added to it, so that we don't have to worry that we forgot or not, as long as we extend from the base form.

Using form view helpers

Instead of the Zend Framework 1 Decorators (where it was a key in the creation and rendering of forms) we now know in Zend Framework 2 that it is better to use different view helpers and renderers to render the forms.

View helpers are very important tools to a developer, here we will discuss how to use them in our code.

Form

We do the following alterations to a view script called `example-viewscript.phtml`:

```php
<?php

// Just open and close the form tag
echo $this->form()->openTag();
echo $this->form()->closeTag();


// Use a form to pull the attributes from
echo $this->form()->openTag($formObject);


/** Do stuff in between **/

// Close the tag again with no form object attached
echo $this->form->closeTag();
```

The rendered output of this would be the following:

```
<form></form>
```

FormButton

We do the following alterations to a view script called `example-viewscript.phtml`:

```php
<?php

// First we create a simple button (this is better done
// inside a form/controller or model of course)
$buttonElement = new \Zend\Form\Element\Button(
  // This is the name of the button
  'somebutton'
);

// Render the button immediately through the button
// element
echo $this->formButton($buttonElement);

// Render the button in 3 steps:
// Step 1, the opening tag: Can be called without a
// parameter, and array of attributes or an instance of
// Zend\Form\Element
echo $this->formButton()->openTag($buttonElement);

// Step 2, the inner HTML: Output our custom inner HTML
// here, like the label of the button
echo '<span>Life is short, click now!</span>';

// Step 3, the closing tag: Close the tag again.
echo $this->formButton()->closeTag();
```

If we now look at the rendered output, it should look like the following:

```
<button name="somebutton"><span>Life is short, click
  now!</span></button>
```

FormCaptcha

We do the following alterations to a view script called `example-viewscript.phtml`:

```php
<?php
$captchaElement = new \Zend\Form\Element\Captcha(array(
  // What is the name of the element
  'name' => 'captcha',
```

```php
  // Now add some captcha specific configuration
  'captcha' => array(
    // The class is necessary for the factory to know
    // what kind of captcha we want. The options are
    // Dumb, Figlet, Image and the famous ReCaptcha
    'class' => 'Dumb',
  )
));


// That's all folks, the $captchaElement needs to be of
// the instance Zend\Captcha\AdapterInterface to make it
// work
echo $this->formCaptcha($captchaElement);
```

FormCheckbox

We do the following alterations to a view script called `example-viewscript.phtml`:

```php
<?php
// Create a simple checkbox with the name someCheckbox
$checkboxElement = new \Zend\Form\Element\Checkbox(
  'someCheckbox');

// The $checkboxElement needs to be of the instance
// Zend\Form\Element\Checkbox to make it work
echo $this->formCheckbox($checkboxElement);
```

The rendered output would be something like the following:

```html
<input type="checkbox" name="someCheckbox" />
```

FormCollection

We do the following alterations to a view script called `example-viewscript.phtml`:

```php
<?php

$object = new \Zend\Form\Element\Collection(
  // The name of the collection
  'someCollection',

  // Some additional options
  array(
    // The label we want to display
    'label' => 'collectionSample',
```

```
        // Should the collection create a template of our
        // template element so that we easily duplicate it
        'should_create_template' => true,

        // Are we allowed to add new elements
        'allow_add' => true,

        // And how many elements do we want to render
        'count' => 2,

        // Define the target element to render
        'target_element' =>array(
          'type' => 'Zend\Form\Element\Text'
        ),
));

    // The $object can be of any class that implements the
    // Zend\Form\ElementInterface
    echo $this->formCollection($object);
```

This has the incredibly vague rendered output like the following:

```
<fieldset><legend>collectionSample</legend><span data-template="&lt;in
put&#x20;type&#x3D;&quot;text&quot;&#x20;name&#x3D;&quot;__index__&quo
t;&#x20;value&#x3D;&quot;&quot;&gt;"></span>
```

This is enough for the collection to know what it needs to do, as in this case it holds the template of our `input` field.

FormColor

We do the following alterations to a view script called `example-viewscript.phtml`:

```php
<?php

// We want a simple text field for our color
$color = new \Zend\Form\Element\Color('someColor');

// The $color can be of any class that implements the
// Zend\Form\ElementInterface
echo $this->formColor($color);
```

FormDate, FormDateTime, and FormDateTimeLocal

We do the following alterations to a view script called `example-viewscript.phtml`:

```php
<?php
// Create a date element
$date = new \Zend\Form\Element\Date('someDateElement');

// The $date can be of any class that implements the
// Zend\Form\ElementInterface
echo $this->formDate($date);
echo $this->formDateTime($date);
echo $this->formDateTimeLocal($date);
```

FormEmail

We do the following alterations to a view script called `example-viewscript.phtml`:

```php
<?php
// Add a simple text field
$element = new \Zend\Form\Element\Text('someElement');

// The $email can be of any class that implements the
// Zend\Form\ElementInterface
echo $this->formEmail($email);
```

FormFile

We do the following alterations to a view script called `example-viewscript.phtml`:

```php
<?php

// The $file can be of any class that implements the
// Zend\Form\ElementInterface
echo $this->formFile($file);
```

FormHidden

We do the following alterations to a view script called `example-viewscript.phtml`:

```php
<?php

// The $hidden can be of any class that implements the
// Zend\Form\ElementInterface
echo $this->formHidden($hidden);
```

FormImage

We do the following alterations to a view script called `example-viewscript.phtml`:

```php
<?php

// The $image can be of any class that implements the
// Zend\Form\ElementInterface
$image->setAttrib('src', '/our/image.jpg');

echo $this->formImage($image);
```

FormInput

We do the following alterations to a view script called `example-viewscript.phtml`:

```php
<?php

// The $input can be of any class that implements the
// Zend\Form\ElementInterface
echo $this->formInput($input);
```

FormLabel

We do the following alterations to a view script called `example-viewscript.phtml`:

```php
<?php
// Create a simple text input
$element = new \Zend\Form\Element\Text('someElement');

// 1. This will declare the label immediately. The
// $element can be of any class that implements
// the Zend\Form\ElementInterface

echo $this->formLabel($element);

// 2. Or we can declare the formLabel like this
echo $this->formLabel()->openTag(array(
    'for' => 'someElement',
));
```

```php
// We are putting some html in between the
// <label></label> tags
echo "Some output in between!";
// Close the tag again
echo $this->formLabel()->closeTag();

// 3. Or as a last method, there is still some other way
// to define the element. This will prepend
// $someOtherElement with our $element's label. Instead
// of prepend we can also use append.
echo $this->formLabel(
    $element,
    $someOtherElement,
    'prepend'
);
```

FormElementErrors

We do the following alterations to a view script called `example-viewscript.phtml`:

```php
<?php

// Create a simple text box
$element = new \Zend\Form\Element\Text('someInput');

// 1. Just display the element errors, with the optional
// attributes added as the second parameter.
// The $element can be of any class that implements the
// Zend\Form\ElementInterface
echo $this->formElementErrors($element, array(
    'class' => 'element-error',
    'id' => 'error_three'
));

// 2. Custom formatted validation error messages.
echo $this->formElementErrors()
        ->setMessageOpenFormat('<a href="/help-me">')
        ->setMessageSeparatorString(
                '</a><a href="/help-me">'
        )->setMessageCloseString('</a>')
        ->render($element);
```

How it works...

The form element view helpers are a great way to render your form elements. In the previous version of Zend Framework this was done by form decorators, which were different to view helpers in ZF2 because they were used before the form reached the view script. The way it now works is that a form is still in its original state when it reaches the view script, which means we can fully manipulate the form to the way our layout looks. This creates a more dynamic output where we can define layouts per view script (something that was very hard to achieve in ZF1).

Because the form element view helpers are in charge of the rendering of the element in the view script, they can also be more in touch with the requirements of the developer. All in all, this is a great way to create a form that looks and works brilliantly.

Various view helpers and/or renderers can be used in order to create the perfect layout. There are a lot of standard view helpers that can be used in order to mark up your form.

Form

This helper renders your `<form />` tag, which can—if wanted—pull some attributes out of our `Zend\Form` object to use as attributes.

The attributes the form helper (by parsing the form) supports is `accept-charset`, `action`, `autocomplete`, `enctype`, `method`, `name`, `novalidate`, and `target`.

FormButton

We can render our `<button />` tag with this helper, and obviously it can work in different ways, just like we want it to. It can either render the button through `Zend\Form\Element` or do it in a three-step way, where we can make up our own stuff in between.

The attributes the `FormButton` helper (by parsing the `Element`) supports are `name`, `autofocus`, `disabled`, `form`, `formaction`, `formenctype`, `formmethod`, `formnovalidate`, `formtarget`, `type`, and `value`.

FormCaptcha

`Captcha` is used to prevent users from submitting forms without validating that they are human. Occasionally, we will get forms that will be spammed with ridiculous amounts of spam. That is why we, nowadays, have this little tool that generates a small image, which is an automated Turing test to find out if we are human or not.

This helper can only be rendered through a `Zend\Element\Captcha` object, so there is not a lot to further explain on that.

FormCheckbox

This helper will render two elements by default:

- The `<input />` element of type `checkbox`
- An `<input />` element of type `hidden`, with the value of the checkbox state

It creates the hidden input because a checkbox will not get posted if it is left unchecked, so we can imagine the consequences of form validation when an element is not there. That is why there is always a hidden field that is rendered before the checkbox element to make sure at least something is posted.

Also, the checkbox element has some other cool options such as using a hidden field. For the developers out there that have any experience with checkboxes, they can sigh in relief as an unchecked checkbox is never posted by the browser in a form.

That is why a hidden field is placed before the checkbox element with the same name as the checkbox element, but filled with the unchecked value. This means that whenever the checkbox isn't checked, it will send the hidden field's value, otherwise the checkbox checked value would override that.

FormCollection

This helper is used, for example, when we want to render a complete form in one instance. If we use a `Zend\Form` object as parameter to this helper, we will get a completely rendered HTML form returned. If we use `Zend\Form\Element\Collection` on the other hand, we will get a fully rendered HTML collection back, with template if required.

FormColor

This is a HTML5 element, which is a `<input />` element with the type color. It creates an input form in which the user can select a color, or when used in a non HTML5 compatible browsers, it will simply display an input field.

FormDate, FormDateTime, and FormDateTimeLocal

Another HTML5 element that outputs an `<input />` element with the type date is FormDate. In an HTML5 compatible browser it will usually output a calendar dropdown where the user can select the date they like, in a non-compatible browser it again just shows a text input field.

FormEmail

This HTML5 field is a nice field that ships in an HTML5 compatible browser with a nifty validation which checks if the typed value is an actual e-mail address or not. It is best not to rely on that too much and still validate the values ourselves just in case the user isn't using an HTML5 compatible browser.

The attributes that can be set on a `FormEmail` are `name`, `autocomplete`, `autofocus`, `disabled`, `form`, `list`, `maxlength`, `multiple`, `pattern`, `placeholder`, `readonly`, `required`, `size`, `type`, and `value`.

FormFile

The `FormFile` helper is helpful for displaying an `<input />` with the type file. Not only does it show the input element, but it can also prepare the element for any upload progress we want to monitor. Like many other element helpers, this helper also supports the attributes: `name`, `accept`, `autofocus`, `disabled`, `form`, `multiple`, `required`, `type`, and `value`.

FormHidden

The hidden `<input />` field is handy for posting information to the application without requiring user input. Nothing fancy about this helper, but it does support the `name`, `disabled`, `form`, `type`, and `value` attributes.

FormImage

The `FormImage <input />` tag is mainly used as a replacement for a **Submit** button in a form. It is simple to use and only requires the `src` attribute (the location of the image). It also supports the `name`, `alt` (recommended), `autofocus`, `disabled`, `form`, `formaction`, `formenctype`, `formmethod`, `formnovalidate`, `formtarget`, `height`, `type`, and `width` attributes.

FormInput

A `FormInput` is a simple `<input />` element that renders an element for us by naturally selecting the type. Not necessarily recommended to use this one as it is pretty generic and would have its flaws (for example, when it isn't an `input` tag that is required).

FormLabel

If we want to display a `<label />`, then using this helper is the perfect thing, as we can declare the position of the label (`FormLabel::APPEND` or `FormLabel::PREPEND`) and we can also add the content of the label. It only supports `for` and `form` as attributes.

FormElementErrors

This helper is used for displaying form validation errors. By default, this will be displayed underneath the form element, but with this helper we can customize the display of this error a bit more.

Creating a custom form element and form view helper

Once we keep on developing in Zend Framework 2, and our application keeps on growing, the more it is necessary to stop copy-pasting and just replace all those replicating bits by a class that simply outputs what we want. In ZF2 this can be done easily through view helpers.

How to do it...

In this recipe we'll create our own form element, and corresponding view helper to display it.

Creating the new element

All we have to do is set the type of the element, and that's it. We do the following alterations to the `/module/Application/src/Application/Form/Element/Video.php` file, let's take a look on what the code should look like:

```php
<?php

// Set our namespace just right
namespace Application\Form\Element;

// We need to extend from the base element
use Zend\Form\Element;

// Set the class name, and make sure we extend from the
// base element
class Video extends Element
{
  // The type of the element is video, 'nuff said.
  protected $attributes = array(
      'type' => 'video',
  );
}
```

As we can see this is a pretty easy job to do, and we have now successfully created a new element to use in ZF2.

Creating the new view helper

The view helper will create the HTML element that we just declared, so let's take a look on how the view helper should look like in the `/module/Application/src/Application/Form/View/Helper/FormVideo.php` file:

```php
<?php

namespace Application\Form\View\Helper;

use Zend\Form\View\Helper\AbstractHelper;
use Zend\Form\ElementInterface;
use Zend\Form\Exception;

class FormVideo extends AbstractHelper
{
  /**
    * Attributes valid for the video tag
    *
    * @var array
    */
  protected $validTagAttributes = array(
    'autoplay' => true,
    'controls' => true,
    'height' => true,
    'loop' => true,
    'muted' => true,
    'poster' => true,
    'preload' => true,
    'src' => true,
    'width' => true,
  );
```

First, we added the attributes that this element can have, this is necessary to make sure we are not declaring attributes that don't exist (although that would in most cases not be that much of a problem).

```php
  /**
    * Invoke helper as functor
    *
    * Proxies to {@link render()}.
    *
    * @param ElementInterface|null $element
    * @return string|FormInput
    */
```

```php
public function __invoke(ElementInterface $element = null)
{
  if (!$element) {
    return $this;
  }

  return $this->render($element);
}
```

The preceding __invoke method is created so that we don't have to initialize the class before we want to call the view helper. This way we can use it in the view scripts by using formVideo(), instead of instantiating a new FormVideo() first.

```php
/**
 * Creates the <source> element for use in the <video>
 * element.
 *
 * @param array|string $src Can either be an
 *                          array of strings, or a
 *                          string alone.
 * @return string
 */
protected function createSourcesString($src)
{
  $retval = '';

  if (is_array($src) === true) {
    foreach ($src as $tmpSrc) {
      $retval .= $this->createSourcesString($tmpSrc);
    }
  } else {
   $retval = sprintf(
     '<source src="%s">',
      $src
   );
  }

  return $retval;
}
```

The `createSourcesString` method gets the string or array containing all our video URLs. As said this can be either a string or an array, which in the last case will just iterate through the array and output the string with the source tags.

```php
/**
 * Render a form <video /> element from the provided
 * $element
 *
 * @param ElementInterface $element
 * @throws Exception\DomainException
 * @return string
 */
public function render(ElementInterface $element)
{
  // Get the src attribute of the element
  $src = $element->getAttribute('src');

  // Check if the src is null or empty, in that case
  // throw an error as we can 't play a video without
  // a video link!
  if ($src === null || $src === '') {
    throw new Exception\DomainException(sprintf(
      '%s requires that the element has an assigned'.
      'src; none discovered',
      __METHOD__
    ));
  }

  // Get the attributes from the element
  $attributes = $element->getAttributes();

  // Unset the src as we don't need it right here as
  // we render it separately
  unset($attributes['src']);

  // Return our rendered object
  return sprintf(
      '<video %s>%s</video>',
      $this->createAttributesString($attributes),
      $this->createSourcesString($src)
  );
}
}
```

Adding view helper to the configuration

Now we need to add the view helper to the module configuration to make sure the view helper can be found in the view scripts. We can simply do this by adding another method to our /module/Application/Module.php as shown in the following code:

```
class Module
{
  public function getViewHelperConfig()
  {
    return array(
        'invokables' => array(
        // Add our extra view helper to render our video
        'formVideo' => 'Application\Form\View\Helper\FormVideo',
      )
    );
  }
}
```

We didn't put the whole class in there, as that would be too much useless information for this example. The idea however is that we can simply put this method in our Module.php to make sure our view helper will be located.

Displaying the new element

We do the following alterations to the /module/Application/view/application/index/video.phtml file:

```
<?php
use Application\Form\Element\Video;

// Declare a new video element
$video = new Video();

// Set the attribute src for this element
$video->setAttribute('src', array(
// These are some public video urls from
// w3schools.com
  'http://www.w3schools.com/html/mov_bbb.mp4',
  'http://www.w3schools.com/html/mov_bbb.ogg',
  ));

// We also want to begin auto playing once loaded
$video->setAttribute('autoplay', true);

// Output the formatted element
echo $this->formVideo($video);
```

We have now created a new form element, and a new form view helper!

How it works...

Creating the element

First of all we need to create the new element before we work with it within ZF2. This can be easily done by extending from the base element of `Zend\Form\Element`.

Next up is the view helper as we want to make sure that our element is also rendered correctly to the user. As our element is not of any existing type (otherwise this would be a very boring recipe) we need to make sure that we create a view helper for ourselves.

The last bit of our code is creating the actual render method, which—as the name tells us—renders the actual HTML object.

In our case, we want to trigger an exception whenever the `src` has not been defined, as without it, this would be a pretty useless HTML element. Now, we have everything set up, we can use the element either in a form, or on its own in the view script. In the last example, we just declared the form element in the view script to show how it can work; however using logic in the view script is not something that is advised to do as we want to keep the view as clean as possible, and only output code with it. Anything remotely unrelated to HTML or the output to the user should go in the controller or models.

What did we do

What we did is create a new form element, which was supposed to be a `<video />` tag, a new HTML5 element. This video tag can have several attributes, one of it being an `src`. The `src` in this case tells the video element where we can find the video that we want to play.

A good reason to create our own view helper would be if we have a piece of HTML that is constantly recurring throughout our application (think of a tool tip or a help text), and which only needs to be copy-pasted and changed some properties for it to work. To save us time and space (code and readability wise), we would transform this into a simple view helper class that replicates the exact object, which we can transform by adding options to it.

In the end, we simply use the `formVideo` view helper in the view script to actually render the object for us, which takes a bit of a load off our hands by rendering a piece of code that is easy to replicate.

4
Using View

In this chapter we will cover:

- ► Working with View
- ► Using view helpers
- ► Creating a global layout template
- ► Creating reusable Views
- ► Using view strategies/renderers
- ► Using context switching for a different output
- ► Writing a custom view strategy/renderer

Introduction

In this chapter we are going to talk about using View, something that we have briefly mentioned in a couple of places before. View was created for the benefit of the developer, to strictly separate everything frontend with everything backend. This way backend developers can focus on controllers and models, while frontend developers can work in Views. Another great benefit of View is that View decides how the data is being outputted, so in most cases this would be HTML, in other cases maybe JSON and so on.

We will show you in the last recipe of the chapter how to make our own customizations as well, so that we fully understand how everything works.

Working with View

View can be considered very important as it actually renders the content that is being outputted to the browser of the user. Therefore, we can assume that knowing how View works is very useful when creating web applications.

Getting ready

For this recipe it is beneficial if we have the Zend Framework 2 skeleton set up and ready to work. We will do some basic things to get you started, so no additional extensions are necessary for this.

How to do it...

We are going to output content to the browser by using `PhpRenderer` which is the default view strategy used.

Configure the ViewManager

We make the following alterations to the `/module/Application/config/module.config.php` file:

```php
<?php
return array(
    'view_manager' =>array(
        // We want to show the user if the page is not found
        'display_not_found_reason' => true,

        // We want to display exceptions when the occur
        'display_exceptions' => true,

        // This defines the doctype we want to use in our
        // output
        'doctype' => 'HTML5',

        // Here we define the error templates
        'not_found_template' => 'error/404',
        'exception_template' => 'error/index',

        // Create out template mapping
        'template_map' =>array(
```

```
        // This is where the global layout resides
        'layout/layout' => __DIR__ . '/../view/layout/layout.phtml',

        // This defines where we can find the templates
        // for the error messages
        'error/404' => __DIR__ . '/../view/error/404.phtml',
        'error/index' => __DIR__ . '/../view/error/index.phtml',
    ),

    // The template path stack tells our view manager
    // where our templates are stored
    'template_path_stack' =>array(
        __DIR__ . '/../view',
    ),
  ),
);
```

Set variables in the ViewModel instance

Now we have set up the view manager; we can go to our controller and add the following to the import section of our controller.

```
use Zend\View\Model\ViewModel;
```

Now we can use the `ViewModel` instance for the `PhpRenderer` in our action controller. Let's do that now:

```
public function someAction()
{
  $view = new ViewModel();

  // One way of setting a variable in the view
  $view->setVariable('example', 'Output this to user');

  return $view;
}
```

It is as easy as that; simply return the `ViewModel` instance after we are done defining everything we want.

Mark up the template file

Now it is time for the last part before we are done, and that is to create a template file that needs to be rendered. We can do this by first creating a file (as an example) in the `view/index` folder called `some.phtml` (as our action in the previous example was called like that).

Now we will just do a simple bit where we output the variable we have just declared in the `ViewModel` instance.

```
<h1><?php echo $this->example ?></h1>
```

And that's it. We have now outputted our variable example that we declared in our `ViewModel` instance in the action. There are also more ways of setting variables to the view, for example by declaring the variables as the first argument of the `ViewModel` constructor.

```
$view = new ViewModel(array(
    'variable_one' => 'Some Variable',
    'variable_two' => 'Some other Variable',
));
```

Or, if we want to set multiple variables at the same time, but not during the constructor execution time we can also perform the following:

```
// First we have the view instantiated
$view = new ViewModel();

// And now we assign a lot of variables at the same time
$view->setVariables(array(
    'variable_one' => 'Some Variable',
    'variable_two' => 'Some other Variable',
));
```

Now, as we are experts in outputting variables to the View, I say it is time for some cake!

How it works...

View works with a couple of different methods before the requested output is returned to the user.

The configuration

If we would use the Zend Framework 2 skeleton application, then this would already be in there by default, but let's assume we have nothing configured just yet and we are working blindly. The first thing we want to do is make sure that `ViewManager` is set up through the **Dependency Injection** (**DI**). We can do this by opening the module configuration called `module.config.php` in the `config` folder (assuming that we are using the standard layout) and add the `ViewManager` configuration there.

One more thing before we move on is that `template_path_stack` works by searching for templates in the base directories that are defined in the array. Then it will descend further in those directories searching for the template using the format we described.

For example, `IndexController` with `aboutAction` would resolve, by default to, the path `view/index/about.phtml` in our case.

The ViewModel instance

The `ViewModel` instance is usually only used in the controller and is basically a container that holds all the information that needs to be outputted to the user. Although the `ViewModel` instance is technically possible to use anywhere else, it wouldn't be a good practice to do so, as the controller's main responsibility is handling the models and Views. If we go and change the nature of a controller, the application would become significantly harder to maintain.

The `ViewModel` instance itself has no other purpose than to keep track of all the variables we want to output to the user, and other options like the template we'd like to use, and if we want to render the main layout or not.

What happens next is that the `ViewModel` instance will be picked up by `ViewStrategy` and `ViewRenderer` to be used in the output.

Almost every `ViewStrategy` has its own type of `ViewModel` designed for that specific purpose. That way we can easily use another `ViewModel` instance and create a different kind of output to the user.

The ViewStrategy class

The `ViewStrategy` class is used to determine if and how we are going to output our content to the user. The way this works is that –usually- the `ViewStrategy` first determines if the `ViewModel` instance it receives is compatible with the model they expect it to be. It does this by attaching a `ViewEvent` to the `EVENT_RENDERER` event, which will be triggered when the framework is searching for a suitable renderer.

The `ViewStrategy` at that point checks if the model is compatible, and if it is it will return a suitable `ViewRenderer`, if not, it will return null. Then after the framework has done its thing and rendered the output (more about this in the The ViewRenderer helper section) it will trigger another `ViewEvent` named `EVENT_RESPONSE`.

This event is basically the end point that the `ViewStrategy` class can do before the output is send to the user. In this `ViewEvent` the `ViewStrategy` class can make the last amendments to the response if necessary. We should think about the content type, extra headers, or some other last minute stuff.

A simplified version of the process is displayed as follows:

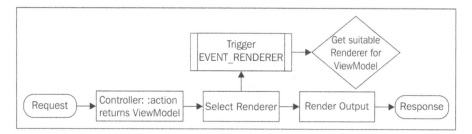

The ViewRenderer helper

The renderer is used in between the two events mentioned in the `ViewStrategy` class before, and it does exactly like you expect it to be; it renders the output. It takes the data from the `ViewModel` instance and renders the output according to that. It usually requires a view script like the PHTML files that `PhpRenderer` uses, but sometimes it doesn't require any script at all and it will just render the output completely by itself (think about outputting in a JSON format for example). We will cover how to use different ViewStrategy and ViewRenderer later in this chapter.

```
Using view helpers
```

The more we add complexity to View, the less we are able to maintain it properly. That is why we get the logic out, and put it in our View outside the view script itself, and place them in the so-called view helpers.

Getting ready

For this recipe it is recommended that the Zend Framework 2 skeleton application is used. We won't require any out of the ordinary extensions for this recipe.

How to do it...

In Zend Framework 2 there are a bunch of default view helpers that comes with the framework. Let's look at a bunch of them to see what they do and how to use them.

The BasePath view helper

The `BasePath` view helper, is a very easy view helper to use, for example:

```
<!--
    The following will prepend the URL with the base path
    which can be /website/public/js/script.js e or /js/script.js.
    The path is something for the basePath to decide.
-->
```

```
<script src="<?php echo $this->basePath('js/script.js'); ?>">
</script>
```

The Doctype view helper

We make the following alterations to the /module/Application/config/module. config.php file:

```
<?php
// This is just a snippet of the code that needs to be
// there for doctype to be defined.
return array(
  'view_manager' => array(
    'doctype' => 'HTML5',
  ),
);
```

Then in the view script, we can do the following to output the well-formed doctype helper:

```
<?php echo $this->doctype(); ?>
```

The URL view helper

The URL view helper is very handy to use if we want to generate a URL for a specific route, for example:

```
<a href="<?php echo $this->url(
    // This is the name we gave the route in our
    //configuration file
    'route-name',

    // Give the parameters for the URL, such as the
    // controller, action or any parameters that should
    // be added to the URL
    array(
      'controller' => 'someController',
      'action' => 'anotherAction',
      'id' => 1234,
    )); ?>">Go to this page!</a>
```

The Partial view helper

First of all it is important to make sure that we actually have a template (/view/ application/index/partial/partial.phtml) that is used as partial content.

```
<div><?php echo $this->partial_variable; ?></div>
```

We then can go to our normal layout and use the `Partial` view helper to add our extra template (`/view/application/index/index.phtml`):

```
<div>Some Content.</div>

<div>
  <?php echo $this->partial(
    './partial/partial.phtml',
    array(
      'partial_variable' => 'Partial content!',
    )
  ); ?>
</div>
```

How it works...

Once we get in to serious development, view helpers cannot be missed. They make sure our code doesn't turn into a spaghetti by keeping the logic as separate as possible (for example) from the HTML. View helpers only work in the view scripts (and if the current view strategy support it, but let's presume it does), so all the examples we give below are only relevant to `.phtml` files in the view directory.

If we have a view helper we can usually instantly use them in the view by calling:

```
$this->someViewHelper('some-parameter');
```

This works because without first instantiating the view helper because the `someViewHelper` class has an `__invoke()` method defined. This means that it can be called without first needing to be instantiated.

However, sometimes we have view helpers that cannot be used through the invocation shown before; they actually need to be constructed first. This can then be done by performing the following:

```
$helper = $this->someViewHelper();
$helper->someMethod('some-parameter');
```

A single view helper can also have multiple public methods available which is mostly used for grouping functionality together. For example a (non-existing in Zend Framework 2) view helper called `Person` might have `getAddress($person)` and `getName($person)` as public methods, which then could be called by using the invoke shown as follows:

```
echo $this->person()->getAddress($person);
echo $this->person()->getName($person);
```

Zend\View\Helper\AbstractHelper

Technically `Zend\View\Helper\AbstractHelper` is not a view helper, but we mention it anyway as this is the class we want to extend with if we would want to create our own view helper. It implements a couple of methods that are required for a view helper class to work correctly.

The BasePath view helper explained

The `BasePath` view helper can be really helpful if we use a custom structure to our application and the public folder is not on the base of a website folder, that is, `/website/public`. We can then use `BasePath` to let it decide where we are. The `BasePath` view helper is usually used more often for static assets such as, images, style sheets, and scripts, which is great to make sure the application stays robust under the change or a root URL.

The Doctype view helper explained

The `Doctype` is a very useful view helper as we tend to forget how those `Doctype` helpers were build up again. Instead of looking on the Internet to find out how to declare them again, we can now just use this little gem.

You can specify the `Doctype` helper whenever you like, but it would be wise to do this in the configuration of your view manager to make sure the rest of the application also knows what `Doctype` we are using (sometimes they just want to output different things then).

The valid `Doctype` view helpers we can use are:

- XHTML11
- XHTML1_STRICT
- XHTML1_TRANSITIONAL
- XHTML1_FRAMESET
- XHTML1_RDFA
- XHTML1_RDFA11
- XHTML_BASIC1
- XHTML5
- HTML4_STRICT
- HTML4_LOOSE
- HTML4_FRAMESET
- HTML5

Setting the `Doctype` helper is essential for other view helpers because they (for example in the case of form elements) make rendering decisions based on the selected type. For example a `HTML4_*` doctype might render an input fields as `<input type="text"></input>` while an `XHTML1_STRICT` would render it as `<input type="text" />`. The `Doctype` helper is more than essential if we want to use the validation service of the W3C.

The URL view helper explained

A nifty little thing the URL view helper is, it builds up URL's depending on named route that we have defined in our configuration. This means that if we want to build up a correctly formed URL we can use this view helper to build it up for us.

The Partial view helper explained

The `Partial` view helper is particularly helpful when we want to divide our layout into different parts, something that is always useful if we want to make sure our templates are maintainable and in a condition to re-use them in multiple places.

The directory we store the partial views in is not strictly set, but it is recommended to place them in a location where we can find them whenever we require them.

There's more...

We only discussed four view helpers which are default in Zend Framework 2, however there are tons more view helpers in the framework by default which are just as useful as well. Personally I would recommend looking through those as well and get to know them a bit as most of them are quite interesting even if you would never use them. Especially the `Cycle`, `Gravatar`, `HeadStyle`, and `HeadTitle` view helpers can come in handy when we are building a HTML page set up.

A complete list of the view helpers is always available in the official Zend Framework 2 documentation.

Creating a global layout template

The view scripts can be very dynamic but most of the time we need a global template that we want to wrap around the output from our `Action` view scripts. This recipe will explain exactly how to do that, and also tells us how that would work.

Getting ready

For this recipe a working Zend Framework 2 skeleton application is needed as we will do some creating and editing of some files which are used in there.

How to do it...

The following is how we set about achieving this:

Creating the main layout file

Let's now create the main file `/module/Application/view/layout/layout.phtml` we use to create our layout:

```
<!-- first of all we want to output the doctype -->
<?php echo $this->doctype(); ?>

<!-- now we add the HTML tag -->
<html>

<!-- enter our head tag -->
<head>
  <!-- we want to output in UTF-8 -->
  <meta charset="utf-8">

  <!-- let's use the headTitle View Helper to output our
       website title -->
  <?php echo $this->headTitle('Awesome website!') ?>

  <!-- make sure mobile browsers get the best of it with
       the use of the headMeta View Helper, and setting
       the viewport -->
  <?php echo $this->headMeta()->appendName(
    'viewport',
    'width=device-width, initial-scale=1.0'
  ) ?>

  <!-- add a favicon.ico file reference for older
       versions of Internet Explorer, as that doesn't
       pick it up by itself -->
  <?php echo $this->headLink(array(
    'rel' => 'shortcut icon',
    'type' => 'image/vnd.microsoft.icon',

    // Use the basePath to find our public folder
    'href' => $this->basePath('/images/favicon.ico')
  )) ?>
```

```
<!-- add a style sheet to our template -->
<?php echo $this->headStyle()->appendStyle(
  $this->basePath('/style.css')
); ?>

<!-- now add a javascript that we need as well, which
     is only used by Internet Explorer version less
     than 9 -->
<?php echo $this->headScript()->prependFile(
  $this->basePath('/script.js'),

  // Non HTML5 browsers need a type set for script
  // tags
  'text/javascript',

  // Add the extra script conditions
  array(
    'conditional' => 'lt IE 9',
  )
); ?>
</head>
```

We have now set up the head tag successfully, and used a lot of the view helpers available to make our lives a little bit easier when it comes to adding head-related tags.

Now let's set up a simple code body and see what we can do there:

```
<!-- let's continue with our body tag now -->
<body>
  <!-- output our main content from our actions -->
  <?php echo $this->content ?>

  <!-- render any inline scripts that we have -->
  <?php echo $this->inlineScript(); ?>
</body>

<!-- we are done here -->
</html>
```

Well that was it, once we output the content variable, it basically renders the content generated from the controller/action output.

Creating the error templates

The error files are easily created as they only require a couple of things. Let's create the /module/Application/view/error/404.phtml file first as that one is fairly straight forward.

```
<h1>404: Page not found!</h1>

<p>
  <!-- show the message of the 404 error, generated by
       the framework -->
  <?php echo $this->message; ?>
</p>

<!-- there is usually also a separate reason attached,
     which (if exists) we want to show as well -->
<?php
  if (isset($this->reason) && $this->reason) {
    switch ($this->reason) {
      case 'error-controller-cannot-dispatch':
        $reason = 'Could not get dispatch controller.';
        break;
      case 'error-controller-invalid':
        $reason = 'Undispatchablecontroller.';
        break;
      case 'error-controller-not-found':
        $reason = 'Controller could not be found.';
        break;
      case 'error-router-no-match':
        $reason = 'URL could not be matched by router.';
        break;
      default:
        $reason = 'Unknown';
        break;
    }

    // Now show the reason to the user
    echo $reason;
  }
```

There are more variables we can use to show the user what went wrong in the routing, and we can also see, for example, what they requested, but usually those are more for development only and not for a production server as we don't want to expose too much data.

Now let's create the file (`/module/Application/view/error/index.phtml`) that
will be shown when we end up having an exception, one of the favorite things of a developer
(not, obviously).

```php
<h1>An error occurred!</h1>

<p>
  <!-- show the error message, that is the least we can
       do -->
  <?php echo $this->message; ?>
</p>

<!-- now show the exception, if we have turned this on
     in the configuration -->
<?php
  if (isset($this->display_exceptions)
    && $this->display_exceptions) :
    // Now let's see if we have an exception, and if it
    // is the right instance as well
    if(isset($this->exception) && $this->exception
      instanceof Exception) :
?>

<!-- Yup, it is an exception all right -->
<div>
  Exception:

  <!--Show which class threw the exception -->
  <?php echo get_class($this->exception); ?>
</div>

<!-- Show the message thrown -->
<h2>Exception message:</h2>
<div><?php echo $this->exception->getMessage() ?></div>

<!-- And the *beautiful* stack trace as well -->
<h2>Stack trace:</h2>

<div>
  <?php echo $this->exception->getTraceAsString() ?>
</div>

<?phpendif; ?><?phpendif; ?>
```

How it works...

The `AbstractActionController` shows the errors when they occur and also selects the right template (which is defined in the `view_manager` configuration) to use for the error messages. The only thing we have to do is to make sure the templates are there.

A global layout is an excellent idea if we would be using the MVC model of Zend Framework 2 and are expecting to use the same layout over and over again, which is what happens in most cases.

Creating a global layout will really make our lives easier, as it is a way of making our code more maintainable, and as a coder that is one of the most important tools in your toolset.

First of all we need to make sure the `view_manager` has been defined properly, this has been described in the *Working with View* recipe, so we assume that we are using the same configuration at this point.

We used the `inlineScript` view helper to make sure the content can also output scripts that are not part of the head tag, but should still be used in the output.

We would like to use `inlineScript` to define any scripts instead of adding them to the template files as we want to separate the JavaScript with the normal HTML content as far as we can (we also want inline scripts to be reusable if we can, and it looks better maintenance wise).

The error template example is a very basic error document that is shown when an exception is happening. There are even more options we could do after this, for example if there were more exceptions, we could get them by doing `$this->exception->getPrevious()` and then parsing through them as an array.

Creating reusable Views

In this time of dynamic applications we have widgets or content that can be used more than once. Instead of getting everything at the same time we want to be able to dynamically load new objects in, or at least not have to do a lot to get functionality working.

Getting ready

For this recipe we need nothing more than a working Zend Framework 2 skeleton application.

How to do it...

In this recipe we'll be discussing how to create reusable templates and the best way of using them in an application.

Use the Action view helper to get the re-usable content

The Action view helper is a great way of calling different actions in our code to retrieve other parts of our application:

```
<div class="left">Some content on the left!</div>

<div class="right">
  <?php
    echo $this->action(
      // The action to call
      'sidebar',

      // The controller to call
      'templates',

      // The module to call
      'application',

      // Parameters to parse along
      array('show' => true)
    );
  ?>
</div>
```

Define a child to the ViewModel instance

First of all we should create a simple view script (/module/Application/view/application/template/sidebar.tpl) to output:

```
Hello from the sidebar!
```

After that we need to be in the controller (/module/Application/src/Application/Controller/IndexController.php).

```
public function indexAction()
{
  // Instantiate our main view model
  $view = new ViewModel();

  // Now let's instantiate our child model
  $child = new ViewModel();

  // For the child we want to render a different
  // template, namely our sidebar.tpl
  $child->setTemplate('template/sidebar.tpl');
```

```
    // Now add the child to our main view model
    $view->addChild($child, 'childModel');

    // Return our view model
    return $view;
}
```

Now we have the controller set up, we would want to output the child as well in our view script. We will be using a similar HTML layout as the first method so that we can spot the differences.

```
<div class="left">Some content on the left!</div>

<div class="right">
  <?php echo $this->childModel; ?>
</div>
```

How it works...

When we are developing web applications, we find ourselves at a point where we need to re-use the content that we already made before, such as the build-up of a form or maybe the layout of a side bar that we want to use on multiple pages.

What we can do in that instance is two things:

▶ Use the `Action` view helper to get the re-usable content

▶ Define a child to the `ViewModel` instance

Both of these methods can be used in different situations, let's explore the both options.

The Action view helper explained

We primarily would want to use this *if the re-usable content is outside the current module*, for example if the content is created by a module that provides page widgets then it can be used anywhere in the application. If we want to use a content that is inside our module, we better use the second option as that is less performance heavy because it doesn't go through the whole routing and dispatching process like the first option does.

What this view helper does is call an action within a view script, and post the results of that action call to the current view script.

If we look at the first example, it makes the call to the action and renders the output inside the current view script. The difference between this and the use of a partial view script is that this will go through the whole routing and dispatching process, while a partial simply displays the rendered output. If we, for example, need to get records from the database, a partial just wouldn't cut it.

Defining a child to a ViewModel instance explained

This method of rendering re-usable content is primarily used *when the re-usable content is inside the current module*, for example when we would like to use a specific overview table that relies on requires more intelligence than, for instance, a view helper would be able to provide. The content we are rendering would not require us to mess around in different modules, we'd rather stay away from relying on other modules from within our controller. We generally want to keep the modules as separate as possible so that we are able to run the application, even if one of the other modules is not available.

If we look at the example shown in *How it works* now, we can see that it has slightly more work to do in this method instead of the view helper class, but the difference is that the view helper class needs to do more in the background to get it all to work.

Pros and cons

Some might disagree when we say that we primarily should use the `Action` view helper outside the current module, and there are probably good reasons for why we should. One of the arguments against it is that it is simpler for the developer (or designer in most cases) to get the content from different locations without being bound by adding it as a `ViewModel` child in the controller. However, the view helper class does require the framework to find the action, controller and module first, render them, and then output them.

Although simpler in set up, it does strain the web application more if we use this option without good reason. Sometimes it is just better to code more and use the benefit of the speed of the application, then be lazy and let the application reduce its speed.

Sure everything has its pros and cons, so we should always consider the situation first to make sure we get the most maintainable and re-usable code possible.

Using view strategies/renderers

Normally we will use the View to output HTML, but sometimes we want a more diverse way of outputting for example JSON or XML. This recipe will provide us with enough information to accomplish this easily.

Getting ready

We simply require the Zend Framework 2 skeleton application to get us going with this recipe. Nothing exotic is required.

How to do it...

Using different view strategies and renderers is a common practice in an application. In this recipe we'll explain how to do that.

Adding a view strategy

We can easily add a view strategy to our application by simply appending the `view_manager` configuration in the module configuration file (`/module/Restful/config/module. config.php`) as shown as follows:

```php
<?php

return array(
  'view_manager' =>array(
    'strategies' => array(
      // This could also be ViewFeedStrategy if we want
      // to output as a feed
      'ViewJsonStrategy',
    ),
  ),
);
```

The JSON strategy

If we receive output from the JSON strategy, it might look very much like the following:

```
{
  "hello": "My name is",
  "first": "Terrible Richard",
  "address: {
    "street": "12 Coronation Street",
    "postcode": "SE1 2PE",
    "city": "London"
  }
}
```

The Feed strategy

Using the Feed strategy is quite similar to the other strategies, as we can see in the following example:

```php
// Assume we have a controller set up wrapped around
// this
public function indexAction()
{
  // Start a new feed
  $feed = new \Zend\Feed\Writer\Feed();

  // Set the feed name/title
  $feed->setTitle('My Awesome Feed!');
```

```
// Set the link to where the feed can be found, and
// the format of the feed
$feed->setFeedLink(
    'http://winter.example.com/rss',
    'atom'
);

// Who is the author of our feed
$feed->addAuthor(array(
    'name' => 'N. Stark',
    'email' => 'ned@winter.example.com',
    'uri' => 'http://winter.example.com',
));

// Add some description to the feed
$feed->setDescription('Loremipsum..');
$feed->setLink('http://winter.example.com');
$feed->setDateModified(time());
```

We have now set up our main data, which will be needed to generate our feed. Now let's add some sample data to the output:

```
$data = array(
    array(
        'title' => 'Post 1',
        'link' => 'http://winter.example.com/post/1',
        'description' => 'Loremipsum..',
        'date_created' => strtotime('2001-01-01 12:03:23'),
        'date_modified' => strtotime('2001-02-12 11:05:24'),
    ),

    // More entries here
);
```

Now we need to parse through the data (I know, it's a bit weird as we just declared it, but in reality this would never happen) and put them in the feed as an entry:

```
foreach ($data as $row) {
    $feed->addEntry(
        $feed->createEntry()
            ->setTitle($row['title'])
            ->setLink($row['link'])
            ->setDescription($row['description'])
```

```
        ->setDateModified($row['date_modified'])
        ->setDateCreated($row['date_created'])
    );
}
```

Now all that is left to do is export the feed to a specific format and add it to the actual `FeedModel` class.

```
// Export our feed to RSS style
$feed->export('rss');

// Instantiate a new feed model
$feedModel = new FeedModel();

// Set the created feed in the feed model
$feedModel->setFeed($feed);

// Action done, return the feed model
return $feedModel;
```

How it works...

The view strategy class

The default view strategy used in the Zend Framework 2 skeleton application is the `PhpRenderer` class, which does nothing more than search for a `.phtml` file in a defined location; by default this would be `/module/ModuleName/view`. The `PhpRenderer` class is able to parse PHP inside the view scripts, which makes it handy (but also very familiar) to perform some last minute scripting for our layout, such as parsing through records to create a table or displaying a username, for example.

 Although PHP is allowed in the `PhpRenderer` class, it should be mentioned that the developer should be wary of putting business logic in the view script. Logic should be placed in the model or at least the controller as it was never intended to reside in the view script.

This strategy will always be used whenever there is no other strategy available.

The default view strategies

There are a small number of view strategies readily available in Zend Framework 2, they are:

- The PHP strategy (default)
- The JSON strategy
- The Feed strategy

The JSON strategy explained

A JSON object is short for JavaScript Object Notation and is a text based, human-readable output format that is mainly used in modern web services around the world. It is derived from the JavaScript language and thus, resembles a lot of its features.

This is probably a nice example as we have put new lines in the output, while the actual JSON strategy will never contain that. But hey, if it is server-to-server talk only, why would we care?

The JSON strategy doesn't require a template or view script as it basically parses through the variables used in the view model, simple!

The Feed strategy explained

The Feed strategy outputs an XML news feed that can be used , for example, by users to subscribe on as an RSS or RSS2 formatted feed. Using the view model of the Feed strategy is a bit different though as directly setting the variables in the view model directly might be a tricky thing to do. Instead of that you can use a `Zend\Feed\Writer\Feed` object to determine the layout of your feed, and then feeding it to the `FeedModel` by passing it as a parameter to the `setFeed` method.

More about view strategies

The nice thing about Zend Framework 2 is that it isn't really hard to change the output, as it comes with a technique called view strategies, and in effect view renderers.

A view strategy is a class that identifies a model and returns a view renderer, which on its turn renders the output of the content. The view strategy will determine which renderer to use and how to use it.

Most of the time view strategies come with their own view model as well, which is to make sure the content we want to output is compatible with the renderer. The view strategy will, upon receiving the model, determine if it can or cannot render a certain model.

For example, the JSON renderer in the framework only renders models of the type `JsonModel` and will, when receiving a `ViewModel`, do nothing as it is technically not compatible with the renderer.

Sometimes we just need to output content in a different way. If we are talking about REST services, RSS feeds, or just something custom, we should always be able to switch between different output formats without needing to do too much work.

Using context switching for a different output

Not only do we want to be able to output the content through different view strategies, we sometimes also want to do this on demand, so that we can switch the output, for example, from HTML to JSON by simply changing the headers in our request.

Getting ready

In some cases (for example, in the REST servers) it is necessary to switch the response output of the content depending on what the user asks for. The user can add an `Accept` header to let the server know which output formats it accepts, for example `application/json`, and `text/html`.

What we are going to do is create a simple website that will output a `text/html` format on default (which is normal), but it will also output a JSON string whenever we have `Accept: */json` in our header.

How to do it...

Sometimes we want to cater not just to the users that view our website, but to a lot of different audiences, for example, the Feed readers or other applications. Therefore we'll discuss how to switch contexts in this recipe.

Define multiple strategies to output

First we want to make sure we have the JSON view strategy lined up so that we can easily switch between views. We can do this by adding `ViewJsonStrategy` in the `/module/Restful/config/module.config.php` as shown as follows:

```php
<?php

return array(
  // Add the JSON strategy to the view manager for our
  // output
  'view_manager' =>array(
    'strategies' => array(
      'ViewJsonStrategy',
    ),
  ),
);
```

Determine the view model based on the Accept header

In the controller there is a nifty little controller plugin called
`AcceptableViewModelSelector`, which can be used to return a view model that is based
on the `Accept` header.

So to make things a bit clear, we first want to define which kind of models we want to
support in our output. Let's create a property in our controller that regulates which view
models we are supporting:

```php
<?php

namespace Restful\Controller;

use Zend\Mvc\Controller\AbstractActionController;

class IndexController extends AbstractActionController
{
  protected $acceptCriteria = array(
    'Zend\View\Model\ViewModel' =>array(
      'text/html',
    ),
    'Zend\View\Model\JsonModel' =>array(
      'application/json',
      'text/json',
    ),
  );
}
```

As we can see here, we will support two models in order of priority. First of all we want the
default view model to use the normal `PhpRenderer` class, so that users will get to see the
normal HTML output. Second of all we want any `application/json` or `text/json` to be
rendered by our `JsonRenderer` class.

Now let's create a simple `indexAction` method and make use of the view model's selecting
abilities there:

```php
public function indexAction()
{
  // Get the right view model that goes with the Accept-
  // header
  $viewModel = $this->acceptableViewModelSelector(
    $this->acceptCriteria
  );
```

```
    // Set the variables in the given view model
    $viewModel->setVariables(array('output' => array(
      'one' => 'Row, row, row your boat,',
      'two' => 'gently down the stream.',
      'three' => 'Merrily, merrily, merrily, merrily,',
      'four' => 'life is but a dream.',
    )));
    // output the view model
    return $viewModel;
}
```

And that's how we do it folks! That was as simple as it can get as `AcceptableViewModelSelector` does all the work for us, and the only thing we have to do is make sure everything is declared in the model.

When we now add a view script for the normal `PhpRenderer` class, so that it renders our normal `text/html` output fine, we can say for sure that everything is done. Please make sure that this view script (`/module/Restful/view/restful/index/index.phtml`) resides in our new `Restful` module.

```
<table>
  <tr>
    <!-- output our variables -->
    <?php foreach ($this->output as $col) : ?>
    <td><?php echo $col ?></td>
    <?php endforeach; ?>
  </tr>
</table>
```

The output for a user with `Accept: application/json` header would look like the following, For this we need no view script as the renderer immediately outputs this.

```
{"output":{"one":"Row, row, row your boat,","two":"gently down the
  stream.","three":"Merrily, merrily, merrily,
  merrily,","four":"life is but a dream."}}
```

The default `PhpRenderer` output will look like the following:

```
<table>
  <tr>
    <!-- output our variables -->
    <td>Row, row, row your boat,</td>
    <td>gently down the stream. </td>
    <td>Merrily, merrily, merrily, merrily, </td>
    <td>life is but a dream.</td>
  </tr>
</table>
```

How it works...

`AcceptableViewModelSelector` looks at the header sent with the request to determine which view model to use. It determines the model by looking in the `array` we parse into it and looking at the different `Accept` headers we have defined that we support.

Next it will take the key of that specific `array` item, and that will be the view model that will be instantiated.

There's more...

To test out different headers, I like to use the Mozilla Firefox browser with the Header Tool add-on (`https://addons.mozilla.org/en-us/firefox/addon/header-tool`) installed, or similar Chrome extensions, or if we are feeling particularly brave, just the command line cURL. There you can just type the header you would like to send along, and turn it either on or off. However, there are different ways of sending headers as well. It depends on how you prefer doing things.

Writing a custom view strategy/renderer

Nothing is more exciting in coding than developing your own bits of custom features that integrate with the framework. In this recipe we will be discussing how to create our own XML view strategy. We will show you how to simply create the basis for a new strategy without too much of a bother.

How to do it...

Sometimes the default strategies and renderers provided are not enough for a specific situation, so let's talk through on how to create our own view strategy/renderer.

Creating the XmlOutput renderer

Let us see first on how our renderer would look like, as that is possibly one of the laziest classes we will ever code. We will do this in a new class located in `/module/XmlOutput/src/XmlOutput/View/Renderer/XmlRenderer.php`.

```php
<?php

namespace XmlOutput\View\Renderer;

use Zend\View\Renderer\PhpRenderer;
```

```
/**
 * This is the XML Renderer, which is as you can see
 * empty as we don't really need
 * to do anything to get this one going, the PhpRenderer
 * basically does everything
 * we need.
 */
class XmlRenderer extends PhpRenderer {}
```

The code for this model is very straightforward as we don't really need to do a lot of coding to get it working, we'll do this in the /module/XmlOutput/src/XmlOutput/View/Model/ XmlModel.php file.

```php
<?php

namespace XmlOutput\View\Model;

use Zend\View\Model\ViewModel;

/**
 * This is the XML View Model
 */
class XmlModel extends ViewModel
{

    /**
     * XML probably won't need to be captured into a
     * a parent container by default.
     *
     * @var string
     */
    protected $captureTo = null;

    /**
     * XML is usually terminal
     *
     * @var bool
     */
    protected $terminate = true;

    /**
     * UTF-8 Default Encoding
     * @var string
     */
```

```php
    protected $encoding = 'utf-8';

    /**
     * Content Type Header
     * @var string
     */
    protected $contentType = 'application/xml';

    /**
     * Set the encoding
     *
     * @param string $encoding
     * @return XmlModel
     */
    public function setEncoding($encoding)
    {
      $this->encoding = $encoding;
      return $this;
    }

    /**
     * Get the encoding
     *
     * @return string
     */
    public function getEncoding()
    {
      return $this->encoding;
    }
```

In the previous code snippet we have a simple getter and setter for the encoding which will usually be UTF-8, as it is also declared as the default value in the property.

```php
    /**
     * Set the content type
     *
     * @param string $contentType
     * @return XmlModel
     */
    public function setContentType($contentType)
    {
      $this->encoding = $contentType;
      return $this;
    }
```

```php
/**
 * Get the content type
 *
 * @return string
 */
public function getContentType()
{
    return $this->contentType;
}
}
```

Now we need to create the more exciting part, the `XmlStrategy` (located in `/module/XmlOutput/src/XmlOutput/View/Strategy/XmlStrategy.php`), which is the part that will actually tell the framework if, what, and how to render the content by handling the two View events (which is required).

```php
<?php

namespace XmlOutput\View\Strategy;

use XmlOutput\View\Model\XmlModel;
use XmlOutput\View\Renderer\XmlRenderer;
use Zend\EventManager\EventManagerInterface;
use Zend\EventManager\ListenerAggregateInterface;
use Zend\View\ViewEvent;

/**
 * This is the XML View Strategy
 */
class XmlStrategy implements ListenerAggregateInterface
{
    /**
     * @var \Zend\Stdlib\CallbackHandler[]
     */
    protected $listeners = array();

    /**
     * @var XmlRenderer
     */
    protected $renderer;
```

Once again we defined all of the properties which we needed. The first one `$listeners` will contain an array of `CallbackHandler` which we will use to attach and detach events to the `EventManager` instance.

The second member variable `$renderer` will store our `XmlRenderer` which we just created.

```
/**
 * Constructor
 *
 * @param XmlRenderer $renderer
 */
public function __construct(XmlRenderer $renderer)
{
    $this->renderer = $renderer;
}
```

Now we have defined our simple constructor, which basically assigns the given `XmlRenderer` class to our local property for safekeeping, which is the typical behavior of a rendering strategy. Next, we'll continue to implement the event handler.

```
/**
 * Make sure we only use our renderer when we are also
 * using our XmlModel.
 *
 * @param ViewEvent $e
 * @return null|XmlRenderer
 */
public function selectRenderer(ViewEvent $e)
{
    if (!$e->getModel() instanceof XmlModel) {
        // This is not our type of model, can't do
        // anything
        return;
    }

    return $this->renderer;
}

/**
 * We can inject the response now with the XML content
 * and the appropriate Content-Type header
 *
 * @param ViewEvent $e
 * @return void
 */
```

```php
public function injectResponse(ViewEvent $e)
{
  if ($e->getRenderer() !== $this->renderer) {
    // The renderer we got is not ours, returning
    return;
  }

  $result = $e->getResult();

  if (is_string($result)) {
    // String is empty, we cannot output anything
    return;
  }

  $model = $e->getModel();
  $response = $e->getResponse();
  $response->setContent($result);
  $headers = $response->getHeaders();
  $charset = '; charset='. $model->getEncoding(). ';';

  $headers->addHeaderLine(
    'content-type', 'application/xml'. $charset
  );
}
```

The last bit we need to do for the strategy is to attach and detach our events. The events methods in this case being `selectRenderer` and `injectResponse`, which will be triggered at different points in the code. The first one will be triggered when the event `ViewEvent::EVENT_RENDERER` happens and the second one will be triggered on `ViewEvent::EVENT_RESPONSE`. Once the framework has used everything it needs, it will call the `detach` method, and we then need to make sure all our events will be detached.

```php
/**
 * Let's attach the aggregate to the specified event
 * manager
 *
 * @param EventManagerInterface $events
 * @param int $priority
 * @return void
 */
```

```php
    public function attach(EventManagerInterface $events,
    $priority = 1)
    {
      $this->listeners[] = $events->attach(
          ViewEvent::EVENT_RENDERER,
          array($this, 'selectRenderer'),
          $priority
      );

      $this->listeners[] = $events->attach(
          ViewEvent::EVENT_RESPONSE,
          array($this, 'injectResponse'),
          $priority
      );
    }

    /**
      * We can detach the aggregate listeners from the
      * specified event manager
      *
      * @param EventManagerInterface $events
      * @return void
      */
    public function detach(EventManagerInterface $events)
    {
      foreach($this->listeners as $index => $listener) {
        if ($events->detach($listener)) {
          unset($this->listeners[$index]);
        }
      }
    }
}
```

Next up is something we didn't use before, which is the `ViewXmlStrategyFactory` class. The factory basically instantiates the `XmlStrategy` class (in this case) and makes sure everything is instantiated correctly. We'll create our new file here: `/module/XmlOutput/src/XmlOutput/Service/ViewXmlStrategyFactory.php`

```php
    <?php

    namespace XmlOutput\Service;

    use Zend\ServiceManager\FactoryInterface;
```

```php
use Zend\ServiceManager\ServiceLocatorInterface;
use XmlOutput\View\Strategy\XmlStrategy;

/**
 * Creates the service for the Xml Strategy.
 */
class ViewXmlStrategyFactory implements FactoryInterface
{
  /**
   * Creates and returns the XML view strategy
   *
   * @param ServiceLocatorInterface $serviceLocator
   * @return XmlStrategy
   */
  public function createService(ServiceLocatorInterface
  $serviceLocator)
  {
    return new XmlStrategy($serviceLocator-
  >get('ViewXmlRenderer'));
  }
}
```

That's it, as we can see it is not a lot, and only the `createService` method is being defined in the class. In that method the only thing we do is get the `ViewXmlRenderer` parameter and make sure the `XmlStrategy` class is constructed with that renderer as a parameter.

Now let's take a look at `ViewXmlRendererFactory`(located in `/module/XmlOutput/ src/XmlOutput/Service/ViewXmlRendererFactory.php`), which is also a factory but now for the renderer.

```php
<?php

namespace XmlOutput\Service;

use XmlOutput\View\Renderer\XmlRenderer;
use Zend\ServiceManager\FactoryInterface;
use Zend\ServiceManager\ServiceLocatorInterface;

/**
 * Creates the service for the Xml Renderer.
 */
```

```php
class ViewXmlRendererFactory implements FactoryInterface
{
  /**
   * Creates and returns the XML view renderer
   *
   * @param ServiceLocatorInterface $serviceLocator
   * @return XmlRenderer
   */
  public function createService(ServiceLocatorInterface
  $serviceLocator)
  {
    $renderer = new XmlRenderer();

    // Set the View resolvers and helper managers.
    $renderer->setResolver(
      $serviceLocator->get('ViewResolver')
    );

    $renderer->setHelperPluginManager(
      $serviceLocator->get('ViewHelperManager')
    );

    return $renderer;
  }
}
```

Although this `createService` method was more work than the one before, it is still a very light method. The only thing that really happens here is that the `XmlRenderer` class is instantiated, and it made sure `ViewResolver` and `ViewHelperManager` are set.

Now we have set up our basic functionality, let's tie it all together so that we can start using it!

First of all we need to create the `/module/XmlOutput/config/module.config.php` file to make sure our services are instantiated properly, and our view manager knows the new strategy we offer.

```php
<?php
  return array(
    // Set our factories, so our service manager can find
    // them
    'service_manager' =>array(
      'factories' => array(
        'ViewXmlStrategy' =>
  'XmlOutput\Service\ViewXmlStrategyFactory',
```

```
        'ViewXmlRenderer' =>
          'XmlOutput\Service\ViewXmlRendererFactory'
    ),
  ),

  // Add our strategy to the view manager for our output
  'view_manager' =>array(
    'strategies' => array(
      'ViewXmlStrategy',
    ),
  ),
);
```

That was rather painless, as we can simply tell `serviceManager` where everything is located and it will work immediately.

The last thing we need to create in our new `XmlOutput` module is the `Module.php` file, which is basically the same as the default `Module.php` that comes with the Application module. We can simply copy that one over, change the namespace in the file and we are done. The file should be located in `/module/XmlOutput/Module.php`.

```php
<?php

namespace XmlOutput;

use Zend\Mvc\ModuleRouteListener;
use Zend\Mvc\MvcEvent;

class Module
{
  public function onBootstrap(MvcEvent $e)
  {
    $eventManager= $e->getApplication()->getEventManager();

    $moduleRouteListener = new ModuleRouteListener();
    $moduleRouteListener->attach($eventManager);
  }

  public function getConfig()
  {
      return include __DIR__ . '/config/module.config.php';
  }
```

```php
public function getAutoloaderConfig()
{
    return array(
        'Zend\Loader\StandardAutoloader' =>array(
            'namespaces' => array(
                __NAMESPACE__ => __DIR__ . '/src/' .
                __NAMESPACE__,
            ),
        ),
    );
}
}
```

Now the `/config/application.config.php` file needs to have our new module added, so that the framework will try to instantiate that module as well. We can just add `XmlOutput` to the modules array and we are done, nothing else needs changing in there.

```php
return array(
    // This should be an array of module namespaces used
    // in the application.
    'modules' => array(
        'Application',

        // Add our module to this array
        'XmlOutput',
    ),

    // After this comes the rest of the file, but that is
    // irrelevant at the moment.
);
```

Everything is ready and set up for use, so now it is time to actually get the ball rolling and output something to XML. First up is using `XmlModel` in our `indexAction` of the `IndexController` (located in `/module/Application/src/Application/Controller/IndexController.php`). We will just assign some variables to `XmlModel` and return this immediately, no need for anything fancy now.

```php
<?php

namespace Application\Controller;

use Zend\Mvc\Controller\AbstractActionController;
use XmlOutput\View\Model\XmlModel;
```

```
class IndexController extends AbstractActionController
{
  public function indexAction()
  {
    return new XmlModel(array(
      "some_variable" => "Awesome!",
      "why_not_another_one" => "While we are here?"
    ));
  }
}
```

Once we have done that, we can build up our view script (located in `/module/`
`Application/view/application/index/index.phtml`) with the necessary XML.

```
<nodes>
  <variable_1><?php
    echo $this->some_variable;
  ?></variable_1>
  <variable_2><?php
    echo $this->why_not_another_one;
  ?></variable_2>
</nodes>
```

And that is it! Once we run it, we can now see that our HTTP headers are set to
`application/xml` and that the output is the XML we have just put in. Obviously this is
nothing fancy, but it is to show how easy it is to just create our own view strategy.

How it works...

Because we added our factories to the `ServiceManager`, we can easily get them to use
by their aliases `ViewXmlStrategy` and `ViewXmlRenderer`. And because we told the
`ViewManager` that our new strategy `ViewXmlStrategy` exists, we can get the ball rolling.

As we would use the `XmlModel` in our controller, the framework will iterate through all the
view strategies to determine the proper strategy to use. Once it has found the strategy it
needs, it will trigger the `EVENT_RENDERER` and `EVENT_RESPONSE` events, which in turn will
trigger our strategy methods. These methods will determine the output of our content.

Our renderer makes sure the content is rendered properly. In our case we took the lazy way
out and let `PhpRenderer` basically do all the work, this can however vary per renderer.

We are creating this new view strategy as a separate module, with separate namespaces
so that we can easily transfer this to another application if we ever need to. And of course it
comes with greater maintainability when we separate pieces of functionality as well.

When we are done we can easily extend the classes further as we wish, but for now let's keep it basic.

There are five files that need to be created before we can have at least the most basic form of a custom view strategy; the files need to be of the following forms:

- Renderer
- Model
- Strategy
- Strategy Factory
- Renderer Factory

The first three we already know as we've discussed in this chapter, the last two Factory ones', however, are new to us.

The XmlRenderer and XmlModel

Because we just want to output XML as a string, we will be using the `PhpRenderer` as that does the exact same thing as we want it to do.

Next up is coding the model. As described earlier, the model will be used in the controller to store variables which we can then use in the View. We will be creating the XmlModel so that when we use this model in our controller our framework knows we want to output with our `XmlStrategy`.

As we can see we made all the properties in the `XmlModel` protected, because these properties are protected in the class we are trying to extend (`ViewModel`) as well. It is necessary while extending a property to give it the same access level or lower. In this case it is protected, which means the lower option would be public. Private, however, would result in a fatal error shown as follows:

```
PHP Fatal error:  Access level to XmlOutput\View\Model\
XmlModel::$captureTo must be protected (as in class Zend\View\Model\
ViewModel) or weaker in /var/www/module/XmlOutput/src/XmlOutput/View/
Model/XmlModel.php on line 0
```

The last bit we need to do in the `XmlModel` is create the getter and setter for the content type, which in our case would become `application/xml`, because we want to output XML, not plain text.

The XmlStrategy

In `selectRenderer` we want to make sure that the model we have is also the model we expect it to be. If this is not the case we cannot return a renderer, meaning that the framework needs to search for a different kind of renderer. For example, the use of a `ViewModel` instance would result in `selectRenderer` returning null, which would tell the framework to search for another suitable strategy. In this case it might be the `PhpStrategy`, which in this case would accept `ViewModel` as a valid model, and that is how the view strategy communicates to the framework to tell it if he can use the model or not.

The `injectResponse` is a method that will ready the content for output, and makes sure that the content type is set in the headers as well. The `ViewEvent` given as a parameter that contains all the collected information we need, such as the `XmlModel`, and also its Response. The next bit of code will tie the last two methods we just created together and use them as handlers for the respective `ViewEvent::EVENT_RENDERER` and `ViewEvent::EVENT_RESPONSE` events.

There's more...

We said before we were a bit lazy with the renderer, basically putting off any of the work by putting all of the work in the hands of the `PhpRenderer`, which in turn basically rendered the view script containing the XML. Naturally one would desire a renderer which makes the use of view scripts obsolete, and just creates the XML from an array in the `XmlModel`.

So yes, there is a lot more that can be said, but the real fun starts if we start exploring the different ways of rendering content.

5
Configuring and Using Databases

In this chapter we will cover:

- ▶ Connecting to a database
- ▶ Executing simple queries
- ▶ Executing queries using the TableGateway
- ▶ Optimization with a DB profiler
- ▶ Creating a Database Access Object

Introduction

Obviously databases are essential if we want to store data, and with all the different kinds of database engines around, it is sometimes hard to see the wood through the trees. Zend Framework 2, however, brings us a bit of hope of standardizing the way we work with databases. In this chapter, we will be showing loads of examples from database connections to optimizing the performance of our queries.

Default database engines available

Zend Framework 2 has a default collection of database drivers available to use, and obviously it also supports the PHP PDO extension for a more standardized way of using databases.

IBM DB2 driver

IBM DB2 is a database server designed by IBM and is the second most used DBMS according to IDC's report of 2009 (http://www.marketresearch.com/IDC-v2477/Worldwide-Database-Management-Systems-Forecast-2393193/view-stat/ibm-14.html). The database engine can be traced back to the 1970's and was mainly only available for the IBM mainframe until the 1990's when it started supporting other more widely used operating systems.

Nowadays, the DB2 is mainly used in ZF2 for the IBM i Power Systems such as the AS/400, but remains a very powerful database engine.

Requirements:

▸ The IBM DB2 Universal Database client needs to be installed on the PHP machine

▸ PHP configured either with the `--with-IBM_DB2` option or enabled (and installed) the `ibm_db2` extension in `php.ini`

MySQLi driver

For PHP developers, this is probably the most used database engine, the **MySQLi** instead of the normal MySQL driver gives the extension several advantages over modern MySQL system versions (4.1.3 and newer). This improved extension supports the following modern MySQL functionality:

▸ Enhanced server support

▸ Transaction support

▸ Prepared statements support

▸ Object-oriented interface

▸ Multiple statements support

▸ Enhanced debugging availability

The requirements for MySQLi driver is that the PHP is configured either with the `--with-mysql` or `--with-mysqli` option or enabled (and installed) the `mysql` and `mysqli` extension in `php.ini`.

OCI8 driver

OCI8 driver supports Oracle Database 11g, 10g, 9i, and 8i (according to the PHP manual), and is widely used in the PHP community.

Requirements:

▸ Oracle 9ir2, 10g, or 11g Client libraries on the PHP machine

▸ PHP configured either with the `--with-oci8` option or enabled (and installed) the `oci8` extension in `php.ini`

PGSQL driver

PostgreSQL is an object-relational database and is my personal favorite, this database has been around since 1995 and is used by websites such as Reddit, Instagram, and Yahoo!.

The requirement for this is that the PHP is configured either with the `--with-pgsql` option or enabled (and installed) the `pgsql` extension in `php.ini`.

SQLSRV driver

Microsoft SQL Server (and SQL Azure) is a database that works exclusively on Microsoft Windows, and is widely considered being a very good and stable database engine. Versions 3.0 or higher of the PHP extension support SQL Server 2005.

Requirements:

> ▸ The Microsoft SQL Server 2012 Native Client needs to be installed on the PHP machine
> ▸ The extension `php_sqlsrv_5*_nts.dll` or `php_sqlsrv_5*_ts.dll` should be enabled (and installed) on the PHP machine

PDO driver

The PDO extension in PHP is probably the best method of connecting to a database available. Not only does it have a wide selection of database engines it supports, but also a more standardized way of working with them, which makes it easier to support in the long run (and that is a pro in the long run).

Not only is it easier to support, for example, its standardized way of connecting to databases and executing queries makes it much easier for us developers to switch.

The requirements for this is that at least one `pdo` extension needs to be enabled in the `php.ini` file or otherwise it won't work.

All the drivers communicate with PHP through either as the built-in compilation or used as an extension on the library. Without these extensions PHP would be unable to figure out how to communicate with the specific libraries. Some extensions (such as the Oracle one) require even more, like client libraries to make it work.

We should always check the php.net documentation for the requirements of the specific extension we try to enable.

Connecting to a database

After seeing all the database types that Zend Framework 2 supports, we can finally start connecting to them. In this recipe, we will connect to a MySQL server and show different ways of doing this.

Getting ready

To make full of the following recipe, a Zend Framework 2 skeleton application should be used, with a MySQL server available to connect to. Don't forget that connecting to a MySQL server requires the `mysql` and `mysqli` extensions enabled in PHP.

How to do it...

In this recipe we'll give some examples of how to connect to a single database or multiple databases.

Connecting to a MySQL database through the configuration

We can make the following change to the `/config/autoload/global.php` file:

```php
<?php

return array(
  // Set up the service manager
  'service_manager' => array(

    // Initiate the connection at the start of the
    // application
    'factories' => array(

      // Use the service factory to start up our db
      // adapter
      'Zend\Db\Adapter\Adapter' =>
      'Zend\Db\Adapter\AdapterServiceFactory',
    ),

    'aliases' => array(
      // Use this db alias in the controllers to get the
      // initialized connection. The value of the db key refers to
      // the factories key with the same name.
      'db' => 'Zend\Db\Adapter\Adapter',
    ),
  ),
  'db' => array(
    // We want to use the PDO to connect to the database
    'driver' => 'pdo',
```

```
// DSN, or data source name is a connection url that
// shows the driver (in this case the PDO) where to
// connect to. The first bit is the driver to use,
// then follows the database name and the host. More
// information on the dsn options can be found here:
// http://php.net/manual/en/pdo.construct.php
'dsn' => 'mysql:dbname=some_db_name;host=localhost',

// Username and password (or at the very least the
// password) should NOT be in the global.php. This
// file usually will be committed to a version
// control, which means your password will be
// publicly available.
'username'  => 'aGreatUser',
'password'  => 'somePassword',
    ),
);
```

As we can see in the example, setting up the database configuration is quite easy. Now, if you were wondering how to use a configuration like this in a real world example, let's consider the following controller:

```php
<?php

namespace Application\Controller;

use Zend\Mvc\Controller\AbstractActionController;

class SomeController extends AbstractActionController
{
  public function indexAction()
  {
    // Get the db adapter through our service manager
    $db = $this->getServiceLocator()->get('db');

    // Now we can execute queries
    $query = $db->query('SELECT * FROM table');
  }
}
```

As we can see it is very easy to get it going now in the controller.

Connecting to multiple databases through the configuration

Some applications require us to connect to multiple databases at the same time, and we can easily achieve that in Zend Framework 2 as well by doing the following in the `/config/autoload/global.php` file:

```php
<?php
return array(
    'db' => array(
        'adapters' => array(
            // The first (default) database connection
            'db_one' => array(
                'driver' => 'pdo',
                'dsn' => 'mysql:dbname=db_1;host=localhost',
                'username'  => 'someUser',
                'password'  => 'aGreatPassword',
            ),

            // Now the second database connection
            'db_two' => array(
                'driver' => 'pdo',
                'dsn' => 'mysql:dbname=db_2;host=localhost',
                'username'  => 'someOtherUser',
                'password'  => 'anotherGreatPassword',
            ),
        ),
    ),
    'service_manager' => array(
        // Let's make sure our adapters get instantiated
        'abstract_factories' => array(
            'Zend\Db\Adapter\AdapterAbstractServiceFactory',
        ),
    ),
);
```

In our controllers (or anywhere where we can access the service manager) we can easily get the db DBAdapter now by doing the following:

```php
<?php

namespace Application\Controller;

use Zend\Mvc\Controller\AbstractActionController;
```

```php
class SomeController extends AbstractActionController
{
  public function indexAction()
  {
    // Get the first db adapter
    $dbOne = $this->getServiceLocator()->get('db_one');

    // Get the second db adapter
    $dbOne = $this->getServiceLocator()->get('db_two');
  }
}
```

Connecting to a MySQL database through code

Although it is less clean than the method we showed before, sometimes it is just necessary to connect through good old instantiation.

First let's see an example if we want to connect to a MySQL server:

```php
<?php

// We need to import this to use the Db Adapter
use Zend\Db\Adapter\Adapter;

class someClass
{
  // This is the property where our database adapter will be
  // stored in
  private $db;

  // First we want to connect to the database on instantiation of
  // this class
  public function __construct()
  {
    // Create the new database adapter
    $this->db = new Adapter(array(
      'driver' => 'Pdo_Mysql',
      'hostname' => 'localhost',
      'database' => 'example_database',
      'username' => 'developer',
      'password' => 'developer-password'
    ));
  }
```

```
// This method will execute a query on the database, to show
// how easy it is to now make use of our database
public function someData()
{
  // Create a statement where we select everything from our
  // tableName table
  $statement = $this->db->createStatement(
    "SELECT * FROM tableName"
  );

  return $statement->execute();
}
}
```

We now can easily execute the queries on the instantiated $db.

How it works...

In Zend Framework 2 there are many ways of defining a database connection, in this section we will discuss three of them.

Connecting to a MySQL database through the configuration

The first method we are going to show is connecting to a (could be of any type) database through the configuration files. This is probably the easiest to do, but would obviously not always be what we want. However, in the case of less code is better maintainability, we should always consider the option of connecting to a database like this.

We should refrain from putting business logic in the controller, as that is not what a MVC is for, we just showed it here as an example only. We can get the db adapter from anywhere where we have the service manager in reach.

Connecting to multiple databases through the configuration

As we can see we now have our adapters defined in the db => adapters array instead of the db array directly. This functionality can be achieved in any version of Zend Framework 2 greater or equal to 2.2.

About the ServiceManager

When we use the `ServiceManager` for connecting to our database, the `ServiceManager` first checks if it has the key we need. If the key is found it first checks in its internal registry if there is already an instance for the requested service. If not, it will use the `config` data to instantiate it. After instantiation is completed it will stash away the reference in its internal registry, which can be retrieved again the next time we request it. This way the database adapter (or any other service) will be only instantiated once by the `ServiceManager`. Instantiating the database connection this way has a couple of pros:

▶ We always have one connection to the database, which is usually limited on the server side

▶ We don't spend valuable time connecting and reinitializing the connection constantly

▶ No memory is wasted on multiple instances

Executing simple queries

Querying the database is obviously something that we need to do once we are connected to the database. This recipe explains how this can be done, and the different methods available.

Getting ready

To make full of the following recipe, a Zend Framework 2 skeleton application should be used, with a MySQL server available to connect to. Don't forget that connecting to a MySQL server requires the `mysql` and `mysqli` extension enabled in PHP.

We have configured a database called `book`, with the table `cards` that has the columns `id`, `color`, `type`, and `value`. The SQL query to create the database and table are included in the code that comes with the book.

How to do it...

Queries come in all sort of forms, and in this recipe we will discuss some basic querying.

Using raw SQL

We'll be editing in the `/module/Application/src/Application/Controller/IndexController.php` file for this example:

```php
<?php

namespace Application\Controller;

use Zend\Mvc\Controller\AbstractActionController;
```

```
class IndexController extends AbstractActionController
{
  public function indexAction()
  {
    // Let's assume there is a service called 'db' that connect to
    // the database
    $connection = $this->getServiceLocator()->get('db');

    // We now start to build up our query
    $query = $connection->query(
      // We will put our raw SQL statement in here, and
      // every variable we want to put in we replace with
      // a question mark. This means we will fill in the
      // blanks later.
      "SELECT * FROM cards WHERE type = ?",

      // We don't want to execute the statement yet, just
      // prepare it.
      Adapter::QUERY_MODE_PREPARE
    );

    // These are the parameters that will replace the question
    // marks (?) in the SQL statement above, in the defined order
    $replacements = array('number');

    // Now execute the query with the parameters attached to
    // replace
    $result = $query->execute($replacements);

    // Iterate over the results
    foreach ($result as $res) {
      // Do something with the result, in this case a raw echo
      echo '<pre>'. print_r($res, true). '</pre>';
    }
  }
}
```

An example using an array or the `ParameterContainer` object for passing variables:

```
// We now start to build up our query
$query = $connection->query(
```

```
    // We will put our raw SQL statement in here, and
    // every variable we want to put in we replace with
    // a question mark. This means we will fill in the
    // blanks later.
    "SELECT * FROM cards WHERE type = ?",

    // These are the parameters that will replace the question
    // marks (?) in the SQL statement above, in the defined order
    array('number')
);
```

Using the prepared statements

We'll be editing in the `/module/Application/src/Application/Controller/IndexController.php` file for this example:

```php
<?php

namespace Application\Controller;

use Zend\Mvc\Controller\AbstractActionController;

class IndexController extends AbstractActionController
{
  public function indexAction()
  {
    // Let's assume there is a service called 'db' that connect to
    // the database
    $connection = $this->getServiceLocator()->get('db');

    // Now let's create a prepared statement
    $statement = $connection->createStatement();

    // Set up the prepared statement
    $statement->setSql("
      SELECT
      *
      FROM cards
      WHERE type = :type
      AND color = :color
    ");

    // Create a new parameter container to store our where
    // parameters in
```

```php
$container = new ParameterContainer(array(
  // These are the variables used in the same order as
  // displayed in the where condition
  'type' => 'picture', 'color' => 'diamond'
));

// Set the container to be used in our statement
$statement->setParameterContainer($container);

// Prepare the statement for use with the database
$statement->prepare();

// Now execute the statement and get the resultset
$result = $statement->execute();

// Iterate over the results
foreach ($result as $res) {
  // Do something with the result, in this case a raw echo
  echo '<pre>'. print_r($res, true). '</pre>';
  }
 }
}
```

Quote identifier

This method will quote an identifier that is going to be used in a SQL query in a safe way:

```php
<?php

// Adapter is of type Zend\Db\Adapter\Adapter
echo $adapter->getPlatform()->quoteIdentifier('some_var');
```

The preceding code will give the following output:

```
"some_var"
```

Quote identifier chain

The `quoteIdentifierChain` method will quote multiple identifiers and glue them together with the identifier separator (see method `getIdentifierSeparator()`):

```php
<?php

// Adapter is of type Zend\Db\Adapter\Adapter
echo $adapter->getPlatform()->quoteIdentifierChain(array(
  'some_table', 'some_column'
));
```

The preceding code will give the following output:

```
"some_table"."some_column"
```

Quote (trusted) value

quoteValue and quoteTrustedValue are used for quoting values used in for example WHERE clauses. quoteTrustedValue() should only be used when we trust the value (for example if we put it in ourselves): The following is an example of quoteValue and quoteTrustedValue:

```php
<?php

// You can either use quoteValue or quoteTrustedValue,
// quoteValue will log an error in the PHP error log if
// there is no driver or module available to quote the
// value. Both methods output the same value.
echo $adapter->getPlatform()->quoteValue("great-value");

// Adapter is of type Zend\Db\Adapter\Adapter
echo $adapter->getPlatform()->quoteTrustedValue("great-value");
```

The preceding code will give the following output:

```
'great-value'
```

Quote value list

Quote value list quotes an entire list of values and returns them, separated by a comma. Comes in handy, for example, if we want to use a list in a WHERE clause where we use an IN operator. There is no method that handles trusted values, so we should be aware that this could trigger errors in our PHP error log if there are no drivers or modules available to quote the value, however, it will always return the expected values. The following is an example of quoteValueList:

```php
<?php

// Adapter is of type Zend\Db\Adapter\Adapter
echo $adapter->getPlatform()->quoteValueList(array(
  "value_one", "value_two"
));
```

The preceding code will give the following output:

```
'value_one', 'value_two'
```

Quote identifier in fragment

The `quoteIdentifierInFragment` method plucks out the identifiers by a RegEx pattern, and makes sure only the right identifiers are quoted. If we are using characters outside the following characters: A-z,0-9, *, "." or 'AS', we will need to give them up as a safe word by using the second parameter.

```php
<?php

// Adapter is of type Zend\Db\Adapter\Adapter
echo $adapter->getPlatform()->quoteIdentifierInFragment(
  '(fork.* AS spoon)',

    // Use the braces as a safe word so that they
    // will not be quoted.
    array('(', ')')
);
```

The preceding code gives the following output:

```
`fork`.* AS `spoon`
```

How it works...

Let's understand the operations we just did.

Using raw SQL

The first method of executing SQL is by simply using the `query()` method on the database connection. This is the simplest form of querying, and it has it pros and cons, one pro is that the queries are quick and easy, the con is that it isn't really useful for reuse as the query constantly needs either new input every time we execute it, or needs the variables passed into it every time we want to execute it.

As we can see in the example, we created a query first with the mode set to `QUERY_MODE_PREPARE`, which in effect means that the query isn't executed straight away, but just prepared for execution. When we come to execute the query, we see that we parse the variables for the `WHERE` clause with the `execute()` method. The `execute()` statement then executes the query and gives the result back.

Instead of the second parameter to `query()`, we could also do either `QUERY_MODE_EXECUTE` to immediately execute the query (and thus returning the result set straight away) or parse an array with parameters or `ParameterContainer`. For more information on `ParameterContainer` see the following section.

If we parse either an array or a `ParameterContainer` object as the last option of `query()`, it would both lead to the query parameters being filled and the query mode to be put on `QUERY_MODE_PREPARE`. This means that because we already parsed the parameters for our query into the `query()` method, we don't have to add them again in the `execute()` method.

Using prepared statements

The `query()` method is described as a convenience function and is not really usefully when we want to protect ourselves against SQL injection or want to use a single query multiple times with different parameters. The `createStatement()` function on the other hand provides a great way of storing and preparing a SQL before use in a safe and responsible way.

As seen in the example, we have executed a similar statement such as the `query()` method, however this method is much more maintainable and reusable than the `query()` method. By using `ParameterContainer` we can easily inject our variables into the SQL and manage them simply because of the container nature of the object.

Because we used `:type` and `:color` the statement knows that our parameter array (`ParameterContainer` implements the `ArrayAccess` class) should contain the keys `type` and `color` to match them to the SQL statement.

Quoting in our SQL

Usually where there is database access there is user input, and if there is one thing we should never trust it is user input. Although the majority of people have no intention of hacking your website, a malicious few will try to do so.

Zend Framework 2 offers a range of quote methods which we can use to protect ourselves from any harm. We should note however that these are just a small set of tools that you can use in prevention of a disastrous situation, and we advice that a full range of utilities is used to prevent SQL injection.

Using createStatement

When we use `createStatement()` the result objects are instantiated through the driver, so the workings of a statement for MySQL can be different from Oracle (can, and will I think). Once we create a statement it will also automatically connect to the database, which is handy but we must be wary that we are not creating the statement on places where we might not need the database. If we omit such a thing it might create a leak that isn't necessary in the first place, although probably not such a big leak but a leak nonetheless.

The `query()` method works directly on the connection adapter, and although quick in use isn't recommended to use in 'real life' situations as it doesn't promote reusability (in my personal opinion). If in doubt, it is always best to do `createStatement()`, unless we are simply testing some things out then we can use `query()` instead.

Executing queries using TableGateway

After we have seen how to execute simply queries, it is now time to tell you about the `TableGateway`, and it's incredible functionality. This recipe is all about querying the database through this and showing off its capabilities.

Getting ready

To make full of the following recipe, a Zend Framework 2 skeleton application should be used, with a MySQL server available to connect to. Don't forget that connecting to a MySQL server requires the `mysql` and `mysqli` extension enabled in PHP.

How to do it...

What we are going to do first is insert a record in our sample table. After that we will check that it was inserted successfully. Next, we will update the record with some new data, and if that worked we will delete it again from the table.

Inserting a new record

Before we go about updating a record, it might be handy if we actually have a record that we can use to update first. Zend Framework 2 has some new nifty database tools that make our lives a little easier when it comes to data handling.

The cards table has the following columns:

- `id` (primary key)
- `color`
- `value`
- `type`

Let's consider the following example (`/module/Application/src/Application/Controller/IndexController.php`):

```php
<?php

namespace Application\Controller;

use Zend\Mvc\Controller\AbstractActionController;
use Zend\Db\TableGateway\TableGateway;

class IndexController extends AbstractActionController
{
```

```php
public function indexAction()
{
  // Let's assume there is a service called 'db' that connect to
  // the database
  $connection = $this->getServiceLocator()->get('db');

  // Let's make this object for examples later on
  // $sql = new Sql($this->connection);

  // Create a new Zend\Db\Sql\Insert object
  // You can also do $sql->insert();
  $insert = new Insert('cards');

  // Define the columns in the table, although not
  //required, it is best practice
  $insert->columns(array(
    'id',
    'color',
    'type',
    'value',
  ));

  // Assign the values we want to insert, the column
  // names are in the keys so that the code knows what
  // to insert where.
  $insert->values(array(
    'color' => 'diamond',
    'type' => 'picture',
    'value' => 'Goblin'
  ));

  // Create a new table gateway to perform our SQL on
  $tableGateway = new TableGateway(
    'cards', $connection
  );

  // We will now use the TableGateway to insert our
  // statement in the table.
  // The insert() / insertWith() method throws an
  // exception whenever the query goes wrong. We need to
  // make sure we catch that.
  try {
    $tableGateway->insertWith($insert);
```

```
      // If we reach this point we can assume that the
      // query went fine.
      echo "Insert success!";
      $hasResult = true;
    } catch (Exception $e) {
      echo "Insert failed.";
    }
  }
}
```

That concludes the table insert, and obviously this is only one way of inserting data in the table. Another way to execute the insert statement would be to use the `$sql` object we created before. If we do that we can get rid of `TableGateway` and just use that instead.

If we would prefer that we could go about it like this:

```
// This will prepare a StatementInterface for us to use
$statement = $sql->prepareStatementForSqlObject(
  // Put the insert object in here
  $insert
);

// Now we simply execute the statement to insert the
// record.
$statement->execute();
```

Updating a record

We can now go on with checking if the insertion went fine, and following that we will update the record with some new data:

```
// If an Exception happened, we will have a false in our
// result.
if (isset($hasResult)) {
  // Let's get the primary key from our last insert for
  // later use.
  $primaryKey = $tableGateway->getLastInsertValue();

  // Now let's update our record
  // You can also do $sql->update();
  $update = new Update('cards');
```

```
// Set the new values (and column names as keys) for
// the data we want to update.
$update->set(array(
   'color' => 'spade',
   'value' => '10',
   'type' => 'number',
));

// Now create a where statement
$where = new Where();

// We want to match our record on the primary key that
// we got back from our insertion.
$where->equalTo("id", $primaryKey);

// Set the where in the update statement so that we
// use that when executing the update. We can add as
// many where statements as we like, but we only match
// on one here.
$update->where($where);

// Now update the record
$updated = $tableGateway->updateWith($update);
```

The result of the update will be the amount of rows affected by our update statement. In our case that would only be one record as we match exactly with the primary key of the table.

Deleting a record

Now, we are done with all our updates we want to begin deleting this record again, so let's look at the following code snippet:

```
// Delete everything again
// You can also do $sql->delete();
$delete = new Delete('cards');

// We can use the same where statement as before!
$delete->where($where);

// Now let's delete it, as there is nothing else to it.
$deleted = $tableGateway->deleteWith($delete);
```

Well that was easy. We could just use the same where statement as it already defined the clause to filter on our primary key from before.

Advanced selects – joins conditions

When developing web application we will require more than one table in our queries for most of the time, this is because we just need to pull a lot of data from everywhere to get the results we need. One way of doing this is by using join conditions in our `select` statement.

Let's just take a look at the following table composition, we are going in our virtual environment:

The `people` table will have the following columns:

- `Id` (primary key)
- `First_name`
- `Last_name`
- `Age`
- `Gender`
- `Address_Id` (foreign key to `addresses` table)

The `addresses` table will have the following columns:

- `Id` (primary key)
- `Street`
- `Number`
- `Postcode`
- `City`
- `Country`

What we want to achieve here is to retrieve the address that belongs to a person and show that in our result.

Let's look at an example (`/module/Application/src/Application/Controller/ IndexController.php`) of how we could achieve that in the best possible way:

```php
<?php

namespace Application\Controller;

use Zend\Mvc\Controller\AbstractActionController;
use Zend\Db\TableGateway\TableGateway;

class IndexController extends AbstractActionController
{
    public function indexAction()
    {
```

```php
// Let's assume there is a service called 'db' that connect to
// the database
$connection = $this->getServiceLocator()->get('db');

// First create our Zend\Db\Sql\Sql object, and let's
// assume $connection has a Zend\Db\Adapter defined.
$sql = new Sql($connection);

// Now create a Zend\Db\Sql\Select statement with
// 'people' as the table we want to select from.
$select = $sql->select('people');

// By default we will select all the fields, but let's
// just change that a bit for sake of the example
$select->columns(array('first_name', 'last_name'));

// Now set up our join condition
$select->join(
    // We want to join the 'addresses' table
    'addresses',

    // We now define the join condition to match the
    // records on
    'addresses.id = people.address_id',

    // We want to select different columns than the
    // default wildcard selection.
    array('street', 'number', 'city', 'postcode'),

    // We want to do a LEFT JOIN on the table
    Select::JOIN_LEFT
);

// Now we are ready to execute the statement.
$statement = $sql->prepareStatementForSqlObject(
    $select
);

// .. And finally execute it
$records = $statement->execute();

// Output to the screen for convenience
echo '<pre>'. print_r($records, true). '</pre>';
    }
}
```

This is how simple it is to create a `join` condition on a `select` statement. Piece of pie!

How it works...

In Zend Framework 2 they have separated all the actions such as `Insert`, `DropTable`, `Update`, `Delete`, and `Where` into classes of their own, which makes it very reusable for developers. The great thing about it is that it also makes the code much clearer.

`TableGatewayInterface` defines a minimum selection of methods that are implemented by `AbstractTableGateway` and also `TableGateway`, as that extends from `AbstractTableGateway` in the first place. `TableGateway`, for short, implements most common features needed to do table operations.

The `TableGatewayInterface`, therefore, defines the following methods:

- `getTable()`
- `select($where = null)`
- `insert($set)`
- `update($set, $where = null)`
- `delete($where)`

Optimizating with a DB profiler

One of the most common bottlenecks in an application is the querying to the database, as sometimes we just don't know how much is being queried, or we can't find out why something is going wrong. This recipe provides us with the tools to find even the smallest query used.

Getting ready

A database profiler is used to find bottlenecks in query performance and is a great tool to debug the queries that are executed in a session and of course the time it takes for them to execute. Once we develop bigger applications we tend to forget when and how certain pieces of code execute, which sometimes can lead to unnecessary complexity in our code.

How to do it...

Profiling an application's database usage can give a clear overview on the performance of our application, in this recipe we will discuss how to set up a simple profiler.

Setting up a new profiler

Setting up a new profiler is really easy as at the moment there is only one class in Zend Framework 2 that can be used as a profiler. This class is called `Zend\Db\Adapter\Profiler\Profiler` and can be instantiated right away. Let's take a look at the following snippet:

```php
<?php
use Zend\Db\Adapter\Profiler\Profiler;

// Instantiate the Zend\Db\Adapter\Profiler\Profiler
$profiler = new Profiler();

// Let's assume $connection is an active Db\Adapter,
// we then need to set the profiler to be used by the
// adapter.
$connection->setProfiler($profiler);
```

That's it; this is basically all that is needed to start profiling everything from the database. The only thing that is left to do for us is to get the profiles back whenever we are done with querying (or whenever we need it really). Let's consider the following example:

```php
<?php
// This will return all the statements that have been
// executed by the adapter.
$results = $profiler->getProfiles();
```

The `$result` variable will now be filled with the statistical information about the statements executed. This result could look similar to the following:

```
array(3) {
    [0] => array(5) {
      ["sql"] => string(77)
         "INSERT INTO `cards` (`color`, `type`, `value`)
         VALUES (:color, :type, :value)"
      ["parameters"] => object(
  Zend\Db\Adapter\ParameterContainer)#255 (3) {
          ["data":protected] => array(3) {
          ["color"] => string(7) "diamond"
          ["type"] => string(7) "picture"
          ["value"] => string(6) "Goblin"
      }
      ["positions":protected] => array(3) {
        [0] => string(5) "color"
        [1] => string(4) "type"
        [2] => string(5) "value"
      }
```

```
        ["errata":protected] => array(0) {
      }
    }
    ["start"] => float(1372316727.1188)
    ["end"] => float(1372316727.1209)
    ["elapse"] => float(0.0020461082458496)
  }
}
```

How it works...

The database profiler is first being attached to the database adapter, making the adapter aware of the existence of the profiler. The adapter will start profiling (it does this by using the `Profiler::profileStart()` method) the statement every time it executes a statement, making sure that everything important will be logged about the statement.

When the database adapter has finished executing the statement, it will let the profiler know that the statement is done (it will execute the `Profiler::profileFinish()` method).

As we can see from the previous example we can view the SQL statement executed and also the parameters used. After that the start time, end time, and time elapsed are also added so that we can spot any potential bottlenecks in the code easily.

All in all this is very useful tool that requires almost nothing in code to work, and is still efficient for developers who want to find faults in their databases' performance.

There's more...

Another great little tool we can take a look at is the Zend Developer Tools, which is a module made by Zend that fits in Zend Framework 2 that provides very useful debugging tools. If we want to know more, we can find the tools at `https://github.com/zendframework/ZendDeveloperTools`.

Creating a Database Access Object

Although we can use a dozen different methods to standardize our database functionality, a Database Access Object (or DAO) can be used efficiently to achieve this. This recipe is a working example of how to make your own, and begin organizing your functionality.

Database Access Object (from now on DAO) is used to simplify functionality to and from our database(s). The idea behind a DAO is to create mapping classes that have a single responsibility on their functionality. This means that, for example, we have a table called `cards`, which also has a mapping called `Cards`. This `Cards` mapping will then contain all the functionality we need to use in that table.

This could include, for example, the CRUD (Create, Read, Update, and Delete) functionality, but also more complex methods such as calculations. The idea behind a mapping class is that we are able to hide the layout of the database and provide an interface for the rest of the application, which is reliable and consistent without the application needing to know how the database is structured.

For the recipe we will use the database layout that has a table called `cards`, with the following columns:

- `id` (primary key)
- `color`
- `value`
- `type`

How to do it...

A DAO is a great way of organizing our database functionality in the application, so that we will always have a clear structure of our logic. In this recipe, we'll show how to make one of our own.

Creating our new module and configuration

Our DAO is going be in a completely separate module, as that is the best way of separating the different pieces of code. So, we go ahead to create a new module DAO, which should have the following directory structure:

```
module\DAO\
  config\
    module.config.php
  src\
    DAO\
  Connection\
    Connector.php
  DTO\
    Cards.php
```

```
Mapper\
  Cards.php
  MapperAbstract.php
  MapperInterface.php
  Module.php
```

Once we have created the necessary folders, we can copy the default `Module.php` from the `Application` module over to our `DAO` folder. We then open our new `Module.php`, and make sure the `namespace` is set to `DAO` as well.

Now, it is time to create a new `/module/DAO/config/module.config.php` file and add the following lines:

```php
<?php

return array(
    // This is going to be the configuration from which we
    // will read. Obviously the username/password should
    // be in the local.php but we will just put it here
    // example wise.
    'dao' => array(
        'hostname' => 'localhost',
        'username' => 'some_user',
        'password' => 'some_password',
        'database' => 'book',

        // This mapper will contain all of our mapper
        // classes such as DAO\Db\Mapper\Cards and let them
        // know which table they need to connect to.
        'mapper' => array(
            'Cards' => 'cards',
        ),
    ),

    // Initialize our service manager so that we can reach
    // our mappers from anywhere else in the application
    // (every mapper should have its own entry) and our
    // connector which should be reached only by the
    // mappers and not anywhere else
    'service_manager' => array(
        'invokables' => array(
            'DAO_Connector' =>'DAO\Db\Connection\Connector',
            'DAO_Mapper_Cards' =>'DAO\Db\Mapper\Cards',
        ),
    ),
);
```

This pretty basic configuration will be used by our database connector later on to get the connection details from.

Creating a connector

Next, we want to create our connector, which is basically a class that will create a database adapter and set everything up for us. It will not do anything else than that, so we should be able to code one easily.

Let's now create a file called `/module/DAO/src/DAO/db/Connection/Connector.php` in the `DAO\Db\Connection namespace` and add the following code:

```php
<?php

// Set the correct namespace
namespace DAO\Db\Connection;

// We will be using the following classes
use Zend\ServiceManager\ServiceLocatorAwareInterface;
use Zend\ServiceManager\ServiceLocatorInterface;
use Zend\Db\Adapter\Adapter;

// We are going to make this as a Service, so make sure
// we implement the ServiceLocatorAwareInterface
class Connector implements ServiceLocatorAwareInterface
{
    // Our service locator will be placed in here
    protected $serviceLocator;

    // Now set our service manager instance required by the
    // ServiceLocatorAwareInterface
    public function setServiceLocator(ServiceLocatorInterface
    $serviceLocator)
    {
        $this->serviceLocator = $serviceLocator;
    }

    // And add our getter for the service manager, as is required by
    // the ServiceLocatorAwareInterface
    public function getServiceLocator()
    {
        return $this->serviceLocator;
    }
```

```php
/**
 * Initializes a connection and returns a fresh
 * adapter.
 *
 * @return \Zend\Db\Adapter\Adapter
 * @throws \Exception
 */
public function initialize()
{
  // Get the configuration from the module.config.php
  $dao = $this->getServiceLocator()->get('config');

  // The following array of configuration items should
  // be in there
  $configItems = array(
    'hostname',
    'username',
    'database',
    'password'
  );

  // Check if everything is there in the configuration
  foreach ($configItems as $required) {
    if (!in_array($required, array_keys($dao['dao'])))
    {
      // If there is a config item missing, just let
      // the develop know
      throw new \Exception("{$required} is not in the DAO
configuration!");
    }
  }

  // We can assume we have everything, now set up our
  // MySQL connection
  return new Adapter(array(
    'driver' => 'Pdo_Mysql',
    'database' => $dao['dao']['database'],
    'hostname' => $dao['dao']['hostname'],
    'username' => $dao['dao']['username'],
    'password' => $dao['dao']['password'],
  ));
}
}
```

That is it for the class definition; we are now able to initialize the connection if we have the right items available in our configuration. If not, the method will throw an exception and let us know anyway.

Creating a mapper interface

We want to create a mapper interface now on which we will base all our future mapper classes. We do this because we want to make sure that all our mapper classes contain at least some of the methods we want. Our mapper interface will, therefore, define a small selection of methods we want our mapper classes to have.

Now, let's create file called `/module/DAO/src/DAO/Db/Mapper/MapperInterface.php` in the `DAO\Db\Mapper` namespace and add the following code:

```php
<?php

// Make sure we have the namespace right
namespace DAO\Db\Mapper;

// Note that this is an interface, and not a regular
// class.
interface MapperInterface
{
  // We need an insert method in our mapper.
  public function insert($data);

  // And obviously we want to update data
  public function update($data);

  // If we want to update, we also want to delete data
  public function delete($id);

  // And of course we want to load one specific record
  public function load($id);

  // Last but not least we also want a method to get all
  // the records in the table
  public function getAll();
}
```

As we see this is a pretty straightforward file as interfaces don't actually do any implementation of the code at all.

Creating an abstract mapper class

Although the interface doesn't implement any of the code, an abstract class can. We want to create a file called `/module/DAO/src/DAO/Db/Mapper/MapperAbstract.php` in the same `DAO\Db\Mapper` namespace, which will contain a method that will create a connection to the database, point to the right table, and return a freshly baked `Zend\Db\Sql\Sql` object:

```php
<?php

// Namespace, do I need to say more ;-)
namespace DAO\Db\Mapper;

// Use the following classes
use Zend\ServiceManager\ServiceLocatorAwareInterface;
use Zend\ServiceManager\ServiceLocatorInterface;
use Zend\Db\Sql\Sql;

// Note that we are again using the
// ServiceLocatorAwareInterface and therefore need to
// implement the getServiceLocator and setServiceLocator
// (not shown here).
class MapperAbstract implements ServiceLocatorAwareInterface
{
  // Our sql object will be put here
  private $sqlObject;

  // We'll just put our service locator in here
  protected $serviceLocator;
```

Everything set up, now let's create the method we need for our connection (don't forget to create `setServiceLocator` and `getServiceLocator` methods as well!):

```php
// This method will set up our connection, initialize
// the right table and return a Sql object
protected function getSqlObject()
{
  // We only want to set up our connection once, no
  // point in doing it more, right?

  if ($this->connection === null) {
    // Get our configuration from the
    // module.config.php
    $config = $this->getServiceLocator()->get('config');
```

```
// Get our class name
$class = explode('\\', get_class($this));

// Now check if our class name is defined in the
// mapper configuration of the dao configuration,
// so that we can get our table name. Looks more
// complicated than it is really.
if (isset($config['dao']['mapper']) === true
&& isset($config['dao']['mapper'][end($class)])) {

    // Get the database adapter from our connector
    $adapter = $this->getServiceLocator()
                    ->get('DAO_Connector')
                    ->initialize();

    // We have a configuration, now return our SQL
    // object with the right table name included
    $this->sqlObject = new Sql(
      $adapter,
      $config['dao']['mapper'][end($class)]
    );
      } else {
        // Make sure the developer knows not all the
        // configuration is set.
        throw new \Exception("Configuration dao\mapper\\".
          end($class). " not set.");
  }
  }

    // Now return our sql object
    return $this->sqlObject;
  }
}
```

Our freshly created connection method can now be used by mappers to get a `Zend\Db\Sql\Sql` object, which is relevant to the table they want to work in.

Creating a Data Transfer Object

Now, let's create a new **Data Transfer Object** (**DTO**) file called /module/DAO/src/DAO/Db/DTO/Cards.php in the DAO\Db\DTO namespace and add the following code:

```php
<?php

// Namespace, quite essential
namespace DAO\Db\DTO;

// We should name our class simply Cards, as that is
// used in the mapper later on as well
class Cards
{
  // Our 'cards' table exists of an id column, color,
  // type and value, let's just define them as private
  // properties.
  private $id;
  private $color;
  private $type;
  private $value;
```

Now that we have set our private properties, we will also create some basic getters and setters for them. Use the following code for getters:

```php
public function getId() { return $this->id; }
public function getColor() { return $this->color; }
public function getType() { return $this->type; }
public function getValue() { return $this->value; }
```

The getters are now done, which was pretty easy, now let's do the setters:

```php
// The id will only be set if we update a record, or
// when we retrieve a record from a database. Never
// when we want to insert a record.
public function setId($id) {
  $this->id = $id;
}

// Make sure we can only use colors that are valid in
// our table.
public function setColor($color)
{
  $validColors = array('diamond', 'spade', 'heart', 'club');
```

```
    if (in_array($color,$validColors)== false) {
      throw new \Exception(
        "Type can only be 'diamond', 'spade', 'heart'".
        "or 'club'."
      );
    }

    $this->color = $color;
}

// Make sure only a valid type is entered.
public function setType($type)
{
    $validTypes = array('number', 'picture');

    if (!in_array($type, $validTypes)) {
      throw new \Exception(
        "Type can only be 'number' or 'picture'."
      );
    }

    $this->type = $type;
}

// A value can only have a maximum of 6 character
public function setValue($value)
{
    $maxValue = 6;

    if (strlen($value) >$maxValue) {
      throw new \Exception(
        "Maximum length of value is 6."
      );
    }

    $this->value = $value;
}
```

The setters were obviously a little more complicated as we also wanted to make sure the data we put in is valid for our database. This way we can safely parse object to the mapper later on and be sure that everything will go all right.

Now, create the last method which is a construct so that we can easily set the properties without needing to do that manually afterwards:

```php
public function __construct($type, $value, $color, $id = null)
{
    // Id is optional, so see if it is parsed or not
    if ($id !== null) $this->setId($id);

    $this->setColor($color);
    $this->setType($type);
    $this->setValue($value);
}
}
```

We now created a simple DTO which we can use to communicate to some methods in our mapper. Now, last but not least let's create the mapper class!

Creating a mapper class

The mapper will be the main DAO class that we will use in the application because it will be the class that has the methods for `insert`, `getAll`, and so on.

Let's start by creating a `/module/DAO/src/DAO/Db/Mapper/Cards.php` file in the `DAO\Db\Mapper` namespace and add the following code:

```php
<?php

namespace DAO\Db\Mapper;

use Zend\Db\Sql\Where;
use DAO\Db\DTO\Cards as CardsDto;
use DAO\Db\Mapper\MapperInterface;

// This class will extend and implement both our
// Abstract as our Interface class
class Cards extends MapperAbstract implements MapperInterface
{
```

Let's create a method for deleting a row first:

```php
/**
 * Delete a specific row.
 *
 * @param int $id
 */
```

```php
public function delete($id)
{
  // Get our fresh Sql object from our Abstract method
  $sql = $this->getSqlObject();

  // Create a new WHERE clause
  $where = new Where();

  // When deleting we want to match on an id
  $where->equalTo('id', $id);

  // Statements can throw exceptions, so make sure we
  //catch them in time.
  try {
    // Create a new delete object with our where class
    // attached and then immediately turn it into a
    // statement. That is called pure laziness
    $statement = $sql->prepareStatementForSqlObject(
      $sql->delete()->where($where)
    );

    // Execute the statement
    $result = $statement->execute();

    // If there is more than 0 rows deleted return
    // true, otherwise false
    return $result->getAffectedRows() > 0;
  } catch (\Exception $e) {
    // Something went terribly wrong, just ignore it
    // for now ;-)
    // TIP: Don't do this in real life, at least log your
    //exceptions.
    return false;
  }
}
```

We have created a simple `delete` method, now let's continue and create our `getAll` method, which will retrieve all the records in the database:

```php
/**
 * Returns all the records in the database.
 *
 * @return \DAO\Db\DTO\Cards
 */
```

```php
public function getAll()
{
  // Get the SQL object
  $sql = $this->getSqlObject();

  // Prepare a select statement
  $statement = $sql->prepareStatementForSqlObject(
    $sql->select()
  );

  // Execute the freshly made statement
  $records = $statement->execute();

  // Create our return array
  $retval = array();

  // Loop through the records and add them to the
  // result array
  foreach ($records as $row) {
    // Create a new Cards DTO and assign our record
    $retval[] = new CardsDto(
      $row['type'],
      $row['value'],
      $row['color'],
      $row['id']
    );
  }

  return $retval;
}
```

After we have created our `getAll`, which returns an array with Cards DTO's we will now create the method to insert a record:

```php
/**
 * Inserts a record.
 *
 * @param \DAO\Db\DTO\Cards $data
 */
public function insert($data)
{
  // We can easily insert this as we know the DTO has
  // already taken care of the validation of the values.
```

```php
if (!$data instanceof DAO\Db\DTO\Cards) {
  throw new \Exception(
    "Data needs to be of type DAO\Db\DTO\Cards"
  );
}

// Get our SQL object
$sql = $this->getSqlObject();

try {
  // Create our insert statement with the values
  // assigned into it.
  $statement = $sql->prepareStatementForSqlObject(
    $sql->insert()
      ->values(array(
        'color' => $data->getColor(),
        'type' => $data->getType(),
        'value' => $data->getValue()
      ))
  );

  // Execute our statement
  $result = $statement->execute();

  // Return our primary key after insertion
  return $result->getGeneratedValue();
} catch (\Exception $e) {
  // Something went wrong, handle exception and
  // return false
  return false;
  }
}
```

Now, let's continue to our `load` method, which will return only one record:

```php
public function load($id)
{
  // Get the SQL object
  $sql = $this->connection();

  // A fresh WHERE clause
  $where = new Where();
  $where->equalTo('id', $id);
```

```
    try {
      // Prepare a select statement with the where
      // clause attached.
      $statement = $sql->prepareStatementForSqlObject(
        $sql->select()->where($where)
      );

      // Execute the statement and return the first row
      $record = $statement->execute()->current();

      // Now let's return a fresh Cards DTO object
      return new CardsDto(
        $record['type'],
        $record['value'],
        $record['color'],
        $record['id']
      );
    } catch (\Exception $e) {
   return false;
    }
  }
```

We now created the `load` method, which will return a Cards DTO object for us to use, now last but not least the `update` method:

```
  public function update($data)
  {
    // We can easily insert this as we know the DTO has
    // already taken care of the validation of the
    // values.
    if (get_class($data) !== 'DAO\Db\DTO\Cards') {
      throw new \Exception(
        "Data needs to be of type DAO\Db\DTO\Cards"
      );
    }

    if ($data->getId() === null) {
      throw new \Exception(
          "Can't update anything if we don't have a card id!"
      );
    }

    // Get the connection
    $sql = $this->connection();
```

```php
    try {
      // Create the WHERE clause
      $where = new Where();
      $where->equalTo('id', $data->getId());

      // Create the update class
      $update = $sql->update();

      // Set the where clause
      $update->where($where);
      $update->set(array(
        'color' => $data->getColor(),
        'type' => $data->getType(),
        'value' => $data->getValue()
      ));

      // Create the statement
      $statement = $sql->prepareStatementForSqlObject($update);

      // Execute the statement
      $result = $statement->execute();

      // If more than 0 rows were updated return true,
      // otherwise false
      return $result->getAffectedRows() > 0;
    } catch (\Exception $e) {
      return false;
    }
  }
}
```

We have now successfully created a mapper class and that also concludes our DAO. We can now easily get the mapper through the service manager in (for example) a controller (/module/Cards/src/Cards/Controller/CardController.php) by using the following code:

```php
<?php

namespace Cards\Controller;

use Zend\Mvc\Controller\AbstractActionController;

class CardsController extends AbstractActionController
{
```

```php
 public function viewAction()
 {
   if (!$this->getParam('id'))
       throw new \Exception("Missing id");

   // Get the record to load from the query string
   $id = $this->params()->fromQuery('id');

   // Get the card mapper from the service manager
   $cardMapper = $this->getServiceLocator()
                   ->get('DAO_Mapper_Cards');

   // Load the requested card
   $card = $cardMapper->load($id);

   // Dump the loaded record to the screen
   echo '<pre>'. Print_r($card, true). '</pre>';
 }
}
```

And, because we created an abstract and interface it is really easy for us to create new mappers as well. Obviously it requires us to be consistent, but that is a good thing.

How it works...

About the DAO

A DAO or Database Access Object is a design pattern that creates an abstract environment for developers to access their database related methods. This means that we create a standardized environment for us to work in, which is not only consistent but also very stable. Because, we limit ourselves in our way of working with database queries and objects we create a piece of code which is very easy to work with.

In this recipe, we created a very simple DAO, which (to my personal opinion) is a good basis, but probably not the most efficient way of creating one. We just took one example how a DAO can be implemented, but we should never shut our eyes to the literally dozens of different ways of implementing it.

About the recipe

Because our configuration contains a mapper array with all the mapper class names (DAO\Db\Mapper\Cards becomes simply cards in the configuration) we cannot go wrong. This separates the local configuration of the database environment from the code. So if we were to change the table name to 'books' we only have to change the configuration and the code would still work!

We are going to create a DTO so that we can easily insert/update and return records through a standardized way. So instead of returning an array in our selections we can then return an object which will contain everything we need. This way we make sure our data is filtered and simply transferrable.

As we can see in the `insert` method in the Mapper class we assume the DTO object contains the right information for us to insert our record. Although this method is far from perfect, it is a good method of separating our checking and validating of the data to another object (in our case the DTO) so we can just concentrate on inserting the record. This separation is essential to a good working DAO.

6
Modules, Models, and Services

In this chapter we will cover:

- ▶ Creating a new module
- ▶ Using modules as a widget
- ▶ A Model and a Hydrator
- ▶ A basic service

Introduction

This chapter is all about making the most of our module, models, and services and their configuration. As Zend Framework 2 is a modular framework, the modules are obviously one of the most important features of it all. We will talk about customizing the configuration of the modules and how to go about working with models and services as well.

Creating a new module

The core of the Zend Framework 2 library is modular and everything is based around a module based system. That's why we will explain this thoroughly in this recipe, so that we can use it in its best way possible.

Getting ready

We will be using the Zend Framework skeleton application for creating new modules. As a reminder, the Zend Framework 2 skeleton application can be found at `https://github.com/zendframework/ZendSkeletonApplication`.

How to do it...

Creating a new module is like starting a new drawing, it is exciting and fun to create a new functionality, but there are always rules we need to obey. In this recipe we will discuss what the rules are for setting up a new module.

Creating the Module.php

We can start off with just a simple class file (that is, `/module/Sample/Module.php`) in the right namespace (`Sample`) with nothing in it, which is basically the only requirement there is for the module.

```php
<?php

namespace Sample;

class Module {}
```

We can add the following method to our `Module` class:

```php
public function getConfig()
{
    return include __DIR__ . '/config/module.config.php';
}
```

Let's just create a `/module/Sample/config/module.config.php` file now which will return an empty array for now, as we don't really have anything to configure at the moment.

```php
<?php

return array();
```

To hook up to the bootstrap event, a module just have to have an `onBootstrap` method in our `Module.php` file which does all the bootstrapping for us, or we can define bootstrap events that are executed when the bootstrap has been called (my personal favorite).

Let's see both ways, beginning with the onBootstrap method:

```php
public function onBootstrap(MvcEvent $e)
{
  // Let's do something on the bootstrap!
}
```

As we can see a simple method is enough to create bootstrapping, it bootstraps the module as soon as the bootstrap event of the application is being triggered.

Attaching to the loadModules.postevent

The following example makes use of the /module/Application/Module.php file:

```php
<?php

namespace Application;

// Use the following classes
use Zend\ModuleManager\ModuleManager;
use Zend\ModuleManager\ModuleEvent;

class Module
{
  public function init(ModuleManager $moduleManager)
  {
    // We can get the event manager from our module manager
    $eventManager = $moduleManager->getEventManager();

    // Now we will attach ourselves to the event manager's event
    $eventManager->attach(
      ModuleEvent::EVENT_LOAD_MODULES_POST,
      function(ModuleEvent $event)
      {
        // Do something with our event, for example print the name
        // of the module to the screen.
        echo '<pre>'. $event->moduleName. '</pre>';
      },
      // Make sure the rest of the triggers all have been
      // triggered already
      -1000
    );

  }
}
```

Implementing the getAutoloaderConfig

The following example is part of the `Module.php` Module class:

```php
public function getAutoloaderConfig()
{
  return array(
    'Zend\Loader\StandardAutoloader' => array(
      'namespaces' => array(
        __NAMESPACE__ => __DIR__ . '/src/'. __NAMESPACE__
      ),
    ),
  );
}
```

Let's consider the following updated code snippet:

```php
public function getAutoloaderConfig()
{
  return array(
    'Zend\Loader\ClassMapAutoloader' => array(
      __DIR__ . '/autoload_classmap.php',
    ),
    'Zend\Loader\StandardAutoloader' => array(
      'namespaces' => array(
        __NAMESPACE__ => __DIR__ . '/src/'. __NAMESPACE__
      ),
    ),
  );
}
```

An example of a class map file (file `/module/Application/autoload_classmap.php`) is as follows:

```php
<?php
return array(
  'Sample\Model\Test' => __DIR__ . '/src/Sample/Model/Test.php',
  'Sample\Model\Test2' => __DIR__. '/src/Sample/Model/Test2.php',
);
```

Implementing the getControllerConfig, getControllerPluginConfig and getViewHelperConfig

Take a look at the following implementation of the `getViewHelperConfig` (in the `/module/Application/Module.php` file):

```php
<?php

namespace Application;

// We need this for the view helper config to be picked up
use Zend\ModuleManager\Feature\ViewHelperProviderInterface;

class ModuleViewHelperProviderInterface
{
  public function getViewHelperConfig()
  {
    // See if the class exists first, to show off that we can use
    return array(
      'invokables' => array(
          // This is a non existing view helper, but is just to
          // show off how to use it.
          // Note: You cannot use a closure as an invokable.
          'exampleHelp' => 'Application\View\Helper\Example',
      )
    );
  }
}
```

How it works...

Modules are instantiated by the framework once they are introduced in the `application.config.php` file. Adding a module's name the file will make the framework look for the `Module.php` file in a directory bearing the name of the module. The `Module.php` file has a selection of methods which will then be called by the framework at certain times, such as loading the configuration or running the module's bootstrap.

For our example we will create a module called `Sample`, which will have a simple controller and an action that outputs some text.

To make sure the `ModuleManager` of Zend Framework 2 picks up our new module, we need to understand how the `ModuleManager` works. What the `ModuleManager` does is fulfill three operations:

- It collects the enabled modules
- It initializes the module, if necessary
- It collects the configuration from all the modules

Although we can automatically create a whole new module with the `ZFTool`, it is still recommended that we know how to make and structure a module without it. We will now begin to create a module that makes sure the `ModuleManager` is happy with it.

Creating a new module directory

When creating a new module, we will follow the recommended way as much as possible, so that we get the clearest view on how it all works. First things first, create a new directory in the module directory with the name `Sample`. This directory will be our main directory when it comes to code relating to the Sample module's namespace, that way we will have every related piece of code enclosed in this directory.

Creating the Module.php

The most important file of every module is the `Module.php` file, which is not only required, but also feeds the framework with important information about things such as; where to find the code, and what the configuration is.

Although it won't actually initialize anything in the module, it is the basic requirement to have a module. Note that because of the lack of code inside `Module.php`, it is impossible for our application to reach any of the code inside the module as well.

The first thing we want to do is to make sure that the framework will read our configuration for our module. This can be done by defining a `getConfig` method in our `Module.php`. which requires an array as a return value.

Because laziness is a skill, we will simply return the complete `module.config.php` file to the `ModuleManager`. We don't have to do this, we can also just return an array with the configuration in as well, but for the purpose of maintainability it is best to keep the actual configuration separate from the code. This way we don't have to edit the code to edit the configuration.

Now we know that our `ModuleManager` will load our configuration, it is time to go over the bootstrapping of the module, which is sometimes necessary to initialize more after the configuration has loaded. This can be done either by using the `onBootstrap` method in the `Module.php` or attach to the `ModuleManager` events.

Optionally act on ModuleManager events

Another way of making sure additional pieces of code will be executed is by attaching them to one of the four other strategic events, namely: `loadModules`, `loadModules.resolve`, `loadModule`, and `loadModules.post`.

To explain them all a bit better, let's go through all of them briefly.

Understanding the loadModules event

The `loadModules` event will be triggered when the framework is loading the modules, so for initializing a module, this event is pretty much useless as it will never be called in the `Module.php` file (the event has already passed at that point).

At this point the framework is still loading the modules up and nothing has happened for our module yet. That is why this event is primarily used on the internal side of the framework and not on our development side. However, as this event is active throughout the whole process of loading the modules, it also does some extra things when all the other events have been done.

This event triggers the following functionality by default:

- `Zend\Loader\ModuleAutoloader::register`: This makes sure that the `Module` class can be found and initiated (It doesn't initiate it just yet, just checks).

- `Zend\ModuleManager\Listener\ConfigListener ::onLoadModulesPre ::onLoadModulesPost`: This functionality merges the configuration files with the local configuration files found by the defined `glob()` in the application configuration when all the modules have been loaded, but only if the configuration is not cached internally (which is not the case by default).

- `Zend\ModuleManager\Listener\LocatorRegistration::onLoadModulesPost`: This attaches the service of the modules to the `ServiceManager`, if the `Module` class implemented the `LocatorRegisteredInterface` interface, which will immediately add the `Module` class to the DI. This is done when all the modules are loaded up.

The loadModules.resolve event

Another internal event and not an event a module can make use of is this event, which is triggered for each module that is defined in our `application.config.php`. This event will actually try to find the `Module` class in the `Module.php` file of our module, so although not useful (yet) to our module, it is coming close!

This event triggers the following functionality by default:

  ▶ `Zend\ModuleManager\Listener\ModuleResolverListener::__invoke`: This initiates the `Module` class

The loadModule event

Now the object (of the `Module` class) has been created; the `loadModule` event will pass it along the other listeners.

This event triggers the following functionality by default:

  ▶ `Zend\ModuleManager\Listener\ConfigListener::onLoadModule`: This merges the configuration by getting all the getConfig() of the Module classes.

  ▶ `Zend\ModuleManager\Listener\AutoloaderListener::__invoke`: This calls the `getAutoloaderConfig` in the `Module` class if available, so that we can get the autoloading going for our new module

  ▶ `Zend\ModuleManager\Listener\InitTrigger::__invoke`: This calls the init method in the `Module` class if available.

  ▶ `Zend\ModuleManager\Listener\OnBootstrapListener::__invoke`: This attaches the `onBootstrap` method of the `Module` class to the bootstrap event of the application, so it will be run at that time.

  ▶ `Zend\ModuleManager\Listener\ServiceListener::onLoadModule`: This calls the following methods in the `Module` class if they exist (we will discuss these methods more extensively a bit further on in this recipe):

    ❏ `getServiceConfig`: This gets the `ServiceManager` configuration from the Module class.

    ❏ `getControllerConfig`: This gets the controller configuration from the `Module` class.

    ❏ `getControllerPluginConfig`: This gets the controller plugin configuration from the `Module` class.

    ❏ `getViewHelperConfig`: This gets the view helper configuration from the `Module` class.

The flow chart showing a simplified version of the module loading is as follows:

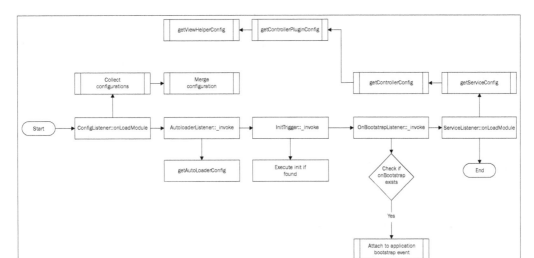

The loadModules.post

The `loadModules.post` event is triggered when the modules have successfully been loaded and the last bits are needed to be done to complete it all.

This event triggers the `Zend\ModuleManager\Listener\ServiceListener::onLoad ModulesPost` functionality by default and instructs the `ServiceManager` to create more services if needed.

Attaching to the loadModules.post event

The `loadModules.post` event is the first event we can attach a handler to in our application, as events before this one can only be used by the internal listeners of Zend Framework 2. That means there is not a good way of hooking up to those events without making extensions to the framework ourselves.

However, the `loadModules.post` event can still be useful, for example, to make sure that our modules are loaded correctly, or for something else modules config related. The best way of attaching ourselves to this event is by doing that as high up as we can get with the `EventManager`. In this case that would be in the `init()` method of the module, as that is being called during the `loadModule` event, and is the first one to contain an `EventManager`.

More specific non configuration file Module configuration

Sometimes we choose not to use the `module.config.php` file all the time and we require a more dynamic instantiation, for example, of services or configurations. Luckily Zend Framework 2 fully supports any dynamic configuration functionality. As discussed before, there are five extra methods we can add to our `Module` class, which are picked up during the module instantiation, namely the `getAutoloaderConfig`, `getServiceConfig`, `getControllerConfig`, `getControllerPluginConfig`, and the `getViewHelperConfiguration`.

The getAutoloaderConfig method

The `getAutoloaderConfig` method will load in the autoloader configuration for our module and expects an array that is compatible with the `AutoloaderFactory`. There are generally two accepted ways of autoloading in Zend Framework 2. The first one is to use the `StandardAutoloader`, which requires a namespace to load and a directory to recur in to. The second one is to use a `ClassMapAutoloader`, which is basically a file with an array where every full domain and class name is mentioned with a reference to a specific file.

Both of them are displayed in the examples, so please take a look at them to see the differences.

We use the `StandardAutoloader` in the first example because we just want our framework to load all the classes in the namespace `__NAMESPACE__` (which is `Sample` for our module) through the directory structure in the `[current directory]/src/Sample` directory. This means that a class that is fully called in `Sample\Model\Test`, will be searched in `/src/Sample/Model/Test.php`. Although this is very handy in a development environment, it isn't handy in a production environment because a large application will put a lot of strain on searching for the class names we need. In that case we can use this `StandardAutoloader`, but in addition (with a higher priority) we will also be using a `ClassMapAutoloader` that loads in a static file with all the class names mapped to a specific directory.

This tells PHP that when we search for the class `Sample\Model\Test`, it can be found in `/src/Sample/Model/Test.php` (or wherever really, as we point the PHP directly towards our file anyway). Both of the autoloaders are PSR-0, where PSR stands for PHP Standards Recommendation compliant.

In the second example we can see we prioritized our `autoload_classmap.php` file over our `StandardAutoloader`, which means that it will look first in our class map file before trying to find it on its own.

To make the framework use the `getAutoloaderConfig` method, we must make sure our `Module` class implements the `Zend\ModuleManager\Feature\AutoloaderProviderInterface` class as well as it consists of the single public method `getAutoloaderConfig()`, otherwise it will not try to execute it. Remember that simply implementing the method is not enough to make it fire as it specifically looks if we are implementing the interface.

The getControllerConfig, getControllerPluginConfig, and getViewHelperConfig methods

Instead of loading the controller configuration through the `module.config.php` or as an override, we can also do it through the `get***Config` method. We can create the method the same way as the `getServiceConfig` method, as the return object can either be of the instance `Zend\ServiceManager\Config` or simply an array with the configuration like in the `module.config.php`.

If we want to use these methods, we should not forget to implement our class with the respective interfaces:

For the getControllerConfig method we need to implement the Zend\
ModuleManager\Feature\ControllerProviderInterface interface.

For the getControllerPluginConfig method we need to implement
the Zend\ModuleManager\Feature\ControllerPluginProviderInterface
interface.

And lastly for the getViewHelperConfig method we need to implement
the Zend\ModuleManager\Feature\ViewHelperProviderInterface interface.

Using modules as a widget

Widgetizing is a great method to use modules on different places in our applications. That's why this recipe will explain everything we need to know about doing this in the best way possible.

Getting ready

A working Zend Framework 2 skeleton application is needed to make full use of this recipe.

How to do it...

Widgets, they even sound great! We will explain in this recipe what they do and how they can be used.

Creating the Comment/Controller/Index

We will create a small controller that will return some example comments, which are static and hardcoded for example only. First we should make sure we have a `Comment` module, so we create the following directories and files:

```
module/
    Comment/
        config/
            module.config.php
        src/
            Comment/
                Controller/
                    IndexController.php
        view/
            comment/
                index/
                    index.phtml
        Module.php
```

Once we have the structure in place, we put the simplest code in the `/module/Comment/Module.php` as possible to initialize the module, which is shown as follows:

```php
<?php

namespace Comment;

class Module
{
  // Get our module configuration
  public function getConfig()
  {
    return include __DIR__
        . '/config/module.config.php';
  }

  // Initialize our autoloader to load in our sources
  public function getAutoloaderConfig()
  {
    return array(
      'Zend\Loader\StandardAutoloader' => array(
```

```
            'namespaces' => array(
                __NAMESPACE__ => __DIR__ . '/src/'
                                . __NAMESPACE__,
            ),
        ),
    );
    }
}
```

As we can see this is the most basic `Module` class because we don't need it more advanced than this. Now let's quickly create our `module.config.php`configuration file in the `/module/Comment/config` directory:

```php
<?php

return array(
    // Set up a quick route to our comment output
    'router' => array(
        'routes' => array(
            'comment' => array(
                'type' => 'Zend\Mvc\Router\Http\Literal',
                'options' => array(
                    'route'    => '/comment',
                    'defaults' => array(
                        'controller' => 'Comment\Controller\Index',
                        'action'     => 'index',
                    ),
                ),
            ),
        ),
    ),

    // Make sure the controllers are invokable by us
    'controllers' => array(
        'invokables' => array(
            'Comment\Controller\Index' =>
                        'Comment\Controller\IndexController'
        ),
    ),
```

```
    // Set the path to our view templates
    'view_manager' => array(
      'template_path_stack' => array(
          __DIR__ . '/../view',
      ),
    ),
);
```

Now that we have set up a quick configuration with a route that responds to the /comment and maps to Comment\Controller\IndexController::indexAction, we can continue with the actual controller (present in the file /module/Comment/src/Comment/Controller/IndexController.php):

```php
<?php

namespace Comment\Controller;

use Zend\Mvc\Controller\AbstractActionController;
use Zend\View\Model\ViewModel;

class IndexController extends AbstractActionController
{
  // This is the action that will be called whenever we
  // browse to /comment
  public function indexAction()
  {
    // Initialize our view model
    $view = new ViewModel();
    $comments = array();

    // Create some static comments and put them in our
    // comments array
    for ($i = 0; $i < 10; $i++) {
      $comments[] = array(
          'name' => 'John Doe ('. $i. ')',
          'comment' => 'Lorem ipsum dolor sit amet...'
      );
    }

    // Return our view with the comments and make sure
    // the renderer doesn't output our layout
```

```
        // (setTerminal(true) does that)
        return $view->setVariable('comments', $comments)
                    ->setTerminal(true);
    }
}
```

After creating our controller, the only thing we still need to create is the view script (found in the file `/module/Comment/view/comment/index/index.phtml`) to actually output the data in an HTML table:

```
<?php /* loop through the comments to display them */ ?>
<?php foreach ($this->comments as $comment) : ?>
  <tr>
    <td>
      <?php echo $comment['name'] ?>:
    </td>
    <td>
      <?php echo $comment['comment'] ?>
    </td>
  </tr>
<?php endforeach; ?>
```

Now that we have our module completely set up, we can go forth and display the comments in widget form.

Using a view helper to display the comments statically

First we want to create the view helper itself, let's do this in the `Comment` module (the file is `/module/Comment/src/Comment/View/Helper/Comments.php`) as the data comes from there anyway:

```
<?php

namespace Comment\View\Helper;

use Zend\View\Helper\AbstractHelper;
use Comment\Controller\IndexController;

class Comments extends AbstractHelper
{
  public function __invoke()
  {
```

```
        // Instantiate the controller with the comments
        $controller = new IndexController();

        // Execute our indexAction to retrieve the
        // ViewModel, and then add the template of that
        // ViewModel so it renders fine
        $model = $controller->indexAction()->setTemplate(
                'comment/index/index'
        );

        // Now return our rendered view
        return $this->getView()
                ->render($model);
    }
}
```

Now all we need to do is add this view helper to our module configuration (the file is /module/ Comment/config/module.config.php) before we are able to use it in our views:

```
    // Add our custom view helper to the configuration
    'view_helpers' => array(
        'invokables' => array(
            'comments' => 'Comment\View\Helper\Comments',
        ),
    ),
```

Obviously we omitted the rest of the configuration here because we didn't want to repeat ourselves. All that is left now is to actually use the new view helper in the code. We can do that to put the following code line in our view script:

```
    <?php echo $this->comments() ?>
```

Using the forward to render the comments statically

Let's take a look at a code snippet of the action of a forward() in our CommentController (the file is /module/Application/src/Application/ Controller/CommentController.php):

```
    public function forwardAction()
    {
        $view = new ViewModel();
```

```
    // Get the comments from the index action
    $comments = $this->forward()
                        ->dispatch(
        // Which controller do we want to invoke
        'Comment\Controller\Index',

        // Any specific options we want to give it
        array('action' => 'index')
    );

    // If we keep this on true it will return an
    // exception, so let us not do that
    $comments->setTerminal(false);

    // Return the view model with the comments as child
    return $view->addChild($comments, 'comments');
}
```

This gets the dispatched state of a action in a specific controller (our `Comment\`
`Controller\Index::indexAction`) and returns it to us as `$comments`, which is a
`ViewModel` instance. We add that as a child to our current `ViewModel` instance and then we
can simply output it in the view script with the following code snippet:

```
<?php echo $this->comments ?>
```

This is the same as outputting a normal variable, and although this gives the feeling of a clean
solution, the `forward()` method is known to be horrible under stress.

Getting the comments through AJAX

Let's see what our view script looks like with JavaScript:

```
<!-- our comments will load in here -->
<table class="comments"></table>

<!-- first we want to make sure that we load in the jQuery script that
comes with the Zend Framework 2 skeleton application -->
<script src="<?php echo $this->basePath('/js/jquery.min.js') ?>"></
script>

<!-- this is the JavaScript bit -->
<script>
```

```
        // This means jQuery will execute this code whenever
        // the document is done loading
        $(document).ready(function() {
          // We want to do a GET request in the background
          $.get(
            // We want to get this URL
            '/comment',

            // This function will be executed when the
            // data comes back from the server
            function(data) {
              // Put our data (the comments) in our
              // comments table
              $('table.comments').html(data);
            }
          );
        });
      </script>
```

How it works...

This is the scenario: We have a page that contains a little story on which users should be able to comment. The comment section however is used at several other locations in the code and should therefore be reusable. There is one proviso though, the comment section doesn't change in layout, it will always need to be displayed in the same way.

What we are going to do is create three different but valid implementations of a module that is being used as a widget. The first two will give a more static feel to it all, while the third one will use JavaScript (jQuery to be exact) to load in the comments. We will also discuss a theoretic fourth solution that should be considered.

But first of all we will set up a small environment, which we will use in the examples of retrieving the comments.

We will set up the `Application/Controller/Comment` controller, which will have the `helperAction`, `forwardAction` and `ajaxAction` method defined. Then we will use this controller and actions to display the comments in the `Comment/Controller/Index` controller and `indexAction` method.

Using a view helper to display the comments statically

The best option to display the comments in a statically way would be to create a view helper specific for this widget. What we are going to do is create a small view helper that will render our comments and return them to our view. This way we can use it everywhere in our view without using a lot of hassle like the `forward()` or the AJAX methods do.

As we can see in the example we instantiate our controller and manually retrieve the output of the action, and after that manually render it and return it to the view. It is not always this easy to do it like this, but it comes close to reality.

Using the forward() method to render the comments statically

A not so great idea but worth mentioning also is getting the comments through the `forward()` method, which is brittle, but at least it doesn't go through the whole MVC initialization like the AJAX functionality does.

Getting the comments through AJAX

Last but not least, a more technical non-PHP solution is also at hand for when we want to be a little bit more creative, or when our environment just calls for an asynchronous AJAX implementation. The idea of this method is that we simply retrieve our comments from the URL through JavaScript, or to be specific the jQuery library.

This only requires us to input a bit of client-side JavaScript in the view script to make it work, which is nice because we don't have to fiddle around much in the code. It has one big con though, and that is that we will go through the whole MVC process again to receive the comments from the database. On the other hand it will speed up the response time from our main action as it doesn't have to load the comments statically. Another con would be that the user visiting the website needs a JavaScript enabled browser to see the comments, but we assume everyone has such browser nowadays.

As we can see from the example this is a pretty easy method of retrieving the comments as well, but it has afore mentioned cons attached to it. However, sometimes this might be the best option performance wise to get the data from somewhere else. It is all due to the architecture of the application.

About Widgetizing

Widgetizing a module is not something that is absolutely native to the framework, but as we can see in the paragraphs above, it is something we can easily achieve by using (not abusing) the framework as much as we can.

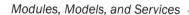

Especially, instantiating controllers and executing actions our self is a great method of dealing with data from other sections of the application. We want to be wary, however, that modules in itself should be independent (or at least as much as possible) from each other and we shouldn't rely too much on their existence.

But to be fair, a perfect situation is never to be found, and we just need to do some concessions some times. In our case this might be relying on modules that might not be there.

A Model and a Hydrator

Models are a great way of providing functionality to our application, and they keep out the Controllers, nice and clean, from any critical logic. A hydrator is also great to transport properties and values from one model to another, that's why we will go into this a bit further to make optimal use of it.

Getting ready

For this recipe a working Zend Framework 2 skeleton application is necessary to make full use of the examples.

How to do it...

In this recipe we will set up a model and a method for hydrating data to and from our model, so that we have easy access of our data.

Accessing the Model

We can access the model anywhere in the application by simply adding a use statement at the top of our document:

```
use Application\Model\SampleModel;

$object = new SampleModel();
```

Or by using the fully qualified name of the class including the namespace, shown as follows:

```
$object = new \Application\Model\SampleModel();
```

If there is already a class `SampleModel` used, but from a different namespace, or if we just want to give it a more identifiable name, we can also use an alias (this is not model specific however, and we can use it in any namespaced class), as shown as follows:

```
use Application\Model\SampleModel as NewModel;

$object = new NewModel();
```

Creating a Hydrator

First thing now is to set up an incredibly simple model (the file is `/module/Application/src/Application/Model/SampleModel.php`), which we will use to hydrate, as shown as follows:

```php
<?php

namespace Application\Model;

class SampleModel
{
  private $engine;
  private $primary;
  private $text;

  public function getEngine() {
    return $this->engine;
  }

  public function setEngine($engines) {
    $this->engine = $engines;
  }

  public function getPrimary() {
    return $this->primary;
  }

  public function setPrimary($primary) {
    $this->primary = $primary;
  }

  public function getText() {
    return $this->text;
  }
```

```php
    public function setText($text) {
      $this->text = $text;
    }
  }
```

This incredibly basic model has nothing more than a couple of properties with the getters and setters for them, simple, but it will work for what we try to achieve next. What we are going to do in the following example is create a `Hydrator` for our imaginary database table and then we will hydrate our `SampleModel` (the file is /module/Application/src/Application/ Model/Hydrator/SampleModelHydrator.php) with the data from the table:

```php
<?php

// Don't forget to namespace our class
namespace Application\Model\Hydrator;

// We extend from this class
use Zend\Stdlib\Hydrator\AbstractHydrator;

class SampleModelHydrator extends AbstractHydrator
{
  private $mapping = array(
    'id' => 'primary',
    'value' => 'engine',
    'description' => 'text',
  );

  // Extracts the hydrated model
  public function extract($object) {}

  // Hydrates our values to our model
  public function hydrate(array $data, $object) {}
}
```

We have now set up the very basic class of our hydrator, and the methods implemented are now only the definitions that we need to have because of the `AbstractHydrator` class. The next thing we want to do is to get some code in there to actually make it all work. The first thing we will implement further is the `hydrate()` method, which will make our `SampleModel` hydrated:

```php
public function hydrate(array $data, $object)
{
  // If we are not receiving an object, throw an
  // exception
  if (is_object($object) === false) {
    throw new \Exception(
      "We expect object to be an actual object!"
    );
  }

  // Loop through the properties and values
  foreach ($data as $property=>$value) {
    // Check if the property exists in our mapping
    if (array_key_exists($property, $this->mapping)) {
      // Build the setter method from our property
      $setter = 'set'. ucfirst(
        $this->mapping[$property]
      );

      // Set the value of the property
      $object->$setter($value);
    }
  }

  // Now return our hydrated object
  return $object;
}
```

Now let's use the `extract()` method, which extracts values from our `SampleModel` and puts them back in an array which is also formatted in the way we used to hydrate the object in the first place:

```php
public function extract($object)
{
  // If we are not receiving an object, throw an
  // exception
  if (is_object($object) === false) {
    throw new \Exception(
        "We expect object to be an actual object!"
      );
  }
```

```
    $return = array();

    foreach ($this->mapping as $key=>$map) {
      // Build the getter method from our property
      $getter = 'get'. ucfirst($map);

      // Get the property value from the object
      $return[$key] = $object->$getter();
    }

    return $return;
}
```

And that is how we extract values from the hydrated object again.

Creating a Hydrator strategy

If we change the setter of the primary property in the SampleModel (the file is /module/ Application/src/Application/Model/SampleModel.php) a bit so that it reflects in the following code snippet:

```
public function setPrimary($primary)
{
  // Throw an exception if there is no valid integer.
  if (!is_int($primary)) {
    throw new \Exception(
        "Primary ({$primary}) should be an integer!"
    );
  }

  $this->primary = $primary;
}
```

Let's begin by creating our strategy first (the file is /module/Application/src/ Application/Model/Hydrator/Strategy/SampleHydratorStrategy.php):

```
<?php

namespace Application\Model\Hydrator\Strategy;

// We need to implement this interface to make it
// eligible to be a strategy
use Zend\Stdlib\Hydrator\Strategy\StrategyInterface;
```

```php
class SampleHydratorStrategy implements StrategyInterface
{

    // This method is called every time an object is
    // extracted
    public function extract($value)
    {
      // Check if the value is an integer
      if (is_int($value) === true) {
        return (int)$value;
      } else {
        // No integer, just randomly return an integer
        return rand(0, 10000);
      }
    }

    // This method is called just before the property of
    // the object is hydrated
    public function hydrate($value)
    {
      // Check if it is a valid integer
      if (is_int($value) === true) {
        return (int)$value;
      } else {
        // No integer, random integer is returned
        return rand(0, 10000);
      }
    }
}
```

Now we need to change two things in our `Hydrator` class that we created, so that it also supports a hydrator strategy (the file is `/module/Application/src/Application/Model/Hydrator/SampleModelHydrator.php`):

```php
public function extract($object)
{
  [.. current code in between ..]

  $return[$key] = $this->extractValue(
      $key, $object->$getter()
  );
```

```
    [.. rest of the code ..]
}

public function hydrate(array $data, $object)
{
    [.. current code in between ..]

    $object->$setter($this->hydrateValue(
        $this->mapping[$property], $value)
    );

    [.. rest of the code ..]
}
```

As we can see we just have to change the previously shown code lines to make sure it will use the hydrator strategy in our `Hydrator`.

In the next example we will use the `Hydrator` to hydrate our `SampleModel` into our controller (the file is `/module/Application/src/Application/Controller/IndexController.php`):

```php
<?php

namespace Application\Controller;

use Application\Model\SampleModel;
use Application\Model\Hydrator\SampleModelHydrator;
use Application\Model\Hydrator\Strategy\SampleHydratorStrategy;
use Zend\Mvc\Controller\AbstractActionController;

class IndexController extends AbstractActionController
{
    public function indexAction()
    {
        // First initialize our model
        $model = new \Application\Model\SampleModel();

        // Now create a sample array of data to hydrate
        $data = array(
            'id' => 'Some Id',
            'value' => 'Some Awesome Value',
            'description' => 'Pecunia non olet',
        );
```

```
    // Now create our Hydrator
    $hydrator = new SampleModelHydrator();

    // Now add our strategy to it to check when the primary
    // value is set (if we put id, it would be when the
    // value would be retrieved)
    $hydrator->addStrategy(
        "primary",
        new SampleHydratorStrategy()
    );

    // Now hydrate our model
    $newObject = $hydrator->hydrate($data, $model);

    // And if necessary extract the values again
    $extract = $hydrator->extract($newObject);

    // Now output it to the browser
    echo "<pre>". print_r($extract, true). "</pre>";
    }
}
```

If we know to compare the extract with the original values, we can see that the ID has now changed to a random number, telling us that the hydrator strategy did its job.

How it works...

Think about the model's purpose

By definition models should only have functionality related to one very specific bit of the application. This means that if we begin coding a model, we should be wary of this requirement and make our models lightweight and catering to a single purpose.

The idea of having loads of small pieces of code is that we can maintain them a lot easier and we only load in what we like to use. Instead of loading a 40k line long model with all the functionality we need, we would like to split them up into small functional classes that do only the thing they are named after.

Think about the model's location

The location of a model is especially important as we still want to be able to find it among our code. We should give it a name that resembles its functionality, and it should be as specific as possible.

If we name the model we need to put it in a location that makes sense as well, so when we look for certain functionality we can find it by just searching in the location it makes most sense.

For example let's take a look at the following namespace and class name:

```
Api\Model\Db\User\Information
```

If we search for a method that retrieves user information then this class would be a great way to start searching.

Think about the model's methods

The model's methods are obviously the most important part of the model, it is also one that is usually highly overlooked. For example, developers sometimes use the wrong visibility while defining their methods, which then ends up misused by other developers who think they could (or couldn't) use a specific method because of its visibility.

Sometimes the method is named incorrect or the visibility has been set up wrong and in turn we end up refactoring the code. All of which can be avoided by simply thinking about it beforehand.

> It is also wise to name your method right, put the visibility in correctly, and to use a strict naming convention in our application.
>
> Method names should be named through camelCase, and only protected and private methods should be allowed to start with an underscore.

Unit test the model

Testing your model is a great way of making sure the output of the methods always matches with the output we expect it to be. An even greater way (personally) of developing your model is to TDD (Test-Driven Development) the code so that you have an objective test, instead of a subjective one, if you write the test after you have written the method. We will talk more about unit testing and TDD in *Chapter 9, Catching bugs*.

Document your class

Usually documenting a class is overlooked and/or unmaintained while it should be something that exists in your routine. Even if we are the only developer on the project, and we know that in ten years time we would still be the only developer, it still is a great way to let the future us know why we created that method, what it does, and what we can expect back from it.

The PHP DocBlock or in short the PHPDoc is the formal standard of documenting our code in the comment format. First of all a docblocks can be identified by the following syntax:

```
/**
 * This is used to describe the method, file or class.
 *
 * @param string $parameterOne Some description here.
 * @result Boolean
 * @throws Some\Exception
 * @author J. Callaars <bcallaars@gmail.com>
 */
public function someMethod($parameterOne);
```

As we can see, the difference between a normal comment block and a docblock is the two asterisks used at the beginning. After that the first line should always describe the current method, class, or file (whatever the context is). The lines' following that consists of tags, which are used to define certain properties of the docblock. For example, the `@param` tag is used to define parameters to a method, which have a type defined, and the name of the parameter behind it. The `@result` expresses the return value of the method call, and the `@throws` tells us an exception can occur in this method. And last but not least `@author` tells us who initially created the method/file/class.

Obviously there are dozens of other tags to use, of which most of them can be found at `http://en.wikipedia.org/wiki/PHPDoc`.

We would recommend using the `phpDocumenter` syntax to use as the standard of creating method and class documentation as it is an industry standard and gives us the option of generating a technical document quite easily.

Creating a hydrator

Hydrators are the sort classes that can be used to hydrate a specific class with values given to the `Hydrator`.

This can be especially useful when retrieving data from a database table, and when we want to map it to another model, where the model doesn't have to know the mappings of the table and the `TableGateway` doesn't have to know how to map them to the model. In such cases a `Hydrator` is perfect for the job as an intermediary between the model and the data access layers.

The `mapping` property defines the mapping between the received array (which we use to hydrate) and the property on the object side. So, for example, if our array contains a key ID, we will set the property primary in the object. Obviously this is the most basic a `hydrate` method can possibly be as it simply checks if we have a valid object and then checks if we have the property name we want to set and sets it if it does.

Creating a hydrator strategy

Now that we have a simple hydrator, we might want to take a look at another amazing piece of the Zend Framework that is new: the hydrator strategy. The hydrator strategy is simply said a transformation of one value that is being parsed into the `Hydrator`.

We changed the primary setter of the hydrator now, so that when it receives something else than an integer it will throw an exception.

But our `Hydrator` is not familiar with the properties in our model, which in turn means that when an incompatible value is used and exception will be thrown. To overcome this (and many other) problem, we can use a hydrator strategy, which will have the last chance to set a value before it goes to the model.

Now the plan is that we will create a hydrator strategy which will check our primary property and make sure it returns an integer. As we can see further on, we basically created an `extract` and a `hydrate` method, which will check if there is an integer as value, and if not return a random integer. This way we safeguard ourselves so that any value that comes in to our model is at least the type we expect it to be.

About models

Models are just regular classes which differ nothing from any other class. However, the principle behind a model is that all the business critical logic is defined in them. An MVC prefers to have skinny controllers (which means no or almost no logic) and fat models.

Hydrators, on the other hand, are classes that are used in between models, for example, when exchanging data from one model to another, or from a `TableGateway` to a model and vice versa. Obviously not every model we write would require a `Hydrator`, but as applications tend to grow, we like to implement new features without having to change the existing ones, and `Hydrator` can then serve as a key factor as they can serve as a proxy between objects.

There's more...

There is a lot more to write about hydrators, and especially the different kinds of default hydrators that come with Zend Framework 2. If we want to know more about that we should check the documentation for the `Zend\Stdlib\Hydrator\ArraySerializable`, `Zend\Stdlib\Hydrator\ClassMethods`, and the `Zend\Stdlib\Hydrator\ObjectProperty` hydrator.

A basic service

One of the biggest features of Zend Framework 2 is the `ServiceManager`, and its influence in the framework can be seen from the initial bootstrap of our application. We don't need a reason to explain why this recipe goes deeper in this topic, do we?

Getting ready

Again a Zend Framework 2 skeleton application should be running to make the full use of our examples in this recipe.

Before we continue let's get the difference between a service and a model. Although the definition of a service is sometimes a judgment call, it can be safely assumed that a service is a class between the controller and the model, which hides all the nasty logic from the controller, for example, checking the authentication or calling a method in a model. Another thing that is different is that the service in our case will be managed by the `ServiceManager`, and therefore, can be called from any controller (and other service) in our application.

How to do it...

Services are a great way of making sure our functionality can be accessed virtually anywhere in our application, and in this recipe we will show exactly how to do that!

Creating a service

We will create our service in the `/module/Application/src/Application/Service/Example.php` file:

```php
<?php

namespace Application\Service;
```

```
use Zend\ServiceManager\ServiceLocatorAwareInterface,
    Zend\ServiceManager\ServiceLocatorInterface;

class Example implements ServiceLocatorAwareInterface
{
  protected $serviceLocator;

  // This is set by our initialization so we don't
  // actually have to do this ourselves probably
  public function setServiceLocator(ServiceLocatorInterface
  $serviceLocator)
  {
    $this->serviceLocator = $serviceLocator;
  }

  // Retrieve the service locator, handy if we want to
  // read some configuration
  public function getServiceLocator()
  {
    return $this->serviceLocator;
  }

  // Let's create a simple string to rot13 encoder as an
  // example
  public function encodeMyString($string)
  {
    return str_rot13($string);
  }
}
```

Now the only thing that left to do is to add this service to the module configuration (the file is /module/Application/config/module.config.php), so it can be reached by the rest of the application as well:

```
<?php
return array(
  'service_manager' => array(
    'invokables' => array(
      // We are going to call our service through the
      // ExampleService name
      'ExampleService' => 'Application\Service\Example',
    ),
  ),
);
```

Of course, this is again a snippet to show what needs to be added to the configuration. We can now easily retrieve the service in, for example, a controller by performing the following:

```
// This is an example from within a controller and
// returns a rot13 encoded string
echo $this->getServiceLocator()
        ->get('ExampleService')
        ->encodeMyString("Service? Easily created!");
```

Getting a service from within a controller

This example shows that it is very easy to retrieve a service from a controller. From within a service we can also easily get our main application configuration by performing the following:

```
// This is executed from within a service class and will
// return the configuration of the application
$config = $this->getServiceLocator()->get('config');
```

How it works...

We created a very basic service and added it to the configuration of our Application module. The idea behind it is that we can show how easy it is to create a service, activate it, and use it in the application. We will create a service that is going to be managed by the ServiceManager and does nothing more than rot13 encode on a string.

To create a service we only need to implement the Zend\ServiceManager\ServiceLocatorAwareInterface in our class, which predefines two methods, the getServiceLocator and the setServiceLocator. The setServiceLocator is called during instantiation, and most of the time (at least not when we add the service in our configuration) we don't have to do this manually.

The getServiceLocator however is a method we can use to get the ServiceLocator, from which we can get useful things like other services, or perhaps the configuration of the application itself.

Services are instantiated either at the loading of the modules if they are in the module configuration, or just during some place in the application. However, when we instantiate the service, we know that we can always get it through the same easy get() method of the ServiceLocator anywhere else in the application once it has been instantiated.

7
Handling Authentication

In this chapter we will cover:

- ▶ Understanding Authentication methods
- ▶ Setting up a simple database Authentication
- ▶ Writing a custom Authentication method

Introduction

In this chapter we will talk about the different methods of authentication and we will show you some examples on how to authenticate and how to create your own authentication method.

Understanding Authentication methods

In a world where security on the Internet is such a big issue, the need for great authentication methods is something that cannot be missed. Therefore, Zend Framework 2 provides a range of authentication methods that suits everyone's needs.

Getting ready

To make full use of this recipe, I recommend a working Zend Framework 2 skeleton application to be set up.

How to do it...

The following is a list of authentication methods—or as they are called adapters—that are readily available in Zend Framework 2. We will provide a small overview of the adapter, and instructions on how you can use it.

The DbTable adapter

Constructing a `DbTable` adapter is pretty easy, if we take a look at the following constructor:

```
public function __construct(
    // The Zend\Db\Adapter\Adapter
    DbAdapter $zendDb,

    // The table table name to query on
    $tableName = null,

    // The column that serves as 'username'
    $identityColumn = null,

    // The column that serves as 'password'
    $credentialColumn = null,

    // Any optional treatment of the password before
    // checking, such as MD5(?), SHA1(?), etcetera
    $credentialTreatment = null
);
```

The Http adapter

After constructing the object we need to define the `FileResolver` to make sure there are actually user details parsed in.

Depending on what we configured in the `accept_schemes` option, the `FileResolver` can either be set as a `BasicResolver`, a `DigestResolver`, or both.

Let's take a quick look at how to set a `FileResolver` as a `DigestResolver` or `BasicResolver` (we do this in the `/module/Application/src/Application/Controller/IndexController.php` file):

```php
<?php

namespace Application;

// Use the FileResolver, and also the Http
// authentication adapter.
use Zend\Authentication\Adapter\Http\FileResolver;
use Zend\Authentication\Adapter\Http;
use Zend\Mvc\Controller\AbstractActionController;
```

```
class IndexController extends AbstractActionController
{
  public function indexAction()
  {
    // Create a new FileResolver and read in our file to use
    // in the Basic authentication
    $basicResolver = new FileResolver();
    $basicResolver->setFile(
      '/some/file/with/credentials.txt'
    );

    // Now create a FileResolver to read in our Digest file
    $digestResolver = new FileResolver();
    $digestResolver->setFile(
      '/some/other/file/with/credentials.txt'
    );

    // Options doesn't really matter at this point, we can
    // fill them in to anything we like
    $adapter = new Http($options);

    // Now set our DigestResolver/BasicResolver, depending
    // on our $options set
    $adapter->setBasicResolver($basicResolver);
    $adapter->setDigestResolver($digestResolver);
  }
}
```

How it works...

After two short examples, let's take a look at the other adapters available.

The DbTable adapter (again)

Let's begin with probably the most used adapter of them all, the DbTable adapter. This adapter connects to a database and pulls the requested username/password combination from a table and, if all went well, it will return to you an identity, which is nothing more than the record that matched the username details.

To instantiate the adapter, it requires a Zend\Db\Adapter\Adapter in its constructor to connect with the database with the user details; there are also a couple of other options that can be set. Let's take a look at the definition of the constructor:

The second (`tableName`) option speaks for itself as it is just the table name, which we need to use to get our users, the third and the fourth (`identityColumn`, `credentialColumn`) options are logical and they represent the username and password (or what we use) columns in our table. The last option, the `credentialTreatment` option, however, might not make a lot of sense.

The `credentialTreatment` tells the adapter to treat the `credentialColumn` with a function before trying to query it. Examples of this could be to use the `MD5(?)` function, `PASSWORD(?)`, or `SHA1(?)` function, if it was a MySQL database, but obviously this can differ per database as well. To give a small example on how the SQL can look like (the actual adapter builds this query up differently) with and without a credential treatment, take a look at the following examples:

With credential treatment:

```
SELECT * FROM `users` WHERE `username` = 'some_user' AND `password` =
MD5('some_password');
```

Without credential treatment:

```
SELECT * FROM `users` WHERE `username` = 'some_user' AND `password` =
'some_password';
```

When defining the treatment we should always include a question mark for where the password needs to come, for example, `MD5(?)` would create `MD5('some_password')`, but without the question mark it would not insert the password.

Lastly, instead of giving the options through the constructor, we can also use the setter methods for the properties: `setTableName()`, `setIdentityColumn()`, `setCredentialColumn()`, and `setCredentialTreatment()`.

The Http adapter (again)

The HTTP authentication adapter is an adapter that we have probably all come across at least once in our Internet lives. We can recognize the authentication when we go to a website and there is a pop up showing where we can fill in our usernames and passwords to continue.

This form of authentication is very basic, but still very effective in certain implementations, and therefore, a part of Zend Framework 2. There is only one big massive *but* to this authentication, and that is that it can (when using the basic authentication) send the username and password clear text through the browser (ouch!).

There is however a solution to this problem and that is to use the Digest authentication, which is also supported by this adapter.

If we take a look at the constructor of this adapter, we would see the following code line:

```
public function __construct(array $config);
```

The constructor accepts a load of keys in its `config` parameter, which are as follows:

- ▸ `accept_schemes`: This refers to what we want to accept authentication wise; this can be `basic`, `digest`, or `basic digest`.

- ▸ `realm`: This is a description of the realm we are in, for example `Member's area`. This is for the user only and is only to describe what the user is logging in for.

- ▸ `digest_domains`: These are URLs for which this authentication is working. So if a user logs in with his details on any of the URLs defined, they will work. The URLs should be defined in a space-separated (weird, right?) list, for example `/members/area /members/login`.

- ▸ `nonce_timeout`: This will set the number of seconds the nonce (the hash users login with when we are using Digest authentication) is valid. Note, however, that nonce tracking and stale support are not implemented in Version 2.2 yet, which means it will authenticate again every time the nonce times out.

- ▸ `use_opaque`: This is either true or false (by default is true) and tells our adapter to send the opaque header to the client. The opaque header is a string sent by the server, which needs to be returned back on authentication. This does not work sometimes on Microsoft Internet Explorer browsers though, as they seem to ignore that header. Ideally the opaque header is an ever-changing string, to reduce predictability, but ZF 2 doesn't randomize the string and always returns the same hash.

- ▸ `algorithm`: This includes the algorithm to use for the authentication, it needs to be a supported algorithm that is defined in the `supportedAlgos` property. At the moment there is only MD5 though.

- ▸ `proxy_auth`: This boolean (by default is false) tells us if the authentication used is a proxy Authentication or not.

It should be noted that there is a slight difference in files when using either Digest or Basic. Although both files have the same layout, they cannot be used interchangeably as the Digest requires the credentials to be MD5 hashed, while the Basic requires the credentials to be plain text. There should also always be a new line after every credential, meaning that the last line in the credential file should be empty.

The layout of a credential file is as follows:

```
username:realm:credentials
```

For example:

```
some_user:My Awesome Realm:clear text password
```

Instead of a `FileResolver`, one can also use the `ApacheResolver` which can be used to read out `htpasswd` generated files, which comes in handy when there is already such a file in place.

The Digest adapter

The `Digest` adapter is basically the `Http` adapter without any Basic authentication. As the idea behind it is the same as the `Http` adapter, we will just go on and talk about the constructor, as that is a bit different in implementation:

```
public function __construct($filename = null, $realm = null,
    $identity = null, $credential = null);
```

As we can see the following options can be set when constructing the object:

- `filename`: This is the direct filename of the file to use with the Digest credentials, so no need to use a `FileResolver` with this one.
- `realm`: This identifies to the user what he/she is logging on to, for example `My Awesome Realm` or `The Dragonborn's lair`. As we are immediately trying to log on when constructing this, it does need to correspond with the credential file (see *The Http adapter* for the credential file layout).
- `identity`: This is the username we are trying to log on with, and again it needs to resemble a user that is defined in the credential file to work.
- `credential`: This is the Digest password we try to log on with, and this again needs to match the password exactly like the one in the credential file.

We can then, for example, just run `$digestAdapter->getIdentity()` to find out if we are successfully authenticated or not, resulting in `NULL` if we are not, and resulting in the identity column value if we are.

The LDAP adapter

Using the LDAP authentication is obviously a little more difficult to explain, so we will not go in to that in full as that would take quite a while. What we will do is show the constructor of the `LDAP` adapter and explain its various options. However, if we want to know more about setting up an LDAP connection, we should take a look at the documentation of ZF2, as it is explained in there very well:

```
public function __construct(array $options = array(), $identity =
    null, $credential = null);
```

The options parameter in the construct refers to an array of configuration options that are compatible with the `Zend\Ldap\Ldap` configuration. There are literally dozens of options that can be set here so we advise to go and look at the LDAP documentation of ZF2 to know more about that. The next two parameters identity and credential are respectively the username and password again, so that explains itself really.

Once you have set up the connection with the LDAP there isn't much left to do but to get the identity and see whether we were successfully validated or not.

About Authentication

Authentication in Zend Framework 2 works through specific adapters, which are always an implementation of the `Zend\Authentication\Adapter\AdapterInterface` and thus, always provides the methods defined in there. However, the methods of Authentication are all different, and strong knowledge of the methods displayed previously is always a requirement. Some work through the browser, like the `Http` and `Digest` adapter, and others just require us to create a whole implementation like the `LDAP` and the `DbTable` adapter.

Setting up a simple database Authentication

After seeing all the authentication methods available, it is time to see how it will actually work when we have a database authentication in place. This recipe will explain all the ins and outs of this specific method.

Getting ready

A working Zend Framework 2 skeleton application with the PHP sqlite extension loaded and enabled.

How to do it...

Database authentication can very well be the most widely used authentication method there is. In this recipe we will set up our own database authentication.

Setting up the module initialization

We will create our database as soon as possible after initialization of the modules, so we will attach it to an event called route or `MvcEvent::EVENT_ROUTE`. As a template for the `Module.php` we can just copy over the `Application/Module.php` file and change the namespace; we will be working in the `onBootstrap` method anyway, and the rest of the `Module` class can stay the same (but don't forget to change the namespace!).

Let's take a look at the code of our `/module/Authentication/Module.php` file:

```
// We can assume the rest of the Module class file is
// exactly the same as the default
// Application/Module.php file, except of course the
// namespace.
public function onBootstrap(MvcEvent $e)
{
  // This is also default
  $eventManager = $e->getApplication()->getEventManager();
  $moduleRouteListener = new ModuleRouteListener();
  $moduleRouteListener->attach($eventManager);
```

```php
// And now we let the magic happen (this is the bit we
// will insert)
$eventManager->attach(
  // We want to attach to the route event, which means
  // it happens before our controllers are initialized
  // (because that would mean we already found the
  // route)
  MvcEvent::EVENT_ROUTE,

  // We are using this function as our callback
  function (MvcEvent $event)
  {
   // Get the database adapter from the configuration
   $dbAdapter = $event->getApplication()
                      ->getServiceManager()
                      ->get('db');

   // Our example is an in memory database, so the
   // table never exists, but better sure than sorry
   $result = $dbAdapter->query("
        SELECT name
         FROM sqlite_master
        WHERE type='table' AND name='users'
   ")->execute();

    // If we couldn't find a users table, we will
    // create one now (with an in memory db this is
    // always the case)
   if ($result->current() === false) {
     try {
       // The user table doesn't exist yet, so let's
       // just create some sample data
       $result = $dbAdapter->query("
         CREATE TABLE `users` (
            `id` INT(10) NOT NULL,
            `username` VARCHAR(20) NOT NULL,
            `password` CHAR(32) NOT NULL,
          PRIMARY KEY (`id`)
          )
         ")->execute();

        // Now insert some users
```

```
            $dbAdapter->query("
            INSERT INTO `users` VALUES
               (1, 'admin', '". md5("adminpassword"). "')
             ")->execute();

            $dbAdapter->query("
              INSERT INTO `users` VALUES
                 (2, 'test', '". md5("testpassword"). "')
                ")->execute();
          } catch (\Exception $e) {
          \Zend\Debug\Debug::dump($e->getMessage());
        }
      }
    });
  }
```

We have now created an event that will be triggered when we start routing. If we look carefully enough we can find one big mistake that will crash this code for sure. The problem of course being the db key in the ServiceManager, as we refer to a service we have yet to create. So let's get cracking and create that /module/Authentication/config/module.config. php file...

```php
<?php

return array(
  // Let's initialize the ServiceManager
  'service_manager' => array(
    'factories' => array(
      // Create a Db Adapter on initialization of the
      // ServiceManager
      'Zend\Db\Adapter\Adapter' =>
          'Zend\Db\Adapter\AdapterServiceFactory',
    ),

    // Let's give this Db Adapter the alias db
    'aliases' => array(
      'db' => 'Zend\Db\Adapter\Adapter',
    ),
  ),

  // We will now configure our Sqlite database, for
  // which we only need these two lines
  'db' => array(
```

```
        'driver' => 'Pdo_Sqlite',
        'database' => ':memory:',
    ),
);
```

That's it; our basic configuration to get the database going is done, and if we run the code now we can be certain our database is created.

Creating the authentication service

The next thing we want to do is to create our Authentication service, the service that will help our application do all the authentication functionality. Let's create this service in the `Authentication\Service` namespace, and let's call the class `Authentication` (the file is `/module/Authentication/src/Authentication/Service/Authentication.php`).

```php
<?php

// Set the namespace
namespace Authentication\Service;

use Zend\ServiceManager\ServiceLocatorAwareInterface;

// We give this one an alias, because otherwise
// DbTable might confuse us in thinking that it is
// an actual db table
use Zend\Authentication\Adapter\DbTable as AuthDbTable;
use Zend\Authentication\Storage\Session;

// We want to make a service, so we implement the
// ServiceLocatorAwareInterface for that as well
class Authentication implements ServiceLocatorAwareInterface
{
    // Storage for our service locator
    private $servicelocator;

    // Get the ServiceManager
    public function getServiceLocator()
    {
        return $this->servicelocator;
    }

    // Set the ServiceManager
    public function setServiceLocator(
    \Zend\ServiceManager\ServiceLocatorInterface $serviceLocator)
    {
```

```
        $this->servicelocator = $serviceLocator;
    }
```

Well that was easy; we just created our service... which does absolutely nothing at the moment. Let's first create a method that checks if we are authenticated or not. We do this by checking the authentication session, and see if it is empty or not. Assuming that in this case we only have a (authentication!) session when are actually authenticated, we can safely agree that we will be logged in;

```
    /**
     * Lets us know if we are authenticated or not.
     *
     * @return boolean
     */
    public function isAuthenticated()
    {
        // Check if the authentication session is empty, if
        // not we assume we are authenticated
        $session = new Session();

        // Return false if the session IS empty, and true if
        // the session ISN'T empty
        return !$session->isEmpty();
    }
```

We can easily just open a session as the namespace of the session will only be used for authentication purposes.

Let's now create our authentication, which will authenticate a username and password, and return a boolean stating that we are or aren't successful in authenticating:

```
    /**
     * Authenticates the user against the Authentication
     * adapter.
     *
     * @param string $username
     * @param string $password
     * @return boolean
     */
    public function authenticate($username, $password)
    {
        // Create our authentication adapter, and set our
        // DbAdapter (the one we created before) by getting
```

```
    // it from the ServiceManager. Also tell the adapter
    // to use table 'users', where 'username' is the
    // identity and 'password' is the credential column
    $authentication = new AuthDbTable(
      $this->getServiceLocator()->get('db'),
      'users',
      'username',
      'password'
    );

    // We use md5 in here because SQLite doesn't have
    // any functionality to encrypt strings
    $result = $authentication->setIdentity($username)
                             ->setCredential(md5($password))
                             ->authenticate();

    // Check if we are successfully authenticated or not
    if ($result->isValid() === true) {
      // Now save the identity to the session
      $session = new Session();
      $session->write($result->getIdentity());
    }

    return $result->isValid();
  }
```

As we saw in the previous code snippet, we created a simple authentication method that returns either true or false, depending on if we are authenticated or not. What it also does is save the identity to the authentication session, so we can see in our previous method if we were authenticated or not. We also need the identity in the session for when we want to get the username from our logged in user, which will retrieve with the following method:

```
  /**
   * Gets the identity of the user, if available,
   * otherwise returns false.
   * @return array
   */
  public function getIdentity()
  {
    // Clear out the session, we are done here
    $session = new Session();

    // Check if the session is empty, if not return the
    // identity of the logged in user
```

```
        if ($session->isEmpty() === false) {
          return $session->read();
        } else {
          return false;
        }
      }
    }
```

Now that we got our identity, it is also important that we are able to logout. In our case it is as simple as just clearing the session, because why would we make it more difficult than just that?

```
    /**
     * Logs the user out by clearing the session.
     */
    public function logout()
    {
      // Clear out the session, we are done here
      $session = new Session();
      $session->clear();
    }

    // This is our last method, close the bracket for the
    // class as well!
    }
```

We have now created a simple authentication service, and the only part left now is to register it in the service manager so that it will be instantiated when we boot up. We can do this in the `/module/Authentication/config/module.config.php` file as usual, and because we already have a `service_manager` configuration there, we can just plant the invokable in there:

```
<?php
return array(
  'service_manager' => array(
    // [The rest of the service manager configuration
    // comes here]

    // And our new invokable can be put here
    'invokables' => array(
    'AuthService' => 'Authentication\Service\Authentication',
    ),
  ),
);
```

And that's it for the service! All that is left now to do is create the `login/logout` action and then check if we are logged in or not. Let's begin with the `login/logout` action so that we are actually able to login!

Setting up the controller and action

Let's first change the `/module/Authentication/config/module.config.php` file while we are still in there so we can access our `login/logout` action, which is kind of crucial to us:

```php
<?php
return array(
    // [The configuration that we have now resides here..]

    // And our route configuration comes here..
    'router' => array(
        'routes' => array(
            'authentication' => array(
                'type'    => 'Literal',
                'options' => array(
                    'route'    => '/authentication',
                    'defaults' => array(
                    '__NAMESPACE__' =>
                            'Authentication\Controller',
                        'controller'    => 'Index',
                        'action'        => 'login',
                    ),
                ),
                'may_terminate' => true,
                'child_routes' => array(
                    'default' => array(
                        'type'    => 'Segment',
                        'options' => array(
                            'route'    => '[/:action]',
                            'constraints' => array(
                                'action'    => '[a-zA-Z][a-zA-Z0-9_-]*',
                            ),
                            'defaults' => array(),
                        ),
                    ),
                ),
            ),
        ),
    ),

    // Make our controller invokable
    'controllers' => array(
```

```
'invokables' => array(
  'Authentication\Controller\Index' =>
        'Authentication\Controller\IndexController'
  ),
),

// Make sure our template path is set correctly
'view_manager' => array(
  'template_path_stack' => array(
    __DIR__ . '/../view',
  ),
),

);
```

This basic route just makes `/authentication` redirect to our `loginAction` and because of the segment route we can simply do `/authentication/logout` to redirect to our `logoutAction`; if more explanation is required for the routes, we can review *Chapter 1, Zend Framework 2 Basics*, and look in the *Handling routines* recipe.

Let's continue creating our `/module/Authentication/src/Authentication/Controller/IndexController` in the `Authentication\Controller` namespace:

```php
<?php

namespace Authentication\Controller;

use Zend\Mvc\Controller\AbstractActionController;
use Zend\View\Model\ViewModel;

class IndexController extends AbstractActionController
{
}
```

We have simply declared our controller; now let's add the `logoutAction` (we will begin with that, as it is incredibly simple) and the `loginAction`:

```php
public function logoutAction()
{
  // Log out the user
  $this->getServiceLocator()
      ->get('AuthService')
      ->logout();
```

```
    // Redirect the user back to the login screen
    $this->redirect()
        ->toRoute('authentication');
}
```

As we can see this is almost too simple, but we won't complain if it works. Now let us create our `loginAction`, which basically looks if there is a post and if there is tries to login, otherwise shows a login form. Upon successful login we will be redirected to the `/application` route, and if not successful we will just display an error message:

```
public function loginAction()
{
    // See if we are trying to authenticate
    if ($this->params()->fromPost('username') !== null) {
        // Try to authenticate with our post variables from
        // the form we just send
        $done = $this->getServiceLocator()
                    ->get('AuthService')
                    ->authenticate(
            $this->params()->fromPost('username'),
            $this->params()->fromPost('password')
        );

        if ($done === true) {
            $this->redirect()
                ->toRoute('application');
        } else {
            \Zend\Debug\Debug::dump(
                "Username/password unknown!"
            );
        }
    }

    // On an unsuccessful attempt or just a get request
    // show the form.
    return new ViewModel();
}
```

As we can see the `loginAction` is merely checking if we have anything posted, and if we do, it lets the `AuthService` handle it. This way is not perfect as it doesn't check for malicious parameters or anything, but it does show how clean a controller is supposed to be with no login in there except the bare minimum parsing of variables.

The `logoutAction` doesn't contain a view script, as that action only redirects the user and never has a response of its own. The `loginAction`, however, does have view script, as it needs to show a form. Let's quickly build a view script for the `loginAction` now (the file is `/module/Authentication/view/authentication/index/login.phtml`):

```
<form action="/authentication" method="post">
  <label for="username">Username:</label>
  <input type="text" name="username" />

  <label for="password">Password:</label>
  <input type="password" name="password" />

  <button type="submit">Login</button>
</form>
```

A simple form to login and in my opinion doesn't require any explanation.

The last thing that we want to do know is to make sure nobody can access anything in the application other than the authentication if he/she is not logged in. We can do that by a new event in the Module (the file is `/module/Authentication/Module.php`) class of the Authentication module, which will check if we are logged in, and if not redirects us before any output is done to the screen:

```
public function onBootstrap(MvcEvent $e)
{
  // Get the event manager from the event
  $eventManager = $e->getApplication()->getEventManager();

  // Attach the module route listeners
  $moduleRouteListener = new ModuleRouteListener();
  $moduleRouteListener->attach($eventManager);

  // Do this event when dispatch is triggered, on the
  // highest priority (1)
  $eventManager->attach(
      MvcEvent::EVENT_DISPATCH,
      function (MvcEvent $event) {
      // We don't have to redirect if we are in a
      // 'public' area, so don't even try
      if ($event->getRouteMatch()->getMatchedRouteName()
                  === 'authentication') return;

      // See if we are authenticated, if not lets
      // redirect to our login page
```

```
        if ($event->getApplication()->getServiceManager()
                ->get('AuthService')->isAuthenticated() ===
          false)
    {
        // Get the response from the event
        $response = $event->getResponse();

        // Clear current headers and add our Location
        // redirection
        $response->getHeaders()
                ->clearHeaders()
                ->addHeaderLine(
            'Location', '/authentication'
        );

        // Set the status code to redirect
        $response->setStatusCode(302)
                ->sendHeaders();

        // Don't forget to exit the application, as we
        // don't want anything to overrule at this point
        exit;
      }
    },

    // Give this event priority 1
    1);
}
```

That's the event that we need, what happens is that we will simply be redirected to the login page whenever we try to reach a route which is not our authentication route.

How it works...

What we are going to do is create a simple database authentication that works through an in-memory SQLite database. This means that the database isn't stored and that all the tables and records need building up every time we request the page. Obviously this is highly inconvenient to use in a production environment, it is, however, excellent to show off how it works and is really handy to get something going quickly.

Assuming we are working on a default Zend Skeleton application, let's create a new module Authentication. This new module will contain the database connection, the authentication itself and the login and logout actions. When we created the directory for the new module, we should also be wary to add the new module in the application.config.php file, otherwise we might end up having trouble finding out why it doesn't do anything (oh yes, I am talking from experience).

First of all we built our in-memory database in the Module.php for the authentication. We then created a table called users, with a unique ID, username, and password. The ID consist of an integer, the username a variable character of 20 positions, and the password will be a character of 32, as that is the size of an MD5 encrypted string.

Because we set up a user table, and connected that table to the authentication adapter, we were able to authenticate the username and password simply. As an extra measure we made sure the user can't go to any other page than the login page when he isn't logged in, which we did by using an event that happens before the output was send to the user.

Writing a custom Authentication method

Sometimes the standard methods just don't cut it, and that is okay. That is why this recipe gives a clear insight into how to create our own authentication method.

Getting ready

For this recipe it would be preferred if there is a web environment that has SSL enabled. Configuring such an environment is outside the scope but it would be beneficial for the execution of this recipe.

An example of an environment like this would be an Apache 2 web server with mod_ssl correctly configured. To enable the certificate verification on Apache2, one needs to place the following code in their public/.htaccess file:

```
# Only execute the following code when mod_ssl is
# enabled
<IfModule mod_ssl.c>
  # This means the client can present their
  # certificate, but it doesn't need to be verifiable
  # by the server
  SSLVerifyClient optional_no_ca

  # This depth means the certificate can only be self-
  # signed otherwise it will be denied
  SSLVerifyDepth 0
```

```
      # We want to export the standard variables but also
      # the certificate data as well to use in PHP
      SSLOptions +StdEnvVars +ExportCertData
  </IfModule>
```

Another thing that is important to mention is that PHP should be configured (and compiled) with the `--with-openssl` parameter, otherwise the code to parse the certificate will not exist and thus, we would not be able to use the code. More information on how to do this can be found at `http://www.php.net/manual/en/book.openssl.php`.

How to do it...

Authentication by certification might be rare, but it is sometimes used when the level of security is a little bit higher than the average web application. In this recipe we will show an example of a certificate-based authentication.

Creating our adapter

Let's get started by creating our new adapter, which will be an implementation of `Zend\Authentication\Adapter\AdapterInterface` as we want to integrate as much as possible with the current authentication adapters.

As we already have an Authentication module from the previous recipe, we will just take that as the namespace in which we are going to work; just as easy as described earlier.

First let's create the adapter (the file is `/module/Authentication/src/Authentication/Adapter/Certificate.php`).

The adapter outline

We'll first start with our basic class outline:

```
// Set the right namespace
namespace Authentication\Adapter;

// We will use this to implement the right methods
use Zend\Authentication\Adapter\AdapterInterface;

// Out class name, not to forget the implementation
class Certificate implements AdapterInterface
{
  // Currently authenticate is the only method required
  // for the AdapterInterface; lucky us!
  public function authenticate() {}
}
```

Creating a getter and setter for any error messages

Normally we would come up with error messages as we go in development. But as this code is already made, we already have the error messages defined. There is no good way to describe these getters and setters, so we will just show them in the following piece of code so that it is at least clear what is going on (the file is /module/Authentication/src/ Authentication/Adapter/Certificate.php):

```php
// After coding the adapter we found the following
// errors that need to be relayed to the user/developer

// Invalid certificate, there is no certificate set
const AUTH_FAIL_INV_CERT = 0;

// Insecure connection, no HTTPS
const AUTH_FAIL_NO_HTTPS = 1;

// Couldn't parse the certificate, invalid certificate
const AUTH_FAIL_PARSE_CERT = 2;

// Certificate is expired
const AUTH_FAIL_EXP_CERT = 3;

// Not all the required fields we need are in the
// certificate, thus rendering it invalid
const AUTH_FAIL_NOT_ALL_FIELDS = 4;

// No Database adapter was provided
const AUTH_FAIL_NO_DB_ADAPTER = 5;

// An error occurred in the SQL
const AUTH_FAIL_SQL_ERR = 6;

// The user requested couldn't be found
const AUTH_FAIL_NO_USER = 7;

// By default we have no error
private $error = -1;
```

These are the error messages we thought of and will be used somewhere in the code later on. Now let's create the setter for these error messages so that the getter can easily retrieve them later on:

```
/**
 * Sets an error.
 *
 * @param int $error
 */
private function setError($error)
{
  $this->error = $error;
}
```

Well that was exciting. Let's create the getter now, which is slightly more elaborate, but only just a little:

```
/**
 * Gets the latest error message back.
 *
 * @return string
 */
public function getErrorMessage()
{
  switch ($this->error) {
    case self::AUTH_FAIL_SQL_ERR:
      $retval = "SQL error occurred while checking "
              . "for the user.";
      break;
    case self::AUTH_FAIL_INV_CERT:
      $retval = "Certificate provided is invalid.";
      break;
    case self::AUTH_FAIL_PARSE_CERT:
      $retval = "Certificate provided couldn't be "
              . "parsed.";
      break;
    case self::AUTH_FAIL_EXP_CERT:
      $retval = "Certificate has expired.";
      break;
    case self::AUTH_FAIL_NO_DB_ADAPTER:
      $retval = "No Database adapter set.";
      break;
    case self::AUTH_FAIL_NOT_ALL_FIELDS:
```

```
        $retval = "Not all the fields required are "
                . "available.";
        break;
    case self::AUTH_FAIL_NO_USER:
        $retval = "The user could not be found.";
        break;
    case self::AUTH_FAIL_NO_HTTPS:
        $retval = "Connection is not secure.";
        break;
    case -1:
        $retval = "No error occurred.";
        break;
    default:
        $retval = "Unknown error occurred.";
        break;
    }

    // Reset the error
    $this->error = -1;

    // Return the string with the error message
    return $retval;
}
```

Making sure we have a secure connection

Although certificates are only sent when we do have an SSL connection, an extra check isn't that bad as we want to be certain that the user is using a secure connection.

```
/**
 * Returns true if the current connection is through
 * HTTPS.
 *
 * @return boolean
 */
private function isHTTPS()
{
    return isset($_SERVER['HTTPS']) ? true : false;
}
```

Wow, that must have been the best method ever! All joking aside, it is fairly simple as the HTTPS key is given in the $_SERVER variable, whenever a secure connection through HTTPS is set up. When the key is present, we can assume that there is a secure connection.

Checking if the certificate is an actual certificate

Next up is to check if the certificate is valid or not, but before we can do that we should also make sure there is a way to set the certificate as well:

```php
// This property will store our certificate array
private $certificate;

/**
 * Sets (and parses) a certificate, returns false if the
 * certificate couldn't be parsed.
 *
 * @param string $certificateContent
 * @return boolean
 */
public function setCertificate($certificateContent)
{
    // This function is part of the OpenSSL extension in
    // PHP. This means that if OpenSSL is not installed
    // into PHP this function will not exist and thus give
    // a fatal error. This function deciphers the
    // information received in the certificate to a great
    // array with variables.
    $certificate = openssl_x509_parse(
                $certificateContent
    );

    // If the certificate can't be parsed (i.e. it is
    // invalid) the function above will return false
    if ($certificate !== false) {
        // We can be sure the certificate is valid at least
        // in raw state now
        $this->certificate = $certificate;

        // Done here
        return true;
    } else {
        // Use the failure to parse certificate here to make
        // sure the developer/user will know what is going
        // on
        $this->setError(self::AUTH_FAIL_PARSE_CERT);
        return false;
    }
}
```

This method did a basic check to see if we actually got a certificate that is at least valid, even if it is expired or doesn't have any of our fields.

Checking if we have all the certificate fields

As we want to check the e-mail address in our certificate, we need to make sure we actually have an e-mail address in there as well. And while we are at it, we will also check for a couple of other fields that are not relevant to our authentication, but would be nice to have anyway:

```
/**
 * Checks if all our fields (issuer, issuer[O],
 * issuer[CN], issuer[emailAddress], serialNumber) are
 * in the certificate.
 *
 * @return boolean
 */
private function checkRequiredFields()
{
  // First get our certificate
  $certificate = $this->getCertificate();

  // Check if our certificate at least is valid
  if ($certificate !== false) {
    // We want to check if the following fields (and
    // subfields) are in the certificate
    $required = array(
      'issuer' => array('O', 'CN', 'emailAddress'),
      'serialNumber' => null
    );

    // Loop through the primary fields
    foreach ($required as $field=>$value) {
      if (in_array($field, $certificate) === true) {
        // The primary field is in there, check if
        // there are any secondary fields we need to
        // check
        if (is_array($value && is_array($certificate[$field]) {
          // Loop through the secondary fields
          foreach ($value as $key) {
            // Now check of our values are in there
            if (in_array(
              $key,
              array_keys(
```

```
                    $certificate[$field])) === false)
                {
                    return false;
                }
            }
        }
    } else {
        return false;
    }
}


// If we reach this point, we are always ok to go
$retval = true;

unset($required);
}

unset($certificate);

return isset($retval) ? $retval : false;
}
```

We check if the fields are in there, and if the field isn't in there we will return false.

Checking if the certificate isn't expired yet

Now we want to know if the certificate is still valid in terms of time, as certificates usually expire after a set time (this can be months, weeks, years, anything really):

```
/**
 * Checks if the current certificate is valid or not.
 *
 * @return boolean
 */
private function isCertificateValid()
{
    // Get our certificate again
    $certificate = $this->getCertificate();

    // Again make sure it is not false (highly unlikely
    // here, but hey, never be sure
    if ($certificate !== false) {
        // Check if the valid from and to fields are set,
        // because if they are not, we won't be able to
        // check if the certificate is valid or not
```

```
    if (isset($certificate['validFrom_time_t']) === true
 && isset($certificate['validTo_time_t']) === true)
   {
     // Check if the from time is smaller than our
     // current time and the to time is bigger than the
     // current time
   if (time() >= $certificate['validFrom_time_t']
 && time() < $certificate['validTo_time_t'])
     {
        $retval = true;
     }
   }
 }

 unset($certificate);

 return isset($retval) ? $retval : false;
}
```

If this method returns true, we can be sure that we have a certificate that isn't expired.

Creating a getter and setter for the Database adapter

Now we need a simple getter and setter for our database adapter, before we can actually do the authentication:

```
/**
 * Our Database adapter property.
 *
 * @var \Zend\Db\Adapter\Adapter
 */
private $dbAdapter;

/**
 * Sets the Db adapter.
 *
 * @param \Zend\Db\Adapter\Adapter $db
 */
public function setDbAdapter(\Zend\Db\Adapter\Adapter $db)
{
  $this->dbAdapter = $db;
}

/**
```

```
 * Returns the Db adapter.
 *
 * @return \Zend\Db\Adapter\Adapter
 */
private function getDbAdapter()
{
  return $this->dbAdapter;
}
```

Of course this was again very simple, as it requires no logic at all. Now that we have set our database adapter, we can actually begin authenticating the user.

Creating the authenticate method

This method will implement all our previously defined methods and if they are all successful, it will authenticate through the database and see if our user is there (or not). But first, we need another method to get fields from our certificate, which is a neater way, and a method to get our identity once authenticated:

```
// We will store our identity in here, once
// authenticated
private $identity;

/**
 * Retrieves a variable from the certificate, returns
 * null if not found.
 *
 * @param string $variable
 * @return string
 */
private function getCertificateVariable($variable)
{
  if (is_array($this->certificate) === true &&
    isset($this->certificate[$variable]) === true)
  {
    return $this->certificate[$variable];
  } else if (is_array($this->certificate) === true &&
      isset($this->certificate['issuer'][$variable])
  {
    return $this->certificate['issuer'][$variable];
  } else {
    return null;
  }
}
```

```
/**
 * Retrieves the identity of the user.
 *
 * @return array
 */
public function getIdentity()
{
  return $this->identity;
}
```

And now for the supreme moment, after a long wait, finally the `authenticate` method!

```
/**
 * Tries to authenticate the user through the
 * certificate.
 *
 * @return boolean
 */
public function authenticate()
{
  $continue = true;

  if ($this->getDbAdapter() !== null) {
    // Check if we are on a secure connection
    if ($this->isHTTPS() === true) {
      // Check if the certificate is valid
      if ($this->getCertificate() !== false) {
        // Check if the fields we require are available
        if ($this->checkRequiredFields() === true) {
          // Check if the certificate isn't expired
          if ($this->isCertificateValid() === false) {
            // Certificate is expired!
            $this->setError(self::AUTH_FAIL_EXP_CERT);
            $continue = false;
          }
        } else {
          // Not all the fields are available
          $this->setError(
              self::AUTH_FAIL_NOT_ALL_FIELDS
          );
          $continue = false;
        }
      } else {
```

```
          // This is an invalid certificate
          $this->setError(self::AUTH_FAIL_INV_CERT);
          $continue = false;
        }
      } else {
        // Oh, oh, no secure connection
        $this->setError(self::AUTH_FAIL_NO_HTTPS);
        $continue = false;
      }
    } else {
      // We don't have a db adapter
      $this->setError(self::AUTH_FAIL_NO_DB_ADAPTER);
      $continue = false;
    }

    if ($continue === true) {
      // Now we are going to check with the database if
      // the email address is in there
      $statement = $this->getDbAdapter()->createStatement(
        "SELECT * FROM users WHERE email = :email"
      );

      try {
        // Input the email address in the statement and
        // execute it on the database adapter
        $result = $statement->execute(array(
          'email' => $this->getCertificateVariable(
            'emailAddress'
          )
        ));

        // Check if we have one result
        if ($result->count() === 1) {
          // One result found, put it in the identity kit
          $this->identity = $result->current();

          // Because we are super-cool add some of our
          // certificate variables as well
          $this->identity['serialNumber'] =
            $this->getCertificateVariable('serialNumber');

          $this->identity['organization'] =
            $this->getCertificateVariable('O');
```

```
          $this->identity['commonName'] =
            $this->getCertificateVariable('CN');

          // We successfully found our user
          $retval = true;
        } else {
          $this->setError(self::AUTH_FAIL_NO_USER);
        }
      } catch (\Exception $e) {
        $this->setError(self::AUTH_FAIL_SQL_ERR);
        error_log($e->getMessage());
      }
    }

    // Return the retval is we have one, otherwise just
    // false
    return isset($retval) ? $retval : false;
  }
```

And that's it! The `authenticate` method will either return true on successful authentication or false, and will set an error at the same time so that we can see what exactly went wrong!

How it works...

Now that we have created our own `authentication` adapter, it is time to sit back and review what we just did.

What are we trying to achieve

On some websites the access is prohibited on such a level that usernames and passwords are a thing of the past. In environments where we want to check every customer that comes in without them needing to type the username and password themselves, we might use certificate authentication.

Certificate authentication works because the client will send a certificate with every server request they do. This certificate then shows the server *who* the user is, who is trying to browse their pages. Usually one or more fields in the certificate are used to identify the user. In our example we will use the e-mail address, which is a common field to be used for identification.

What we will do first off, is create an adapter that will get the certificate either from manual input (easier testing that way) or the browser, whichever works really. We will then check if the e-mail address exists in our database, and if so we consider the user logged in. Obviously our server will not be configured so strictly that no certificate will be allowed, as in this stage basically every certificate with a right e-mail address gets access. If we want to know how we can prevent users from using any certificate, we can take a look at the *There's more...* section, where we will look in the direction of securing your server a bit further, and restricting the certificate use.

From an application point of view, however, we just presume that all the certificates that we get, are valid.

The `AdapterInterface` only requires us to have an authenticate method. But before we can go ahead we want to make sure that the following items are checked:

- We want to make sure the user is coming through a secure connection (HTTPS)
- We also want to make sure the certificate is valid (obviously)
- While we are checking, we'll make sure our certificate has the fields we require for authentication
- And we need to know if the certificate is still valid and not expired
- Last but not least, we also need to make sure that we have a database adapter to check the values against

About certificates

In general the certificates are validated on the server before they reach the application. The validation usually happens against some sort of CA, or Certificate Authority, which is basically an entity on the server site that issues certificates, and therefore can vouch for any certificates carrying its signature. Of course in real life this is way more complicated than just described, but the idea is the same. So when a certain level of checking is being done on the server to verify the identity of the certificate, and if it is valid against the CA provided by the server, it will then parse it through to our application.

By the time it reaches our application, we usually assume that the user got the certificate from us, and therefore should be allowed in, as he knew the password at the door. But although he knew the password, that doesn't mean we know who it is! That is why a second authentication (the one we just made) verifies if a user actually belongs in our application or not, that is, if it is a valid certificate or not!

There's more...

Securing a server is the most important part of this kind of validation, as we really (really, really) need to be sure that the user carrying the certificate is actually valid. Usually building complex servers like this are done with server engineers and not the task of the developer, but if it is then it would be a great idea to read up on the subject first.

Personally, I am a fan of Apache and would recommend anyone to read up on the `mod_ssl` configuration, as it is very thorough on the subject of securing a server and it has a lot of resources to find out how to configure it just right.

But in the end configuring SSL without the proper know-how is a very tedious and error-prone process and it is likely that properly configuring a server is a bit over the head of a developer. In that case getting a server engineer to do it for us is the best way, and the laziest, which lets us concentrate on our work!

8
Optimizing Performance

In this chapter we will cover:

- ▸ Caching, and when to cache
- ▸ Understanding and using storage plugins
- ▸ Setting up a caching system

Introduction

In a society where we want our data now, it is important to make sure that our websites and applications also deliver it as soon as possible. When we rule out any obvious cause of slow downs, such as network infrastructure or server configuration, we can start looking at caching. This chapter is all about what to cache and how to cache, making our lives a lot faster.

Caching and when to Cache

Caching, everyone knows about it, everybody talks about it, but what is it? In its purest essence caching is all about serving your application as quickly as possible to the user. That's what we will talk in this recipe when and how to cache.

Getting ready

We will be working with the Zend Framework skeleton application again, so it would be wise to have that set up.

How to do it...

When developing an application, caching might not be something that immediately comes up in the design, and most probably this will come up when the application goes live and after a while you find your application responding slower than when you first put it live.

That is the perfect (well not perfect, as that would be during the design phase, obviously) time to consider implementing a cache.

When we talk about caching, a common misunderstanding is that we are solely talking about caching an HTML output. Nothing could be further from the truth, as we have several powerful methods of caching in PHP.

The following list is a collection of some methods available to us to cache different sections of our application:

- Caching the ZF2 configuration
- Caching the rendered output
- Caching the class map

We will now go in further detail of the methods named in the preceding list.

Caching configuration

Probably the most static bit of code in your application will be the configuration. Oh but how we need configuration to properly load our application, but in the meantime we might hate it for all the merging it needs to do before we end up with the final version of the configuration.

But fear not, as we can simply cache the merged configuration so that your application doesn't have to parse through the lot anymore! This is actually such a simple process, that it is almost hilarious to give the example for it (`/config/application.config.php`):

```php
<?php
return array(
   // Look for this ke y in the configuration array.
   'module_listener_options' => array(

     // Enable the config cache.
     'config_cache_enabled' => true,

     // If we want to give the cache a special filename
     // we can just type a name here.
     'config_cache_key' => 'configuration'
```

```
    // The directory where we want to write the cache
    // to. Don't forget that we need read/write access
    // to this directory by the process running the app, which in
    // most cases is the web server process!
    'cache_dir' => 'data/cache/',
  ),
);
```

And that's it. Nothing fancy is needed to make this work as everything that is required to make this work is already built in Zend Framework 2.

This is a very effective way to start caching everything that is static, and although it probably doesn't give the application an enormous speed boost (unless we have literally dozens of modules) it will be a method that shouldn't be forgotten.

Caching output

Caching output is useful when we have a lot of static files that normally don't or rarely change. When we talk about content that doesn't change a lot we can think of blog posts or news items as those usually get generated once and put live indefinitely. There are obviously more output types that are useful to cache, but we will just give an example to show how easy it is to cache output that we deem static.

First we need to create the configuration in our module to make sure the caching is enabled in our `ServiceManager` (`/module/SomeModule/config/module.config.php`):

```php
<?php
return array(
  // We need to define the ServiceManager
  'service_manager' => array(
    // We will call it cache-service
    'cache-service' => function () {
      // Return a new cache adapter
      return \Zend\Cache\StorageFactory::factory(array(
        'adapter' => array(
          // We want to use the cache that is being
          // stored on the filesystem
          'name' => 'filesystem',
          'options' => array(
            'cache_dir' => 'data/cache/',

            // This is the amount in minutes the cache is valid
            'ttl' => 100
          ),
```

```
        ),
      ));
    },
  },
);
```

Now that we created the configuration, let's continue to control the caching in our /module/ SomeModule/Module.php file's onBootstrap method:

```php
<?php
// Don't forget the namespace (obviously)
namespace SomeModule;

// We need this event for the onBootstrap event
use Zend\Mvc\MvcEvent;

// Begin our module class
class Module
{
  // This is going to be run at bootstrap, and will thus
  // create our events that will create our cached
  // output
  public function onBootstrap(MvcEvent $e)
  {
    // We will need a list of routes that we deem
    // cacheable
    $routes = array('blog/pages', 'blog/archives');

    $eventManager = $e->getApplication()->getEventManager();
    $serviceManager = $e->getApplication()->getServiceManager();

    $eventManager->attach(
        MvcEvent::EVENT_ROUTE,
        function($e) use ($serviceManager)
    {
      $route = $e->getRouteMatch()
                  ->getMatchedRouteName();

      // Check if this is a page that we want to cache,
      // if not then just exit this method
      if (!in_array($route, $routes)) {
        return;
      }
```

```
  // Get the cache-service from the configuration
  $cache = $serviceManager->get('cache-service');

  // Define a unique key that we use for the route
  $key = 'route-'. $route;

  // Check if our cache has the key with our route
  // content
  if ($cache->hasItem($key)) {
    // Handle response
    $response = $e->getResponse();

    // Set the content to our cached content
    $response->setContent($cache->getItem($key));

    // Return the response, because when we return
    // the response from a route event, the
    // application will output that response.
    return $response;
  }
},
// Make this priority super low to make sure this
// route has already happened
-1000);

// Now we create an trigger for the render event
// which will come after the route event. This means
// that we didn't have a valid cache, and we will
// now use this opportunity to create a cache of our
// rendered content.
$eventManager->attach(
  MvcEvent::EVENT_RENDER,
  function($e) use ($serviceManager, $routes)
{
  // Get the current route name
  $route = $e->getRouteMatch()
          ->getMatchedRouteName();

  // Check if this is a page that we want to cache,
  // if not then just exit this method
  if (!in_array($route, $routes))
    return;
```

```
        // Apparently we want to cache the content, so
        // here we go!
        $response = $e->getResponse();

        // Get the cache service from the ServiceManager
        $cache = $serviceManager->get('cache-service');

        // Build up our unique cache key
        $key = 'route-'. $route;

        // And now set the cache item
        $cache->setItem($key, $response->getContent());
    },
    // Again the lowest priority to make sure rendering
    // already has happened.
    -1000);
    }
}
```

Now every time we go to our application the route event will check if we might have a cache of the specific route, and if we do, it will return the cache (if not expired, of course). If the route hasn't been cached yet it will do so if necessary once the rendered event is triggered.

Credit for this example goes to *Jurian Sluiman* (*jurian-sluiman*) who is a user on the `stackoverflow.com` website and a significant contributor to Zend Framework 2.

Caching the class map

The class map file is one of those files that are just big, and basically static after the application has done merging it. That it is static and is obviously a great opportunity for us so we can cache it and take a bit of the load from the applications merging away. As for the first method of our caching, this one also only requires us to add a couple of properties in the configuration file.

Let's get this example started (`/config/application.config.php`):

```php
<?php
return array(
    // Look for this key in the configuration array.
    'module_listener_options' => array(

        // Enable the module map cache.
        'module_map_cache_enabled' => true,
```

```
    // If we want to give the cache a special filename
    // we can just type a name here.
    'module_map_cache_key' => 'classmap

    // The directory where we want to write the cache
    // to. Don't forget that we need read/write access
    // to this directory!
    'cache_dir' => 'data/cache/',
  ),
);
```

Again, although this might not be a significant improvement on the overall performance, we can be sure that every little bit helps, and it will certainly help lighten the load for the autoloader process.

How it works...

All that caching does is speeding up the application by keeping everything ready for when it is needed within a certain time (the ttl or also called time-to-live) period. It speeds up the application because it gives the application the data it requires without the application needing to make the connection to the database, or recompiling templates for example.

Caching is usually done on the filesystem, as it is considered to be a very fast option instead of going through a database for example. However, technically the fastest option for caching would be in-memory (this is because the memory or RAM is the closest data storage for the CPU and therefore the fastest). Although memory caching is a great method of caching, it can also become the worst kind if there is just too much to cache.

It is therefore wise to think about different caching methods (filesystem cache, for example, only with blog posts and application configuration, for example, in memory cache) before just generally using a method.

Understanding and using storage plugins

Instead of customizing everything, Zend Framework 2 provides an excellent interface that can manipulate the storing, removing, and retrieving of cache data by using storage plugins.

How to do it...

Storage plugins are used to compliment the storage adapters whenever a developer feels that they need more functionality added to the adapter without necessarily making a custom adapter. Therefore, plugins are the handiest tool to use when we want to modify the way our storage adapters handle the cache.

There are a couple of storage plugins readily available in Zend Framework 2, so let's get cracking on and explain them a bit further.

Using the ClearExpiredByFactor plugin

The `ClearExpiredByFactor` plugin clears the expired cache items once in a while, which are determined by a set factor. The higher the factor integer is, the less likely it will be that the cache will clear its expired items. But don't forget; this being a (pseudo) random process and all chances could be that it will be called every single time. We understand that this is incredibly counterintuitive, so maybe this code snippet taken from the plugin will clear things up.

```
if ($factor && mt_rand(1, $factor) == 1) {
    $storage->clearExpired();
}
```

We should also note that this plugin is only fired when there is cache to be written, it does not fire when cache is read.

`PluginOptions` that can be set is `setClearingFactor`, which sets the clearing factor.

> This plugin requires the storage adapter to be an instance of `ClearExpiredInterface`, otherwise it will not do anything (and we would never know as it doesn't log this error). Only the Filesystem and Memory Storage adapters support this interface.

Using the ExceptionHandler plugin

The `ExceptionHandler` plugin catches any exceptions that are thrown when getting/setting the cache and forwards it to a developer defined callback.

`PluginOptions` that can be set are:

- `setExceptionCallback`: This is a callback function to call when an exception occurs
- `setThrowExceptions`: This is a Boolean (default `true`) value that tells the plugin to re-throw exceptions that it caught

Using the IgnoreUserAbort plugin

The `IgnoreUserAbort` plugin makes sure that the script isn't aborted before the writing has finished to the cache. This way we can be sure we won't get any corrupted data in our cache.

`PluginOptions` that can be set is `setExitOnAbort`, which is a Boolean (default `true`) value that tells us if we can abort the script whenever we want, or if we need to wait until we are done writing.

Using the OptimizeByFactor plugin

You wanted to clear by factor? I am sure you also want to optimize by factor then! This plugin (pseudo) randomly optimizes the cache. The factor determines the chance it has of actually optimizing, the lower the number (between 1 and a high number) the greater chance, the higher the number the lower the chance. We understand that this is incredibly counterintuitive, so maybe this code snippet taken from the plugin will clear things up:

```
if ($factor && mt_rand(1, $factor) == 1) {
    $storage->clearExpired();
}
```

We should also note that this plugin is only fired when there is cache to be removed, it does not fire when the cache is read or written.

`PluginOptions` that can be set is `setOptimizingFactor`, which sets the optimizing factor.

> This plugin only works on storage adapters with an instance of `OptimizableInterface`. If this is not available it will not throw an error, so we will never know. The adapters currently supporting this interface are Dba and Filesystem.

Using the Serializer plugin

The `Serializer` plugin will serialize and unserialize the data when setting and getting it from the cache.

`PluginOptions` that can be set:

- `setSerializer`: This sets the serializer we want to use, it needs to be an class that implements the `Zend\Serializer\Adapter\AdapterInterface` class
- `setSerializerOptions`: If a string is given at the `setSerializer` option (the full class name as a string) then the instantiation options need to be set in this option

Using any plugin

Fortunately plugins are easy to use, and all we have to do is add them to the storage adapter to make it work.

We know that there are several ways of instantiating plugins, but we will just display one method to show off how it basically works:

```php
<?php

// Use the following libraries for our example
use Zend\Cache\Storage\Plugin\Serializer;
```

```
use Zend\Cache\Storage\Adapter\FileSystem;

// Initialize our Serializer plugin
$plugin = new Serializer();

// Initialize our FileSystem adapter
$adapter = new FileSystem();

// Now bind the two together
$adapter->addPlugin($plugin);
```

That's all that needs configuring to make it all work together nicely. In a MVC application (which we probably will use Zend Framework 2 for) plugin can be on very different locations. Normally though we want to configure this in the configuration or in the bootstrap event if we will use it constantly throughout the application, as that will save time compared to instantiating it more than once.

How it works...

Plugins are attached to storage adapters and work because they attach themselves to events of the storage adapters. When these events get triggered, the functionality gets triggered as well. It is really as simple as that, and there is no real further explanation needed for this.

Setting up a caching system

A good example on how to do it is always the best way to learn a new technique quickly. That is why we will show you how to implement a caching system on different parts of our application.

Getting ready

In this recipe we will show off a simple system that makes use of caching. We will also show off some benchmarks so that we can clearly see the differences between a system without caching and a system with caching. The code for this project can also be found with the book, which contain a couple of sample classes so that we can measure the performance a bit better. We will not discuss any of the sample classes (which all can be found in the `/module/Application/src/Application` directory), but we will refer to them in some of the examples.

How to do it...

Setting up a simple caching system is easy enough, but the question most of the time is, where to begin.

Benchmarking our application before cache

For the benchmark we will use an application called `ab`, which is short for ApacheBench. This is a tool which comes standard with the Apache web server on both the Microsoft Windows as the Linux version; for our recipe we will be using the Linux version of the benchmarking tool, don't worry though as both versions do exactly the same.

For our benchmark, we will use no caching at all and we will use the following code in `Application\Controller\IndexController` (/module/Application/src/ Application/Controller/IndexController.php) to generate our ridiculously long output:

```php
<?php

// Don't forget to set our namespace
namespace Application\Controller;

// Use the following classes
use Zend\Mvc\Controller\AbstractActionController;
use Zend\View\Model\ViewModel;

// Define our class name and extend
class IndexController extends AbstractActionController
{
  // We will just use the index for this
  public function indexAction()
  {
    // Initialize our LongOutput class
    $output = new \Application\Model\LongOutput();

    // echo our stupidly long output
    echo '<!-- '. $output->run(1500). ' -->';

    // Just return a view model, it doesn't affect us
    return new ViewModel();
  }
}
```

This action will output a very long string, which is overly complicated, but we don't really care about that as we just want to measure how long it takes to create such a string. We can now commence with the first benchmark.

The following command will be used to do the benchmarking:

```
$ ab -c 4 -n 10 http://localhost/
```

The command stands for a concurrency of four (-c 4) and we want to run the test ten times (-n 10) on the localhost as our website. This means that a total of 40 times our page will be visited, which will give us quite a clear view on the average in response times.

The following is a review of the most important result of the benchmark. Obviously the rest of the result is also somewhat interesting, but we are just interested in the response time at the moment.

```
Time taken for tests:    18.111 seconds
```

We will use the 18.111 seconds as the base to compare all the other results with.

Implementing configuration/class map cache

First we are going to implement the configuration cache as that is the basis of all caching (at least I like to think so).

We can do that by adding the following configuration to the /config/application. config.php file:

```php
<?php
// Lets add our options to the configuration array,
// please be aware that we don't show any other options
// here that could very well be in the configuration
// already.
return array(
  // We should add our options inside this array key
  'module_listener_options' => array(
    // Enable the config cache
    'config_cache_enabled' => true,

    // Give the config cache a file name like module-
    // config-cache.config.php
    'config_cache_key' => 'config',

    // Enable the class map caching
    'module_map_cache_enabled' => true,

    // Give the class map cache a file name like module-
    // classmap-cache.classmap.php
    'module_map_cache_key' => 'classmap',

    // Use our data/cache as the cache directory
    // (remember this directory need to be writeable for
    // the web server).
    'cache_dir' => 'data/cache',
```

```php
        // We don't want to check the module dependencies as
        // that is the job of the developer, it just takes
        // time to do this and is pretty much useless.
        'check_dependencies' => false,
    ),
);
```

We now enabled the configuration/class map caching, which should get us a very (very) small increase in response time. Naturally, this will be a bigger difference when we have a larger application with more modules.

Let's do our benchmark again to see what the difference is:

Time taken for tests: 15.428 seconds

As we can see our result has been significantly different, a staggering 14.2 percent faster actually. We should not forget, however, that our application is incredibly small and this percentage may actually be a lot smaller if our application grows larger in the future. Still, this is a clear sign that caching our configuration and class mapping is a good practice.

 A little bug in the configuration caching system we should wary about is that we cannot use closures (also called anonymous functions). If we do we get a PHP fatal error saying something like the following:

```
Call to undefined method Closure::__set_state() in
your_configuration_cache.php on line XX
```

Implementing the class caching

Because we have this incredibly long output, it is interesting to use the `ClassCache` adapter to cache the output of the single method that generates this output. And we also know our `LongOutput` model has no output that changes, we can safely cache the output.

For this caching method to work we need to make sure that the configuration cache has been turned off, otherwise it will end up in a PHP error.

We are going to change `module.config.php` in the `Application` module first to initialize our cache storage adapter first. After that we will change the `Application\Controller\IndexController` so that we can use our pattern. We can just add the following code to `/module/Application/config/module.config.php`:

```php
<?php
return array(
    // We are configuring the service manager
    'service_manager' => array(
        'factories' => array(
```

```
            // Initialize our file system storage
            'Zend\Cache\StorageFactory' => function() {
              return Zend\Cache\StorageFactory::factory(
                array(
                  'adapter' => array(
                    'name' => 'filesystem',
                    'options' => array(
                      // Define the directory to store the
                      // cache in
                      'cacheDir' => 'data/cache',
                    ),
                  ),
                  // For the file system storage we need to
                  // have the serializer plugin enabled,
                  // otherwise thing just go wrong when we
                  // want to storage a class or so
                  'plugins' => array('serializer'),
                ),
              );
            }
          ),
          // We want to call our cache with the 'cache' key
          'aliases' => array(
            'cache' => 'Zend\Cache\StorageFactory',
          ),
        ),
      );
```

Now we have initialized our cache, we need to make sure our output is cached as well. This will be done in `IndexController` (`/module/Application/src/Application/Controller/IndexController.php`) of our `Application` module:

```php
<?php

// Set the namespace
namespace Application\Controller;

// Define the imports
use Zend\Mvc\Controller\AbstractActionController;
use Zend\View\Model\ViewModel;

// Define the class name and extend
class IndexController extends AbstractActionController
{
```

```php
// Begin our index action again
public function indexAction()
{
  // This time we want to make sure our class is
  // loaded in to the ClassCache pattern so that we
  // can eventually cache the output of our class
  // method
  $pattern = \Zend\Cache\PatternFactory::factory(
          'class', array(
    'storage' => $this->getServiceLocator()->get('cache'),
    'class' => '\Application\Model\LongOutput'
  ));

  // Now call our method through the ClassCache
  // pattern with the same arguments as the previous
  // test
  echo '<!-- '. $pattern->call('run', array(1500)). '-->';

  // Return the view model again because we don't
  // actually do anything with it
  return new ViewModel();
  }
}
```

If we now take a look at the benchmarking, we can see that the following caching has resulted in the following performance improvement:

Time taken for tests: 14.956 seconds

As we can see this is almost a 17.4 percent improvement on the original benchmark, which obviously is a fantastic improvement. It is also a 3.2 percent response increase in comparison to the configuration/class map caching. We know that this doesn't sound too impressive, and we understand your disappointment. However, do understand that in real life a database call or a service call can take a lot longer than this, and the percentage of improvement therefore would be much more!

There is only one slight issue with this method; and that is we won't be able to cache the configuration/class map this way. Because we want to optimize our application the best we can, this is obviously not good practice. Don't panic, however, there is a solution to this issue, and it comes in the form of `StorageCacheFactory`!

We didn't immediately discuss this because it is always best to see more than one way of coding, at least that is my personal choice.

What we'll do is strip the configuration we just added in /module/Application/config/ module.config.php and add the following configuration:

```php
<?php
// We need to assume that we have stripped the previous
// configuration out of here and it is back to the
// default configuration file
return array(
    'service_manager' => array(
        // Instantiate the cache through our storage cache
        // factory. It will look for the 'cache' key to
        // initialize the cache
        'factories' => array(
            'cache' => '\Zend\Cache\Service\StorageCacheFactory',
        ),
    ),

    // And here we go, initializing the cache
    'cache' => array(
        // We want to use the filesystem adapter
        'adapter' => 'Filesystem',
        'options' => array(
            // Of course we need to set the directory to cache
            // in
            'cache_dir' => 'data/cache'
        ),

        // We also want the serializer otherwise it will
        // throw an exception
        'plugins' => array('Serializer'),
    ),
);
```

If we now turn back on the configuration and class map caching and do a benchmark, we get the following result.

Time taken for tests: 14.303 seconds

As we can see this time with both caching systems enabled, we get a 21 percent speed increase in comparison to the original.

How it works...

It is always good to cache the things we use regularly and are sure about their persistence. If we know a class's output doesn't change, but for example merely does some calculations we know that it will be a strong candidate to use for caching. Don't forget that caching methods which rely on third party input, such as databases, are harder to cache as they require a certain time-to-live in which the cache knows the data they have cached is out-of-date.

Another thing to look out for is to cache too much, that way your application actually slows down instead of speeding up as the cache is too busy refreshing/getting and setting the cache instead of actually outputting it. A good way of auto-cleaning and auto-optimizing however, is by setting up a periodic `cron` (much like scheduled tasks for Windows users) process that runs periodically.

9
Catching Bugs

In this chapter we will cover:

- ▶ Handling Exceptions—your partner in crime
- ▶ Logging and how it makes your life easier
- ▶ Unit testing – why would you do it
- ▶ Setting up and using unit testing

Introduction

On 9 September, 1947 the first computer bug was found by Grace Hopper. This computer bug was an actual insect instead of a software bug. Since then we are basically chasing bugs in our software applications, and the more we learn to code the more we begin to appreciate good error handling, and catching bugs in time.

As a coder nothing is more annoying than getting customers on the phone that say "it doesn't work", without us knowing what actually is going on. That is why this chapter is focused on catching bugs early, and finding the cause of the bug more easily.

Handling Exceptions – your partner in crime

To find the source of errors, good error handling should be implemented. In this recipe we'll talk about Exception handling within the Zend Framework 2 and how to optimally use it.

We can safely assume that we all know about try-catch and Exceptions, but to make sure nobody is caught out please take a look at the link to the PHP manual in the *See also* subsection in this section.

How to do it...

Exception handling is not that difficult to use, but it is a very useful tool if used correctly.

Exception classes in Zend Framework 2

Let's take a look at the following example:

```php
<?php

// This non existing method throws a couple of Exception, which
// is a PDOException, BadMethodCallException and probably more.
try {
  $object->executeMe();
} catch(PDOException $e) {
  // We catch the most specific Exception first, as this is an
  // Exception that has to do with a database query that went wrong
} catch(BadMethodCallException $e) {
  // Next up this one, as this tells us that we have done
  // something wrong when calling this method, maybe we forgot
  // some arguments, or the method might not exist?
} catch(Exception $e) {
  // We don't know what is going wrong, but we know something did
  // go wrong. Perhaps we just want to log this, or handle it on
  // another way?
}
```

This implementation of `try-catch` is also called cascading Exceptions.

Handling Exceptions on dispatch or rendering

To implement the trigger on one of these events we should add some code to the `/module/Application/Module.php` file in one of our Modules (it doesn't specifically matter which one).

```php
<?php
  use Zend\Mvc\Application;
  use Zend\Mvc\MvcEvent;
```

```
  // We'll skip the beginning of the file as it has no
  // effect on us
class Module
{
  // We want to add/create the onBootstrap method to put
  // our event attachment in
  public function onBootstrap(MvcEvent $e)
  {
    // Get the event manager from the application
    $eventManager = $e->getApplication()
                        ->getEventManager();

    // Make sure our module router listens to our event
    // manager as well
    $moduleRouteListener = new ModuleRouteListener();
    $moduleRouteListener->attach($eventManager);

    // Get the service manager for later use
    $serviceManager = $e->getApplication()
                        ->getServiceManager();

    // Attach our handler to the events
    $eventManager->attach(
        // What events do we want to attach to
        array(
          MvcEvent::EVENT_DISPATCH_ERROR,
          MvcEvent::EVENT_RENDER_ERROR,
        ),

        // What class and method do we want to trigger
        array($this, 'handleException')
    );
  }

  // This is the method we use to handle the exception
  public function handleException(MvcEvent $event)
  {
    // Make sure the error is an exception, otherwise
    // it might be some other parameter in the event
      if ($event->getError() === Application::ERROR_EXCEPTION) {
      // Now get the exception from the event
      $exception = $event->getParam('exception');
```

```
        // Do whatever with this exception
    }
  }

  // Again, we are not bothered by the rest of the
  // Module class
}
```

How it works...

Now we have seen how to do it, let's see how it actually works in Zend Framework 2.

Exception classes in Zend Framework 2

Zend Framework 2 throws a different Exception for almost every component of the framework, and although different in name they are all the same in functionality.

First of all here is a list of Exceptions that are default to PHP but are overridden by Zend Framework 2 because Zend Framework 2 just likes to use Exceptions that are in the Zend namespace, instead of in the global namespace:

- `BadMethodCallException`
- `DomainException`
- `ExtensionNotLoadedException`
- `InvalidArgumentException`
- `InvalidCallbackException`
- `LogicException`
- `RuntimeException`

Luckily we can use the global `\DomainException` as well as `\Zend\Stdlib\Exception\DomainException` (it is such a mouthful) when catching our Exceptions, as the Exceptions are overridden from the original.

It can however be useful if we are using a chain of catches to know where a specific Exception comes from; for example, when we catch a `RuntimeException` and we know that either `Zend\Cache` or `Zend\Authentication` can throw one. However usually it is quite clear what it might be or reactions to Exceptions might be different per instance.

Zend Framework 2, however, has docblocks for every class and method and luckily for us also has documented `@throws` as well. This means that we can easily look at the documentation and see what that specific functionality throws, that way we can easily wrap our code inside a `try-catch` block and handle the Exceptions.

We can also just catch any `\Exception` that is thrown, instead of specifically targeting a named Exception, but we don't tend to do that as it doesn't give us good control over the errors occurring. In general we would like to be as specific as possible when it comes to Exceptions, and the rule is to catch them from most specific down to least specific.

Handling exceptions on dispatch or rendering

If we don't handle exceptions on either dispatch or rendering, we are in for a bad time. One of the issues that can arise is the white screen issue where we won't see anything on the screen because of an error happening. During the development stage, this only leads to mild frustration for the developer, but think about the user that sees this on a live environment as they want to tell you their nephew/cousin/uncle is a better coder than us. We can't have that.

That is why we need to make sure that we listen to the `Zend\Mvc\MvcEvent::EVENT_DISPATCH_ERROR` and `Zend\Mvc\MvcEvent::EVENT_RENDER_ERROR` events. These events will be triggered when a controller or route is not found or an error occurrs during the rendering of the templates.

As we can see from the example, this event is only triggered when an error occurs, when dispatching, or rendering. The exception retrieved can then be used to either log, or dump to the screen, whatever feels appropriate. The idea here is that we are able to debug effectively even if we don't see the error happening.

For example, if this technique was implemented on the live application, it could log all the exceptions to a log (or e-mail to support) then we would be able to see errors that occur when we are "not around" to see it for ourselves.

About try-catch

The `try-catch` block in PHP is one incredibly useful tool of the trade and we would need to use it as much as possible as chains of Exceptions are much easier to solve than a `return false` or `null` back from a method. Especially in combination of events we are able to catch anything in time, or at least make sure we are able to debug it in a reasonable fashion.

See also

Exceptions manual and the introduction to try-catch: `http://php.net/manual/en/language.exceptions.php`

Logging and how it makes your life easier

Besides good error handling, logging is a good way to make sure you get the most knowledge of what is going on out of your system. Most of time we can even build it so that we can record events that lead up to an error, which can then be traced back to the original issue.

Because we want to go all exotic with the logging in Zend Framework 2, it is required for us to install the FirePHP core on our web server. We can install this library through the Composer tool (we need to assume that we already use this on the server, otherwise it would get a bit too complicated).

We can install the FirePHP library by adding the following lines in the require section of the `composer.json` file:

```
"firephp/firephp-core" : "dev-master"
```

If we now execute `'php composer.phar update'` in the command line, it will install the library for use within our code later on. To make full use of the logger functionality, it would also be wise to use a browser that can understand FirePHP headers. With the Mozilla Firefox browser we need to install the Firebug and FirePHP add-ons to make it work. If we want to use FirePHP logging in Google's Chrome browser or Microsoft Internet Explorer, we need separate extensions/add-ons as well, as none of these support it by default.

How to do it...

In this recipe we will show off examples on how to implement a logger system in our application.

Implementing a really simple file logger

Let's implement a simple file logger first, which can be done in one of our configuration files. We will add our logger to our `/config/autoload/global.php` file as we want it available everywhere in our application:

```
return array(
  // We want to put our logger in the service manager
  'service_manager' => array(
    'factories' => array(
      // We will call our logger 'log' so we can find it
      // easily back in our application
      'log' => function () {
        // Instantiate our logger
        $log = new Zend\Log\Logger();

        // Add the writer to our logger (don't forget to
        // make the data directory writable)
        $log->addWriter(new Zend\Log\Writer\Stream(
            getcwd(). '/data/application.log'
        ));
```

```
        // Return our logger now
        return $log;
    },
  ),
 ),
);
```

That was pretty easy as we can see, and now everywhere we have the `ServiceManager` object to our disposal we can get the logger by doing something like the following Controller (file: `/module/Application/src/Application/Controller/IndexController.php`) code:

```php
<?php

namespace Application\Controller;

use Zend\Mvc\Controller\AbstractActionController;
use Zend\View\Model\ViewModel;

class IndexController extends AbstractActionController
{
  public function indexAction()
  {
    $this->getServiceLocator()
         ->get('log')
         ->debug("A Debug Log Message");
  }
}
```

Implementing a FirePHP logger

The FirePHP logger is the same as the Logger initialization shown before in `/config/autoload/global.php` with one difference, and that is `Zend\Log\Writer` attached to `Zend\Log\Logger`.

```php
// As we can see we can just change (or add if
// we want more loggers) the log writer to FirePHP.
$log->addWriter(new Zend\Log\Writer\FirePhp());
```

How it works...

Logging is one of the most underestimated pieces of code that we kind of forget to implement. And when we implement it, we forget to make use of it regularly enough.

We all know that it is important, but for some reason we are hesitant to implement it on a regular basis.

What we are going to do is install a logger in our basic Zend Framework 2 application, and a more special way of logging with FirePHP.

Implementing a really simple file logger

As we saw in the preceding `indexAction` method, we have simply put a debug statement in our `application.log` file, which will look similar like the following:

```
2013-03-04T13:58:38+02:00 DEBUG (7): A Debug Log Message
```

The log methods we can use are `log()`, `info()`, `warn()`, `err()`, and `debug()`, if we use `log()`, we need to give it a priority first and then pass the message as parameters. As we can also see, assigned to `DEBUG` is the value `7`, this refers to the level of priority used. In our case `DEBUG` has priority `7`, but there are more priorities:

```
/**
 * @const int defined from the BSD Syslog message severities
 * @link http://tools.ietf.org/html/rfc3164
 */
const EMERG   = 0;
const ALERT   = 1;
const CRIT    = 2;
const ERR     = 3;
const WARN    = 4;
const NOTICE  = 5;
const INFO    = 6;
const DEBUG   = 7;
```

Implementing a FirePHP logger

If we now begin logging with the FirePHP writer, we will receive the following entries in our Browser console. (Press *F12* in Mozilla Firefox, Chrome, and Microsoft Internet Explorer.)

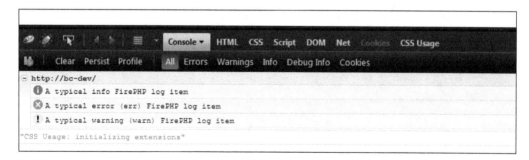

As we can see this gives a quite clear view of the log items sent through the browser.

> Please note that using the debug() log method in Zend Framework 2.2.4 still executes and outputs a trace() instead of the message we want to display when using the FirePHP writer. This is currently reported as a bug, but it hasn't been confirmed yet, so we don't know for sure if it will be ever solved.
>
> However, using this debug() method results in a really (really) big return header and it will slow down the response times of a larger application by literally minutes.

One more thing before we move on, please don't use the FirePHP log() method in a production environment, as everyone (literally) will be able to see what and when you logged in and out; and that is something you don't want.

About the Logger

The Log\Logger holds a collection of methods that can be used to log in a standardized fashion. The Logger has one or more Zend\Log\Writer objects attached to it, to which the Logger writes to. The Writer is the only class that does the actual writing to the requested log method.

With Writer\FirePhp, this is by sending headers to the client browser through the response, with the Writer\Stream it is a physical file (funny how we use physical here isn't it?).

Unit testing – why would you do it

Unit testing is a form of testing that has been widely accepted in the programming world. Unfortunately a lot of PHP developers still lack the knowledge on how to utilize it to their benefit, or they just don't know how to get started. This recipe will try to change that.

Getting ready

To get started with Unit testing a Zend Framework 2 application, it is required that we have PHPUnit 3.7.x installed. We can do this in a couple of different ways, but the easiest and most recommended way is by installing it through Composer, which comes with the Zend Framework 2 application.

To install PHPUnit through Composer we just need to add the following lines to `composer.json`:

```
{
  "require-dev": {
    "phpunit/phpunit": "3.7.*"
  }
}
```

After saving the `composer.json` file, run Composer to update the new requirements.

```
$ php composer.phar update
```

After a short while, the Composer installer will be complete and we will be ready to begin creating our unit tests. We can see that we now have an extra directory in our vendor directory called phpunit.

How to do it...

Before we can show how to really unit test our application, it is best that we show off the concept behind it first.

Pseudo-code examples

We will now examine a couple of pseudo-code examples that display an effective way of coding according to a (sort of) TDD principle (technically it will be PHP, but we won't take it too seriously as we just want to show some example).

For this example we will have a class, called `Person`, with only the `isAdult()` method in there. After we have defined the method, we should write our first test that should let our initial outcome fail.

```php
public function testIsAdult()
{
  // Initialize our Person
  $person = new Person();

  // Our first fail test that makes sure that when no
  // parameters are given the test will result in false
  assertFalse($person->isAdult());
}
```

As we have no code in our method yet, the result will always be null, so this test will immediately fail as we expect a false to be returned back at the moment.

When we execute PHPUnit now, it would (hypothetically) result in the following result:

PHPUnit 3.7.9 by Sebastian Bergmann.

F

FAILURES!

Tests: 1, Assertions: 1, Failures: 3.

Normally seeing a failure would be considered wrong, however in this instance, we would know that our method does what we expect it to do: fail! The next step is to make the test pass, so let's add a simple return `false` to our `isAdult` definition.

```
public function isAdult()
{
    // If the return value is set, return that, otherwise
    // return false; which will always happen at this
    // point
    return isset($retval) ? $retval : false;
}
```

If we know run the test again we will see that the test has now passed:

PHPUnit 3.7.9 by Sebastian Bergmann.

.

OK (1 test, 1 assertion)

Now it is time to continue by making sure that the test fails again, this time we want to make sure that we accept a parameter, `$age` and we want this value always to be an integer and higher or equal to 18, and if not we want to get `false` returned back as result.

So let's continue and edit the `test` script so that it fails again (never was failing so much fun).

```
public function testIsAdult()
{
    // Initialize our Person
    $person = new Person();

    // Our first fail test that makes sure that when no
    // parameters are given the test will result in false
    assertFalse($person->isAdult());
```

```
    // Ok, that works now, let's now parse in an integer
    // parameter so that we get result true back
    assertTrue($person->isAdult(21));
}
```

If we now run the test again, we will see that the test fails, which in this case triggers us to rewrite the following code so that the test will pass again:

```
public function isAdult($age)
{
    // Check if $age is an integer, and if so,
    // make sure the person is above 18
    if (isset($age) && is_int($age) && $age >= 18) {
        $retval = true;
    }

    // If the return value is set, return that, otherwise
    // return false; which will always happen at this
    // point
    return isset($retval) ? $retval : false;
```

And if we now run the test, the test will pass again, which means we can (if we need to) run the cycle again of making the test fail, change the code to let it pass again, etcetera, etcetera! The cycle will continue until we are happy with the result of the method and it exactly does what we planned it to do.

How it works...

When we talk about unit testing, a lot of developers have one of the following thoughts about it:

They simply don't know what it is, or what its use is; or they know they should do it, but they tend to not do it.

Of course there is also the occasional "I don't see any positive side to it" kind of developer, but we will just ignore that comment for now.

What is unit testing

Unit testing is the art of testing the smallest testable part of an application. Unit tests are divided up in test cases, which are compartmentalized tests that should test only one specific part of your code.

This unit test can use other objects through the use of mock objects, fakes and method stubs, but the main part is that only one particular piece of code should be tested in a unit test at any given time. The idea behind this is that we have a small unit test which tests only a small part of the code, so when problems occur we don't have to look far and wide to find out where the problem lies.

In reference to Zend Framework 2 we would usually unit test the models, services and controllers but not the html output (unless we are testing the `ViewRenderer` perhaps).

When should we test? – before, or after code is written

In a pure **TDD** (**test-driven development**) point of view, it is a simple answer: before. The whole idea of TDD is that a test is written before development begins, and therefore it always fails. The reason why it is important that a test fails is that we then know that the test we wrote at least fails. If we write a test that has never failed, how can we know that it will fail when it actually should fail?

Obviously there are also arguments for writing the test afterwards, one of them being that we cannot test code that we haven't designed yet. Although there is a point to that argument, personally I don't view it is a valid one. We can write tests beforehand, but that doesn't mean that we should write the full test before the code is written. The idea is to do the following: write a test, let it fail, write code to let it pass, and repeat the process from the start again. It also forces you to think about the app architecture before you start coding your app.

It is a matter of discipline

Unit testing is a strong matter of discipline, as it requires us to stop being eager to code and write the test first. For a lot of developers this means that we should throw out our current "muscle-memory" coding and really think what we want to code, before we actually start to code.

Of course when we start a new piece of code we have an idea of what we want the functionality to do, for example getting records from the database. However it is important to think about what we want to get as a return from that functionality. Is it an array, or is it a `boolean`, does it throw Exceptions and what if we don't get valid parameters? All of these things are questions that are architecture related, but are usually not defined beforehand.

Unit testing works only because of a strong discipline in the team. If we were the only one in our team that would write the tests for the code, we would surely fail in being able to maintain it as other members of our team would (unintentionally probably) break our unit tests whenever they would change something in the code.

However, it cannot be under estimated that unit testing is an invaluable part of software development, even if done after the code is already written (as you can see I am all for writing tests first).

Setting up and using unit testing

To start using Unit testing in Zend Framework 2 can be a bit of a hassle. But don't worry; help is coming as we fly you through a proper set up of Zend Framework 2 unit testing.

Getting ready

To get started with Unit Testing a Zend Framework 2 application, it is required that we have PHPUnit 3.7.x installed. We can do this on a couple of different ways but the easiest and recommended way is by installing it through Composer which comes with the Zend Framework 2 application.

To install PHPUnit through composer we just need to add the following lines to `composer.json`.

```
{
  "require-dev": {
    "phpunit/phpunit": "3.7.*"
  }
}
```

After saving the `composer.json` file, run Composer to update the new requirements.

```
$ php composer.phar update
```

After a short while the Composer installer will be complete and we will be ready to begin creating our unit tests. We can see that we now have an extra directory in our vendor directory called `phpunit`.

How to do it...

Setting up unit testing with PHPUnit is fairly simple in Zend Framework 2, and fortunately well documented as well.

Setting up the test framework

To get everything to work in order, we need to set up our separate test framework first. For that we will need three new files: `Bootstrap.php`, `TestConfig.php`, and `phpunit.xml`.

Because we basically want to test per module (keeping it all separate from each other, remember) we need to set this up for every module we are testing.

First of all we should create the directory called `test` in the root of the `module` directory. In that directory we create a file called `phpunit.xml` in `/module/Application/test/`, which is used by PHPUnit to determine some configurations.

```xml
<?xml version="1.0" encoding="UTF-8"?>

<!-- we want to bootstrap with the Bootstrap.php file, and we want to
     output in pretty colors. -->
<phpunit bootstrap="Bootstrap.php" colors="true">
  <testsuites>
    <!-- we can just give this a name for our own
         identification -->
    <testsuite name="Application Module Tests">
      <!-- this is the directory we want to use for
           testing -->
      <directory>./Application</directory>
    </testsuite>
  </testsuites>
</phpunit>
```

This first file is used for the general configuration of PHPUnit, and has many more options than the ones we showed here, but these are not relevant for our setup right here.

The next thing we want is to set up the `TestConfig.php` file in `/module/Application/test/`, which is a simple configuration file that loads up the most basic configurations we need to start up the application and run our code. It is basically the same as the normal `application.config.php`, but we need it in a separate file as we want to be able to make changes without it affecting the main application.

```php
<?php

// Just as the normal configuration we simply return the
// array
return array(
    // These are the modules we need to test our module.
    // Normally this only the current module, but if
    // this module has dependencies we need to add them
    // here as well.
    'modules' => array(
        'Application',
    ),
```

```
    // Here we define our default module listener options,
    // nothing special to note here.
    'module_listener_options' => array(
      'module_paths' => array(
        'module',
        'vendor',
      ),
    ),
  );
```

The next and last thing to set up in our testing framework is the `Bootstrap.php` file in `/module/Application/test/` that we referenced in the `phpunit.xml` file as our bootstrap. This bootstrap class is created by *Evan Coury* the primary author of the entire ZF2 module system, but we added the commentary to make it all a bit clearer of what is going on. It is important for us to know how this bootstrap works to ensure we can make optimal use of it.

```php
<?php
// The namespace needs to reflect the namespace of the
// module we want to test.
namespace Application;

// The following imports are needed for our class
use Zend\Loader\AutoloaderFactory;
use Zend\Mvc\Service\ServiceManagerConfig;
use Zend\ServiceManager\ServiceManager;
use Zend\Stdlib\ArrayUtils;
use RuntimeException;

// We want to put the error reporting on, so that we see
// if there is something going wrong
error_reporting(E_ALL | E_STRICT);

// Our current directory is going to be our root
// directory
chdir(__DIR__);

// Begin our bootstrap class here
class Bootstrap
{
    // Here we will define our ServiceManager in
    protected static $serviceManager;
```

```php
// The merged configuration of our application will be
// put in this property
protected static $config;

// This property isn't used, but we copied it for
// originality sake any way
protected static $bootstrap;
```

Now let's start by creating the init() method, which will be used later on to bootstrap the application so that we can use it to test on.

```php
public static function init()
{
  // Read our created TestConfig file, and if it
  // doesn't exist try the TestConfig.php.dist, but
  // that won't exist in our environment
  if (is_readable(__DIR__ . '/TestConfig.php')) {
    $testConfig = include __DIR__ . '/TestConfig.php';
  } else {
    $testConfig = include __DIR__ . '/TestConfig.php.dist';
  }

  $zf2ModulePaths = array();

  // Now we will load in all the module paths from the
  // configuration (if set).
  if (isset($testConfig['module_listener_options']
['module_paths']))
  {
    // Get the module path from the configuration
    $modulePaths = $testConfig
['module_listener_options']['module_paths'];

    // Now loop through the module paths and find out
    // what the parent path is of the module
    foreach ($modulePaths as $modulePath) {
      // This method is defined later in the class
      if ($path = static::findParentPath($modulePath)) {
        $zf2ModulePaths[] = $path;
      }
    }
  }
}
```

```php
// Now make a concatenated string with all the
// module paths separated by a colon.
$zf2ModulePaths = implode(
    PATH_SEPARATOR, $zf2ModulePaths
) . PATH_SEPARATOR;

// See if we defined some module paths outside this
// class or configuration and add them to the
// existing module paths
$zf2ModulePaths .= getenv('ZF2_MODULES_TEST_PATHS')
        ?: (defined('ZF2_MODULES_TEST_PATHS')
        ? ZF2_MODULES_TEST_PATHS : '');

// Make sure that we initiate auto loading so we
// don't have to worry about that (this method is
// defined later in the class)
static::initAutoloader();

// Now create a new configuration array so that we
// can merge it with the loaded configuration.
$baseConfig = array(
    'module_listener_options' => array(
    'module_paths' => explode(
        PATH_SEPARATOR, $zf2ModulePaths
    ),
  ),
);

// Merge our configuration with the base
// configuration that we just generated.
$config = ArrayUtils::merge(
    $baseConfig, $testConfig
);
```

Up until now showed the definition of the configuration file, and it is now all merged for use by our bootstrap. Next up is the definition of the service manager.

```php
// Let's create a new service manager
$serviceManager = new ServiceManager(
    new ServiceManagerConfig()
);

// Set the service manager to load the configuration
```

```
    // so that the ModuleManager can use it to load up
    // the modules and dependencies
    $serviceManager->setService(
        'ApplicationConfig', $config
    );

    // Now get the module manager, and load up the
    // modules plus dependencies
    $serviceManager->get('ModuleManager')
                    ->loadModules();

    // Make the service manager and configuration
    // available as a static in the bootstrap class
    static::$serviceManager = $serviceManager;
    static::$config = $config;
}
```

That's the end of our initialization, and as we can see it is pretty straightforward what is being done. The bootstrap initialization first read out the configuration and then created the service manager. After the service manager was created, we used the module manager to load up the modules (and dependencies) we required for our tests. Now that we have defined our most important part of the class, let's define the rest of the methods that we used in the preceding init() method.

```
    // Not completely unimportant, this is a getter for
    // our servicemanager property.
    public static function getServiceManager()
    {
      return static::$serviceManager;
    }

    // A simple getter for our static configuration.
    public static function getConfig()
    {
      return static::$config;
    }

    protected static function initAutoloader()
    {
      // Get the parent path of the ZF2 library (this
      // method is defined later on)
      $vendorPath = static::findParentPath('vendor');
```

```php
    // Now make sure the ZF2 path is ready to go
    if (is_readable($vendorPath . '/autoload.php')) {
      $loader = include $vendorPath . '/autoload.php';
    } else {
      // The vendor path isn't in the configuration, try
      // to find it ourselves.
      $zf2Path = getenv('ZF2_PATH')
              ?: (defined('ZF2_PATH') ? ZF2_PATH
              : (is_dir($vendorPath . '/ZF2/library')
              ? $vendorPath . '/ZF2/library' : false));

      // If the path is not defined, we cannot continue
      if (!$zf2Path) {
        throw new RuntimeException(
            'Unable to load ZF2.'
          );
      }

      // Include our autoloader from ZF2
      include $zf2Path. '/Zend/Loader/AutoloaderFactory.php';
    }

    // If we come here that means we have a valid ZF2
    // path, and can safely initialize our Autoloader.
    AutoloaderFactory::factory(array(
      'Zend\Loader\StandardAutoloader' => array(
        'autoregister_zf' => true,
        'namespaces' => array(
          __NAMESPACE__ => __DIR__ . '/' . __NAMESPACE__,
        ),
      ),
    ));
  }

  // This method finds the parent path of a given path.
  protected static function findParentPath($path)
  {
    $dir = __DIR__;
    $previousDir = '.';

    while (!is_dir($dir . '/' . $path)) {
      $dir = dirname($dir);
```

```php
        if ($previousDir === $dir) return false;
          $previousDir = $dir;
        }

        return $dir . '/' . $path;
    }
}

// And finally, initialize the application bootstrap
Bootstrap::init();
```

Now we finally set up our testing framework, it is time to write a simple test to see if everything works. What we'll do first is create a small Model (file `Company.php`: `/module/Application/src/Application/Model/`), which we are going to test.

```php
<?php

namespace Application\Model;

class Company
{
  public function hasEmployees() {}
}
```

That's it, no more coding at this point, as we first need to create our unit test (file `CompanyTest.php`: `/module/Application/test/Application/Model/`).

```php
<?php
// Define the namespace like a boss
namespace ApplicationTest\Model;

// We want to use this model for testing
use Application\Model\Company;

// Begin our test class, which needs to be extended from
// the PHPUnit framework test case.
class CompanyTest extends \PHPUnit_Framework_TestCase
{
  /**
   * Test some method.
   * @covers Application\Model\Company::hasEmployees
   */
  public function testHasEmployees()
  {
    $this->markTestIncomplete();
  }
}
```

And there we go, a simple test that does nothing but prints an I (which means one incomplete test) in the terminal if we were to execute it. As we can see we also defined a @covers PHPDoc tag, which is always a good idea for the sake of good documentation to actually document what method you are testing.

> To execute the PHPUnit tests, simple go to the test directory and type phpunit, which will trigger PHPUnit to test every file that ends in Test. php like SomeModelTest.php and look for methods that begin with test like testSomeMethod.

Let's do a simple test now, which tests if our method return value is true or not (file CompanyTest.php in /module/Application/test/Application/Model/).

```
public function testHasEmployees()
{
  // Instantiate our model (remember the use statement
  // in the top of the file).
  $object = new Company();

  // Make sure the method returns true
  $this->assertTrue($object->hasEmployees());
}
```

If we now run PHPUnit again, we'll see that it has printed a nice big red F (which means the test failed) in the terminal. Now we know that the unit test fails, we will modify our model (file Company.php in /module/Application/src/Application/Model/) again to make sure it passes again.

```
public function hasEmployees()
{
  return true;
}
```

If we now run PHPUnit again, a . (which means that the test passed) simply appears in the terminal. We know now that our test worked, and that we can trust the outcome of the unit test as well. We can now use this test framework over and over again for every other method and module that we write.

How it works...

What we did first is set up a small testing framework that would load in anything we need for the module that we want to test. After that we wrote a couple of simple tests for some code that we wanted.

The test framework we set up is a test framework that can be used per module separately, as it is unwise to make one test framework for the whole application. What we are trying to achieve is that our modules are still as independent as they can be (considering of course that some modules will have dependencies), and that we can test them separately as well.

There's more...

The framework we've set up is also available in the official documentation, which means that there is always support available if we are stuck with something.

See also

- The PHPUnit XML configuration file options:`http://phpunit.de/manual/3.7/en/appendixes.configuration.html`
- The PHPUnit cheat sheet: `https://gist.github.com/loonies/1255249`

Setting up the Essentials

In the appendix we will cover:

- Making sure you have all that you need
- Downloading Zend Framework 2 and finding its documentation
- Composer and its uses within Zend Framework 2
- Basic Zend Framework 2 structures
- About storage adapters and patterns

Making sure you have all that you need

The Zend Server is a nice piece of software that takes out a lot of work from our hands by installing everything we need (or at least provide a good platform) to code Zend Framework 2 (and Zend Framework 1!) applications. Although the paid version of Zend Server might not be necessary for production applications, developing in the developer version of the Zend Server is a pure delight as it will give a proper overview of the system, logs, configuration, and everything else we need to know.

We are going the cheap way by installing the Zend Server Community Edition, which installs everything we need to use Zend Framework and Zend Framework 2. The handy thing about the Zend Server is not only the ease of installation, but the immense toolset you get with the server itself. It is a great product to get a good overview of any PHP related configuration and is also able to monitor performance and track events in your system.

To install the Zend Server we need to download it first from the Zend website (http://www.zend.com), at the moment Zend Server 6.2.0 is the latest version of the application, and although we use it, the installation process should be the same for any later versions.

 Zend Server is not needed to run Zend Framework 2, but does, however, provide an excellent platform that needs only minimal configuration to get started.

Installing Zend Server Community Edition on a Linux environment

When we have downloaded Zend Server for Linux (you need a free Zend account to download any of their software), we will have a file called ZendServer-6.2.0-RepositoryInstaller-linux.tar.gz.

Next, to install the Zend Server we need to execute the following command sequence:

```
$ tar -xf ZendServer-6.2.0-RepositoryInstaller-linux.tar.gz
```

This will unpack the Gzipped Tarball (this is a compression method) package and extract it in the ZendServer-RepositoryInstaller-linux directory. Now let's install the Zend Server:

```
$ cd ZendServer-RepositoryInstaller-linux/
$ sudo ./install_zs.sh 5.4
```

We have chosen to install PHP 5.4, and if there is no reasonable explanation why we need PHP 5.3, we recommend keeping it in this version. If we need PHP 5.3, however, we can easily change the 5.4 to 5.3 and it will install the lower PHP version. Once we execute the install_zs.sh command as the root user (hence, the sudo, which tells the system we want to execute a command as a super user) we will get a short confirmation window asking us if we really want to install the Zend Server. Simply press *Enter* to continue the installation.

At some point during the installation, the script will ask if you want to install X amount of new packages. You want to answer Y or yes for that, otherwise the installation will end there.

The installation itself takes a couple of minutes and upon successful installation, the script will display the following message:

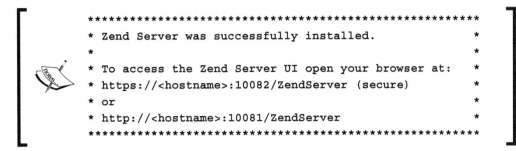

```
***************************************************************
* Zend Server was successfully installed.                     *
*                                                             *
* To access the Zend Server UI open your browser at:          *
* https://<hostname>:10082/ZendServer (secure)                *
* or                                                          *
* http://<hostname>:10081/ZendServer                          *
***************************************************************
```

Security wise it is best to always use the secure version of Zend Server, as you want to make sure that passwords are put in securely. However, while working locally it doesn't really matter that much.

Installing Zend Server Community Edition on a Windows environment

When we have downloaded the Zend Server for Microsoft Windows (you need a free Zend account to download any of their software) and we started up the `ZendServer-6.2.0-php-5.4.21-Windows_x86.exe` file, we find ourselves again with a very simple installation. If we choose the custom installation, we have a few options that we can change, but normally the default options are fine enough for us.

Another great thing about the Windows installation of Zend Server is that the installation program asks us if we want to use an existing IIS web server or install an Apache server instead.

What option you choose is all down to the configuration requirements for the rest of the project, assuming that we have more requirements; otherwise, we would really need to reconsider using Windows for our PHP environment.

After a summary screen of the installation we are about to commence, the installation will continue and configure the system. If the installation has been completed successfully, we get the option to start working with the Zend Server and to add the Zend Server as a desktop icon.

First-time run of Zend Server

If we go to the Zend Server interface in the browser for the first time (please note that the Zend Server in Windows does not have the secure connection built-in like the Linux version has), we will see the license agreement, which we need to accept before we can go on.

In the next screen, depending on the purpose of the Zend Server, we need to choose between the Development, Single Server, or Cluster license. The Single Server and Cluster license come standard with a 30-day trial version, and if we are new to the Zend Server then this is the best option to see the full server capabilities in action.

Next up is setting the administrator and developer password. If we are not the only one working on the server environment, it is best to use separate accounts as that creates a better maintenance structure in the organization; if only one person (or account) is capable of changing the system settings, then we can just skip filling in the developer details as they will not really have any use.

Once we have done all that, we are ready to login for the first time in our brand new system.

By default the login URL to the administration panel is `http://localhost:10081/ZendServer` for the non secure panel and `https://localhost:10082/ZendServer` for the secure administration panel.

The first thing we will see is the overview of the server's health, which also displays the current events that have taken place such as high memory uses, exceptions, and slow execution times.

The main bit we want to view now is the PHP configuration, which can be found in the **Configuration** screen, under **PHP**. It is very important to set the time zone for PHP as otherwise PHP will annoy us(for a reason: as some application developers erroneously believe that the machine is running on their local time zone, and base many of their date and time code on this) with warnings telling us that this should be set. If we search for the `date.timezone` in the search bar in the top right corner of the screen, it will take us (and highlight) immediately to the setting that we need to change. We can easily search on the Internet what the relevant value is for our specific time zone; this can be, for example, `Europe/London` or `America/New_York`.

See also

- PHP manual: This is a list of supported time zones `http://php.net/manual/en/timezones.php`

Downloading Zend Framework 2 and finding its documentation

Let's find out where to get all the essential literature on the Zend Framework.

Finding Zend Framework 2

The main website of Zend Framework 2 is `http://framework.zend.com` and always holds the most updated information on Zend Framework 2. We can easily download the framework from there, as well as some packages, for example the framework including the Zend Server, or the minimal package of Zend Framework.

Downloading only the framework itself, without any context like the skeleton application is a great way of starting an application from scratch without any of the clutter that comes with the default skeleton.

Coding in the phpcloud

A new toy made by Zend that is currently still in beta level is the phpcloud, which allows developers to create a fast reliable development environment for developers to develop on. One of the features of using the phpcloud is that it not only comes with Zend Framework 2, but also runs on the Zend Server which allows spectacular debugging capabilities and application deployment. At the moment sign up for the phpcloud is free, but we can assume that this will change in the future. How this will turn out, however, is not known to us yet.

The documentation and getting started guide

The Zend Framework 2 documentation is luckily much more reliable than the original Zend Framework documentation (which is a good thing, trust me). Zend really committed to creating a framework that is well documented and has an open contribution that is powered by a strong community and tools like Github (instead of Subversion as in the original framework). The documentation and getting started guide can both be found under the **Learn** menu option on the main Zend Framework 2 website.

See also

- The main Zend Framework 2 website found at `http://framework.zend.com`
- The Zend Framework 2 Coding Standards found at `http://framework.zend.com/wiki/x/yQCvAg`
- The latest Zend Framework 2 Documentation PDF found at `https://media.readthedocs.org/pdf/zf2/latest/zf2.pdf`
- The Zend Framework 2 Security RSS Feed found at `http://framework.zend.com/security/feed/`
- The Zend Framework 2 Blog RSS Feed found at `http://framework.zend.com/blog/feed-rss.xml`

Composer and its uses within Zend Framework 2

Composer is a dependency manager tool for PHP, which has been live since the spring of 2011, and is incredibly handy when it comes to getting projects set up with ease.

Composer reads its configuration from a file called `composer.json`, which is a JSON file that is being read by `composer.phar` (PHP archive).

We can use Composer to initialize the Zend Framework 2 library when we are using the Zend Framework 2 skeleton application. Other functionalities within Zend Framework 2 include installing new modules or libraries, which we can use to extend our application.

The composer.json file

If we open up the `composer.json` file we can see that the file has a couple of keys defined, which tells the Composer what it needs to load, and what versions we need. By default, the Zend Framework 2 skeleton application's `composer.json` will look similar to the following:

```
{
    "name": "zendframework/skeleton-application",
    "description": "Skeleton Application for ZF2",
    "license": "BSD-3-Clause",
    "keywords": [
        "framework",
        "zf2"
    ],
    "homepage": "http://framework.zend.com/",
    "require": {
        "php": ">=5.3.3",
        "zendframework/zendframework": ">2.2.0rc1",
    }
}
```

As we can see the file is pretty easy to understand, and the keys are pretty self explanatory, but to be sure we will go through them quickly to make sure we understand what is going on.

- ▸ name: This is the name of the package with the vendor name as the prefix, in this case the vendor is `zendframework` and the `skeleton-application` is the package.

- ▸ description: This short description tells us what the package does.

- ▸ license: This is the license the software is licensed under, normally this is one of the numerous open source/software licenses such as the BSD, GPL and MIT licenses. However, a closed-source software license is also available under the key 'proprietary'.

- ▸ keywords: This is an array of keywords that is used when searching for this package on the getcomposer.org website.

- ▸ homepage: Well this is pretty clear, is it not?

▶ `require`: Now this is getting interesting, as this will tell Composer exactly what we need to run our package. In this case it is an array with PHP, where we need Version 5.3.3 or higher and Zend Framework 2 version 2.2.0rc1 or higher. Please note however, that in production we should always avoid a dev Version or a package with a greater than symbol, as it could potentially break our application. Always (please remember!) to get the exact version required when putting the application live.

Although it doesn't say it here, Composer will always install Zend Framework 2 to the vendor directory, as the required section in the `composer.json` says we need `zendframework/zendframework` to run our application. Composer knows that it needs to be installed to the vendor directory because the `zendframework/zendframework` package is of the type library, and that type is always being copied by Composer to the vendor directory.

Upgrading packages

Sometimes we just want to update our libraries, for example, when we know that a bug has been solved in Zend Framework 2's library, and we really want to have it. Fortunately, Composer comes with a great self-update and update command that we have for our disposal.

To update our libraries automatically through Composer, we should execute the following commands in the terminal (this cannot be done properly through the web browser):

```
$ php composer.phar self-update
```

First we want to make sure that we are using the latest Composer, as using an outdated Composer might give unnecessary errors.

```
$ php composer.phar update
```

This will update all our packages that we have put in the `require` section of the `composer.json` to update to the latest (compatible) version. We should be wary, however, that when we want a new package installed, but without the updation rest of the packages, we should use the following command:

```
$ php composer.phar update vendor-name/package-name
```

Here `vendor-name` and `package-name` are the names of the packages we want to install.

Composer works because all the packages are registered on their website `getcomposer.org`. In the website they keep all the packages together, and whenever we try to update or install, the `composer.phar` will connect to the website and retrieve the newest packages.

When we create our own modules or libraries, we can also submit that to the composer website. Submitting to composer's website will create a better community and a better understanding of the dependencies needed when we begin developing certain applications.

See also

▸ The composer's main website `http://getcomposer.org`

Basic Zend Framework 2 structures

When we consider the Zend Framework 2 structure, we must be aware that Zend Framework 2 doesn't actually care how our directory structure looks like, as long as we tell Zend Framework 2 in our configuration where all the paths can be found.

In the skeleton application we see that our configuration can be found in the `config/application.config.php` file. But that file solely exists there because in the `public/index.php` it is being loaded. If we, for example, want to change the location of that configuration file to somewhere else, we (in this case) only need to change it in the `public/index.php` file. The same goes for the module and vendor directory, as these can be anywhere we like, as long as we tell the `application.config.php` file where exactly that location is.

If we want to change the public directory, we can safely change it to any name we want, as long as we tell our web server where the new `DocumentRoot` is. Obviously making a good structure is of course, the key to a successful application, and therefore the skeleton application was created. That doesn't mean that different structure requirements have to make us stop using Zend Framework 2, as the framework can be fully configured to such requirements.

However, we can assume that because we are using the skeleton made available by Zend, it displays a very optimal structure for us to develop in.

When we list the initial folder of our skeleton application, we note some of the following objects of importance:

▸ `config`
▸ `module`
▸ `public`
▸ `vendor`
▸ `init_autoloader.php`

As we can see there are many objects in our folder, but these have no significant importance to our basic application.

Folder – config

The `config` folder consists of the following objects by default:

- ▸ `autoload/`
- ▸ `global.php`
- ▸ `local.php.dist`
- ▸ `application.config.php`

Probably the most important file in this folder would be the `application.config.php` as it contains all of our main configuration options. If we open this file we can see that it has a couple of options set to make our application work.

The file contains, for example, the `modules` key, which tells the framework which modules we need to load in for our application. It also contains the `module_listener_options - module_paths`, which tells our framework where to find our modules and libraries, which modules and vendor are by default.

The `config` folder also contains an `autoload` folder, which in itself contains two files which are the global configuration override and the local configuration override files. Both files are empty by default.

Folder – module

The default `module` folder consists of the following important objects:

- ▸ `Application/config/`**`module.config.php`**
- ▸ `Application/language/src/Application/Controller/`**`IndexController.php`**
- ▸ `Application/src/Application/Controller/`**`IndexController.php`**
- ▸ `Application/view/Application/index/`**`index.phtml`**
- ▸ `Application/view/Application/error/`**`404.phtml`**
- ▸ `Application/view/Application/error/`**`index.phtml`**
- ▸ `Application/view/Application/layout/`**`layout.phtml`**
- ▸ `Application/`**`Module.php`**

The application module gives away the basic structure that we would like to see when creating a new module. The most important file that we see here is the `Module.php`, which tells the framework how our module is built up, where it can find our controllers, and many more.

Depending on how our application is built up, we would also want to have a configuration file for each module as we would like to keep the application as dynamic as possible. In the skeleton application we can see that our `Module.php` contains a method called `Module::getConfig()`; all it does is a simple include to the `config/module.config.php` file. Although we theoretically could just define the configuration in the `Module.php`, it is nicer if we separate the actual configuration file from our code, as that also brings a lot more maintainability with itself if we don't need to change the code for a simple change in configuration.

We can also see a `language` folder in this folder, which contains all the i18n (short for internationalization as it contains 18 characters between I and N) files needed for translating our application. Although probably used by a lot of developers, not all of our application will require translation, so we might not need this folder at all in our project.

But if we do require `i18n` and `l10n` (localization) then it would be beneficial to do this module wise instead of application wise, again for maintainability as we don't want the application (which is the whole application) to define `i18n/l10n` for all the modules, as theoretically not all of the modules have to be there. That is why working module oriented makes the code a lot more dynamic, but also maintainable as we can safely assume that if an error occurs in one of our modules, the problem also lies in that module.

The next folder `src` might very well be one of the most interesting folders in our module, as it contains—as we might have guessed—the source of our module. The folder `src` only contains another folder called `Application`, which is the defined namespace of the classes inside.

Make sure that you name your subdirectories in `src` to the namespace they are using. Otherwise it might not only lead to conflicts, but also confusion and inconsistencies. For example, if your module is called `Winter`, then our directory should be called `src/Winter`, to make sure that all our `Winter` namespaces are in that directory. That way we can safely assume that all our code for that namespace has been neatly put in that directory and its sub directories.

The subfolder in `Application` is in our skeleton application `Controller`, which contains only the `IndexController.php`. The `IndexController.php` is an extension of the `Zend\Mvc\Controller\AbstractActionController`, which is generally used for our day-to-day controllers; however, there is also the `AbstractRestfulController` in the same namespace, which we can use if we want to create a restful service.

Next up is the `view` folder, which contains all our view scripts. View scripts are basically template files we use to do the actual displaying to the user requesting the page. As we can see in the default `module.config.php` of our `Application` module, we have the view scripts configured to point to the `view` directory, which tells the framework that when it needs to find any view scripts, it should look in that folder.

```
    ),
    'view_manager' => array(
        'display_not_found_reason' => true,
        'display_exceptions'       => true,
        'doctype'                  => 'HTML5',
        'not_found_template'       => 'error/404',
        'exception_template'       => 'error/index',
        'template_map' => array(
            'layout/layout'             => __DIR__ . '/../view/layout/layout.phtml',
            'application/index/index'   => __DIR__ . '/../view/application/index/index.phtml',
            'error/404'                 => __DIR__ . '/../view/error/404.phtml',
            'error/index'               => __DIR__ . '/../view/error/index.phtml',
        ),
        'template_path_stack' => array(
            __DIR__ . '/../view',
        ),
    ),
),
```

As we can see the `view` folder is built up with the same structure as in the configuration file. The `Application` folder refers to the namespace which is using this view script that is, `Application`, then we see that there is also a layout defined, which is used as a global layout for our module—and the rest of the project if none is defined elsewhere—and an `error` folder, that is only used whenever an error occurs in the application. If we want to read up more about how the layouts work in Zend Framework 2, you should take a look at *Chapter 4, Using View*.

The `layout` folder and the `error` folder are usually considered to be the main template files for the project. This does not mean, however, that we can only have one layout defined; all we need to do is just define another layout configuration in our module file, which makes a specific module different to the others.

That concludes the buildup of our `module` folder, and when creating other modules—when using the skeleton application—it requires us to use the same folder structure.

Folder – public

The `public` folder contains all of the files that the public may see. We need to make sure our application is secure, so we will only put images, style sheets, and JavaScript files in here. The only file related to the framework here, will be the `index.php` file, as that is the file that initializes our application, and is used only when an HTTP request is made. Although we can put PHP files here, we would strongly recommend against it, as it can potentially make your project open for vulnerabilities.

Folder – vendor

The vendor folder contains—as the name suggests—libraries that are made by a third party. In our default project this will only contain the Zend Framework 2 libraries, which are needed to run the project (located in the zendframework/library folder). Whenever we are going to use third party libraries like Smarty or Doctrine, these will be placed here.

 If we have a homemade library that is (or can be) non application specific we would recommend putting it in here as well, especially if the library is maintained somewhere else. Once we begin scattering our libraries around in other folders, it is almost impossible to maintain consistency and maintainability.

File – init_autoloader.php

The init_autoloader.php file makes sure our project can find the classes and namespaces we are trying to use. It is called by the public/index.php file.

For the Zend Framework 2 to start up and configure itself, a couple of actions happen. If we use the skeleton application, the following flow of information can be assumed:

- ▸ /public/index.php: This is the first file that is going to be ran as that is the only public script file related to the application. When run, the script is including the init_autoloader.php in the root folder to the script and after that it initializes the Zend Framework 2.

- ▸ /init_autoloader.php: This file does exactly what it says it does, it initializes the autoloader. One of the best features of Zend Framework 2 is the extensity of the autoloader. All this file does is make sure the autoloader has most of the namespaces and classes that we use known (but not loaded up yet) before we go on and initialize the application, that way the autoloader can simply load up the class whenever it is requested. Although the skeleton application has a very lazy autoloader, which we shouldn't use in this form, in a production environment it can be a very powerful tool to create the best performance for your application.

What's next?

After the public/index.php has loaded up the locations of known classes and namespaces, it is ready to start up the Zend Framework 2 MVC application.

1. Get the config/application.config.php file. It actually doesn't do anything with this file at the moment.

2. Run the `Zend\Mvc\Application::init($configurationArray)`, where `$configurationArray` is the variable that contains the read configuration from step 1.

   ❑ Initialization of the `ServiceManager`, which handles all the services in the application.

   Invoke `Zend\EventManager\SharedEventManager`.

   Factory `Zend\ModuleManager\ModuleManager`.

   ❑ Request the `ModuleManager` from the `ServiceManager` and run its `loadModules()` method.

   ❑ This will then resolve all the modules and load in the module-specific configurations.

   ❑ Request the `Zend\Mvc\Application` from the `ServiceManager`.

   ❑ It will run the `bootstrap()` method.

3. The `public/index.php` will now execute the `run()` method on the fully initialized `Zend\Mvc\Application`, which will make the sure the routing, which will trigger the bootstrap, route, dispatch, render and finish events, making sure the application has done what was requested of it.

4. After the `Zend\Mvc\Application` has completed its `run()` method, it will execute the `send()` method, which will send the output made by the `run()` method back to the client.

Here is a flow chart diagram to show how the process goes a bit more graphically:

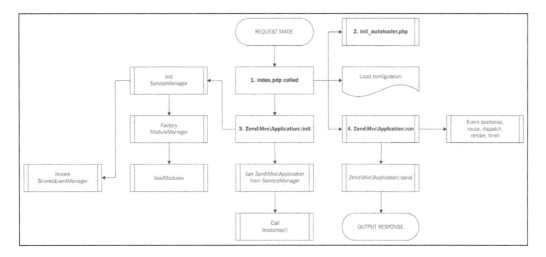

About storage adapters and patterns

The different storage adapters and patterns are a great way of implementing different functionality throughout our cache adapters, and storing them on different platforms, for example, the file system or just in memory. This recipe will tell us all about the default tools available in Zend Framework 2.

Storage adapter's implementations

Storage adapters in ZF2 are adapters used to do the actual caching of our data, meaning they also control how the data is stored. The storage adapters always implement the `Zend\Cache\Storage\StorageInterface`, which contains the basic functionality that the storage adapter needs to comply with. Most of the storage adapters also extend from the `Zend\Cache\Storage\Adapter\AbstractAdapter`, but no guarantee can be given for that. Aside from the `StorageInterface`, storage adapters often implement additional interfaces representing enhanced functionality. These implementations obviously play a crucial role of the functionality of the adapter, so we think it is best to give a short list of implementations that the adapter can use that are defined by the framework.

- `AvailableSpaceCapableInterface`: This interface provides a method to check the available space for the caching.

- `Capabilities`: This interface provides methods to check the capabilities of the Storage adapter, such as the minimum and maximum ttl (time-to-live) of the cache, or the supported data types (boolean, string, object, and so on).

- `ClearByNamespaceInterface`: This interface has a method defined that can clear cache by the given namespace.

- `ClearByPrefixInterface`: This interface defines a method that can clear cache by the given prefix.

- `ClearExpiredInterface`: This interface provides a method to clear expired cache items.

- `FlushableInterface`: This interface is able to flush the whole cache.

- `IterableInterface`: This interface provides functionality to iterate over the cache items. Super handy to `foreach` over them!

- `OptimizableInterface`: This interface gives the ability to optimize the caching.

- `TaggableInterface`: This interface provides methods to get and set tags for a specific cache item, and the ability to remove all the cache items through a certain tag.

- `TotalSpaceCapableInterface`: This interface has a method that returns the total space of the cache.

Storage adapters

Now that we know the interfaces an adapter may implement, it is time to give a comprehensive list of the storage adapters available in the Zend\Cache\Storage\ Adapter namespace.

Apc caching

Apc or Alternative PHP Cache is a well known framework that heavily optimizes the PHP output and stores the compiled PHP code in the shared-memory. This way some of the opcode (operation code) doesn't have to be recompiled again as it is ready for immediate use. The Apc adapter also extends from the AbstractAdapter.

This adapter implements the following interfaces:

- ▶ AvailableSpaceCapableInterface
- ▶ ClearByNamespaceInterface
- ▶ ClearByPrefixInterface
- ▶ FlushableInterface
- ▶ IterableInterface
- ▶ TotalSpaceCapableInterface

> This adapter can only work if the APC extension in PHP has been enabled, please make sure that it is before trying.

Dba caching

You want to store the cache in a pre-relation dbm database, then this is your chance! This adapter can store it all neatly away in a nice database. This adapter also extends from the AbstractAdapter.

This adapter implements the following interfaces:

- ▶ AvailableSpaceCapableInterface
- ▶ ClearByNamespaceInterface
- ▶ ClearByPrefixInterface
- ▶ FlushableInterface
- ▶ IterableInterface

- ▸ OptimizableInterface
- ▸ TotalSpaceCapableInterface

 This adapter needs the dba extension enabled in PHP before it can work, please make sure it is enabled.

File system caching

File system caching is a personal favorite, to store the cache on the good old file system, a fast and usually reliable place to place it. This adapter also extends from the AbstractAdapter.

This adapter implements the following interfaces:

- ▸ AvailableSpaceCapableInterface
- ▸ ClearByNamespaceInterface
- ▸ ClearByPrefixInterface
- ▸ ClearExpiredInterface
- ▸ FlushableInterface
- ▸ IterableInterface
- ▸ OptimizableInterface
- ▸ TaggableInterface
- ▸ TotalSpaceCapableInterface

 It sounds as something really obvious, but make sure we have write permissions on the directory where we want to store the cache.

Memcached caching

The Memcached adapter stores the cache in the memory, which is a great way to store static file that don't change often and can be considered semi-static. This adapter also extends from the AbstractAdapter. Please note that Memcached is not restricted by PHP's memory limit settings, as Memcached stores the memory outside of the PHP process in its own Memcached process.

This adapter implements the following interfaces:

- ▸ `AvailableSpaceCapableInterface`
- ▸ `FlushableInterface`
- ▸ `TotalSpaceCapableInterface`

 We need the `memcached` PHP extension to cache through this adapter. Please make sure it is enabled on your system.

Memory caching

The Memory adapter stores all the cache in the PHP process, in comparison to the Memcached adapter, as that stores all the cache in an external Memcached process. This adapter also extends from the `AbstractAdapter`.

This adapter implements the following interfaces:

- ▸ `AvailableSpaceCapableInterface`
- ▸ `ClearByPrefixInterface`
- ▸ `ClearByNamespaceInterface`
- ▸ `ClearExpiredInterface`
- ▸ `FlushableInterface`
- ▸ `IterableInterface`
- ▸ `TaggableInterface`
- ▸ `TotalSpaceCapableInterface`

Redis caching

The Redis is a key-value data store that stores the data in-memory, which is extremely well done and certainly is a caching method worth using. This adapter also extends from the `AbstractAdapter`.

This adapter implements the following interfaces:

- ▸ `FlushableInterface`
- ▸ `TotalSpaceCapableInterface`

 If we want to use this caching adapter, we need to make sure the `redis` extension is loaded, otherwise this storage adapter cannot be used. Please make sure the extension is installed and enabled.

Session caching

The Session storage adapter uses the session to store our cache in. Although handy for one user at a time, this method isn't really effective for users who view the same pages as it builds up the cache every time a user initiates a session. This adapter also extends from the `AbstractAdapter`.

This adapter implements the following interfaces:

- `ClearByPrefixInterface`
- `FlushableInterface`
- `IterableInterface`

WinCache caching

The WinCache is an excellent adapter that is useful when running PHP on a Microsoft Windows server. WinCache supports opcode caching, file system caching, and relative path caching. This adapter also extends from the `AbstractAdapter`.

This adapter implements the following interfaces:

- `AvailableSpaceCapableInterface`
- `FlushableInterface`
- `TotalSpaceCapableInterface`

 For this method the `wincache` extension needs to be loaded, and if that wasn't all you also need to be on Microsoft Windows to, to use this.

XCache caching

The XCache is an adapter that utilizes the XCache module in PHP, which is another cache adapter like APC and is a fast opcode cacher, which is very useful. This adapter also extends from the `AbstractAdapter`.

This adapter implements the following interfaces:

- `AvailableSpaceCapableInterface`
- `ClearByNamespaceInterface`
- `ClearByPrefixInterface`
- `FlushableInterface`

- IterableInterface
- TotalSpaceCapableInterface

 This adapter requires the XCache extension to be loaded and enabled in PHP. Please make sure this is the case before trying to use the adapter.

ZendServerDisk caching

The ZendServerDisk adapter is a great file system cache adapter provided by the Zend Server application. If we have the Zend Server installed, this adapter is a great way of storing the cache on the file system as it integrates ridiculously good with the Zend Server. This adapter also extends from the `AbstractAdapter`.

This adapter implements the following interfaces:

- AvailableSpaceCapableInterface
- ClearByNamespaceInterface
- FlushableInterface
- TotalSpaceCapableInterface

 To make this adapter work you'll need to have the Zend Server installed, otherwise it will just throw an exception.

ZendServerShm caching

The ZendServerShm adapter also requires us to have the Zend Server installed, but if we have and we want to cache items in the shared memory (shm) then this is an amazing way of doing it, as this adapter integrates very nicely with the Zend Server. This adapter also extends from the `AbstractAdapter`.

This adapter implements the following interfaces:

- ClearByNamespaceInterface
- FlushableInterface
- TotalSpaceCapableInterface

 To make this adapter work you'll need to have the Zend Server installed to make this adapter work, otherwise it will just throw an exception.

Cache patterns

When we start caching, we will quickly find ourselves in situations that are counteractive to the performance while we just wanted everything to go faster. That is why there are classes in ZF2 that are called Cache patterns, which are there for us to use when we want to overcome some common problems.

Like the adapters, patterns are also always implementations of an interface; in this case the `PatternInterface`. And because we usually also want some basic functionality, most of the patterns also extend from the `AbstractPattern` class.

Options for the patterns are defined through the `PatternOptions` class, which is explained a bit further on as well.

The CallbackCache pattern

What do we want, a callback or the cache? Sometimes we just don't know for sure, so we'll let the pattern to figure it out itself! The `CallbackCache` pattern first makes sure if there is a result for our callback already defined in the cache, and if so, returns that. If the result is not in the cache yet, it will call our callback function, put our output in the result and then return that. Either way, the second time that callback is being handled, we will get our cache back. So if this is a long running method, it will be considerably faster when we don't have to execute the code again.

This pattern also takes the arguments for that callback in consideration, which means you don't really have to worry much about the callback providing you with the wrong results!

This Pattern uses the `AbstractPattern` class.

The CaptureCache pattern

The `CaptureCache` pattern captures the output we are sending to the browser by initiating an `ob_start()` and `ob_implicit_flush()`. We can then do a check if the cache exists every time we sent the output out, so that instead of generating it we just display the output.

This pattern uses the `AbstractPattern` class.

This pattern does not automatically output cache once defined, the developer needs to get the cache themselves first before using the start method. If we want to output cache when it exists before generating new content we should use the `OutputCache` pattern.

The ClassCache pattern

The `ClassCache` pattern caches the output of a class method call and returns that instead of the actual call. But of course, this only happens when the cache is actually available, otherwise it will just do the method call and cache the results. The class name (not the object) needs to be set in the `PatternOptions::setClass` to make it work.

This pattern uses the `AbstractPattern` class.

The ObjectCache pattern

The `ObjectCache` pattern caches the object and can be used to call methods upon its retrieval, very handy if we have objects that need to persistent for a very long time. The object needs to be set in the `PatternOptions::setObject` to make it work.

This pattern uses the `AbstractPattern` class.

The OutputCache pattern

The `OutputCache` pattern outputs the cache if it is defined. If not, then OutputCache caches the output and sets the cache upon script end (or call to the end method, whichever comes first).

This pattern uses the `AbstractPattern` class.

The PatternOptions pattern

The `PatternOptions` pattern can be used to set options or get options from and to the patterns (`setOptions` and `getOptions` respectively). For most patterns some form of options need to be set before the pattern can be used. Think here about the `setStorage` method for example, because the pattern needs to know the storage adapter before it can actually store things.

Explaining the difference

Storage adapters store and retrieve the cache data. We can set options to determine the length of the validity or perhaps check if the cache is full or not, but we can't determine how it is stored, as that is part of the adapter's job description.

Patterns however don't store anything themselves. They determine if they need to store anything by checking if the cache already exists, or if the cache is what we expect it to be (for example, when we use a different method call or different arguments to that call). They do tell the adapters what they want to retrieve and store, so that the adapter then can find out how to retrieve it from the actual storage again.

In a developer's eye we would rather be using patterns before we would want to use the adapters, as we'd not want to interfere with the adapters too much if there are already patterns doing most of the work for us.

Index

Thank you for buying
Zend Framework 2 Cookbook

About Packt Publishing

Packt, pronounced 'packed', published its first book "*Mastering phpMyAdmin for Effective MySQL Management*" in April 2004 and subsequently continued to specialize in publishing highly focused books on specific technologies and solutions.

Our books and publications share the experiences of your fellow IT professionals in adapting and customizing today's systems, applications, and frameworks. Our solution based books give you the knowledge and power to customize the software and technologies you're using to get the job done. Packt books are more specific and less general than the IT books you have seen in the past. Our unique business model allows us to bring you more focused information, giving you more of what you need to know, and less of what you don't.

Packt is a modern, yet unique publishing company, which focuses on producing quality, cutting-edge books for communities of developers, administrators, and newbies alike. For more information, please visit our website: www.packtpub.com.

About Packt Open Source

In 2010, Packt launched two new brands, Packt Open Source and Packt Enterprise, in order to continue its focus on specialization. This book is part of the Packt Open Source brand, home to books published on software built around Open Source licences, and offering information to anybody from advanced developers to budding web designers. The Open Source brand also runs Packt's Open Source Royalty Scheme, by which Packt gives a royalty to each Open Source project about whose software a book is sold.

Writing for Packt

We welcome all inquiries from people who are interested in authoring. Book proposals should be sent to author@packtpub.com. If your book idea is still at an early stage and you would like to discuss it first before writing a formal book proposal, contact us; one of our commissioning editors will get in touch with you.

We're not just looking for published authors; if you have strong technical skills but no writing experience, our experienced editors can help you develop a writing career, or simply get some additional reward for your expertise.

[PACKT] open source
PUBLISHING
community experience distilled

Zend Framework 2.0
by Example

A step-by-step guide to help you build full-scale web
applications using Zend Framework 2.0

Beginner's Guide

Krishna Shasankar V   [   ] open source

Zend Framework 2.0 by Example: Beginner's Guide

ISBN: 978-1-78216-192-9   Paperback: 228 pages

A step-by-step guid to help you build full-scale web
applications using Zend framework 2.0

1. Master application development with Zend
   Framework 2.0

2. Learn about Zend Framework components and
   use them for functions such as searching, image
   processing, and payment gateway integrations

3. Integrate third-party services for media sharing
   and payment processing

PHP Application Development
with NetBeans

Boost your PHP development skills with this step-by-step
practical guide

Beginner's Guide

M A Hossain Tonu   [   ] open source

PHP Application Development with NetBeans: Beginner's Guide

ISBN: 978-1-84951-580-1   Paperback: 302 pages

Boost your PHP development skills with this step-by-step
practical guide

1. Clear step-by-step instructions with lots of
   practical examples

2. Develop cutting-edge PHP applications like never
   before with the help of this popular IDE, through
   quick and simple techniques

3. Experience exciting features of PHP application
   development with real-life PHP projects

Please check **www.PacktPub.com** for information on our titles

Expert PHP 5 Tools

ISBN: 978-1-84719-838-9   Paperback: 468 pages

Proven enterprise development tools and best practices for designing, coding, testing, and deployment PHP applications

1. Best practices for designing, coding, testing, and deploying PHP applications – all the information in one book

2. Learn to write unit tests and practice test-driven development from an expert

3. Set up a professional development environment with integrated debugging capabilities

4. Develop your own coding standard and enforce it automatically

Magento 1.4 Development Cookbook

ISBN: 978-1-84951-144-5   Paperback: 268 pages

Extend your Magento store to the optimum level by developing modules and widgets

1. Develop Modules and Extensions for Magento 1.4 using PHP with ease

2. Socialize your store by writing custom modules and widgets to drive in more customers

3. Achieve a tremendous performance boost by applying powerful techniques such as YSlow, PageSpeed, and Siege

Please check **www.PacktPub.com** for information on our titles

www.ingramcontent.com/pod-product-compliance
Lightning Source LLC
LaVergne TN
LVHW062305060326

832902LV00013B/2056